LITERARY THEORIE

AWN

Literary Theories

A CASE STUDY IN CRITICAL PERFORMANCE

EDITED BY JULIAN WOLFREYS AND
WILLIAM BAKER

First published 1996 by
MACMILLAN PRESS LTD
Houndmills, Basingstoke, Hampshire RG21 6XS and London
Companies and representatives throughout the world

ISBN 0–333–66301–2 hardcover
ISBN 0–333–66302–0 paperback

A catalogue record for this book is available from the British Library.

10 9 8 7 6 5 4 3 2 1
05 04 03 02 01 00 99 98 97 96

Printed in Hong Kong

Contents

v

Preface and Acknowledgements

Arguably, today most teachers of literature, most academics and researchers in literary studies, are in some way 'theorized' in their approaches, to a greater or lesser extent, whatever the school of thought to which they claim affinity, to which they are seen as adhering. Their – and our – pedagogical approaches and their interpretive techniques are informed by disciplines and fields of thought not having originated in Departments of English and literary studies. Furthermore, it is now quite commonplace to find in Departments of English Literature in universities throughout the English-speaking world courses for undergraduates which, in some manner or other, address the subject of 'literary theory'. This broad heading, which we shall go on to reject as an unhelpful umbrella term in our introduction, serves to gather together discourses from numerous disciplines outside the immediate field and traditional concerns of literary study as is well known, discourses which range from the obviously political – feminism, Marxism – to the quasi-scientific (psychoanalysis, semiotics, structuralism). What often emerges on the positive side from such interaction is a series of sophisticated, fertile, hybrid interpretive techniques importing useful analytical methods into the service of critical reading and interpretation. On the negative side – unfortunately the side on which the student seems to be positioned frequently, albeit inadvertently – and because of the sheer proliferation of published theoretical analysis over the last 25 years, students are left bewildered through not comprehending the contexts of the thought which they are required to apply to poems, novels or plays. Another potentially negative effect of the importation of theoretical models from outside the field of English Studies is that theories (can) get watered down, ideologies hidden, positions reified, seemingly not positions at all but merely the 'natural' assumptions of that particular discourse.

At the same time as the development of diverse theoretical approaches to literary analysis there have, inevitably, appeared a range of explicatory texts, histories, overviews and anthologies, aimed at various areas of the student market, from the undergraduate to graduate student, with the idea of providing introductions to what is commonly called 'literary theory'. Amongst these we might include Terry Eagleton's *Literary Theory: an Introduction*, Catherine Belsey's *Critical Practice*, Jonathan Culler's *Structuralist Poetics*, Philip Rice and Patricia Waugh's *Literary Theory: A Reader*, Frank Lentricchia's *After the New Criticism*, Josué Harari's *Textual Strategies*; we might even include the entire Methuen 'New Accents' series. All have their good and bad points, all are conceived with different student groups in mind, from first-year undergraduates, to doctoral students. No one text, however, can claim to be 'definitive' or authoritative', the field of 'literary theory' being just too diverse, too broad. (This should not, of course, suggest that any of the texts mentioned in the paragraph claim authority. We are merely pointing out a significant problem of introducing the student to 'literary theory'.)

More recently, there have also appeared 'casebooks', combining editions of familiar texts (Bram Stoker's *Dracula*, Mary Shelley's *Frankenstein*, James Joyce's *The Dead*) with a range of critical essays from different theoretical perspectives treating the text in question. Clearly such books have developed partly out of the experience of teaching 'theory', teaching from theoretical positions, and applying that theory – those theories – to textual exegesis; such casebooks have also appeared, it can be suggested, partly out of a sense of a desire to provide the student with an immediate example of the multi-layered condition of textual meaning when viewed through the lens of 'theory' in a single volume, oriented around a single work. This current volume is one such casebook, although not entirely similar to those already mentioned.

How, then, might we suggest that this volume is different? How might we justify yet one more collection of literary-theoretical essays? What might be our arguments be for such a volume, aimed at undergraduates encountering theoretically oriented interpretive approaches, if not for the first time then with a sense of unfamiliarity?

Our purpose in this collection is to allow the student to witness various literary theories performing acts of reading and theoretically grounded interpretation around a single short story, a recently discovered, never before published manuscript by Richard Jefferies. Furthermore, we do not suggest to the student that this is a pluralist collection. We want the student to witness the development of certain tensions between the essays. We argue, in the introduction, that there is no *one* literary theory, not some absolutely totalizable, comprehensible approach to literature which is termed 'theoretical'. If it is commonplace to find courses entitled 'literary theory' taught throughout English departments today, as we suggested above, it is equally easy for undergraduates to find such a hydra daunting, off-putting, *monstrous*, in its being presented as a discernible multi-headed body, distinct from literature. The student may well end up disagreeing with a particular theoretical model; but surely, isn't the rejection better coming from a position of knowledge, rather than one of ignorance? and, equally, isn't it better to let the students in, if only in order that they can find their own way out? As possible answers to such questions this collection seeks to provide as accessible and approachable an introduction as possible, without diluting or obscuring either the theoretical or ideological issues.

With these concerns in mind we have adopted the casebook approach, but have chosen to offer to the student a fairly short text. A number of the casebooks available for undergraduates feature novels. The novels and stories chosen for such critical attention are usually defined as being *overdetermined*: In the case of narratives such as those of *Frankenstein, Dracula,* or *Dr Jekyll and Mr Hyde*, the teacher of literary theories can use the familiarity of such stories – many students will know something of the story of these novels, even though they may not have read them – to play off students' expectations and doxical beliefs against different theoretical readings. The student's excitement can be engaged precisely because the various theoretical modes confound her or his expectations and presuppositions through the new insights which such modes allow. This in turn can lead to a direct questioning and discussion of literary value, what constitutes literature, and how the literary canon is formed, all of which is both valuable to the student and an intrinsic element in the more politicized forms of literary-theoretical thinking.

The disadvantage of such primary texts – a minor disadvantage, yet still an important one – is one of *length*. The student can be overwhelmed when having to read, sometimes simultaneously, a long and quite convoluted narrative *and* a number of quite abstract texts. Furthermore, the student, in keeping up with the theoretical material, would not necessarily have the opportunity of reading the primary text more than once or, at the most, twice.

On the other hand, the student can read a short story in a relatively short space of time; unlike a novel, a short story allows the reader the possibility of re-reading each time s/he encounters a new theoretical approach. A short story also shows, because of its brevity, how different readings can be developed with full attention to many of the same details. With a multi-layered novel, critics working from different critical positions may not touch on the same material. A short story, however, affords the opportunity for close discussion of the same points. This, we believe, allows the student reader the opportunity of seeing more precisely how literary theories serve to enrich the reading process. A short story such as 'Snowed Up' is particularly exciting, then, because it provides the critic and the student alike the chance to encounter a new, hitherto unpublished text, and one moreover which is highly overdetermined, richly, often densely communicative and yet both brief and clear. When one adds to this the fact that Richard Jefferies himself is relatively unknown, both teacher and student are presented with some potentially fascinating interpretive possibilities. If a story *is* well known, if there are sufficient numbers of critical evaluations around which dazzle with their virtuosity and impress with their authority, then what access does the student have to such a work or criticism of it? A relatively unknown author and a completely unknown story change the stakes of interpretation. For the critics here this story has provided an opportunity of examining their own pedagogical procedures while putting to work their theoretical knowledge. Without exception, each writer found it exciting to work with what was, to them, an initially unknown text. We can only hope the excitement and enthusiasm is conveyed to the student reader through each of these essays.

•

We would like to thank Margaret Bartley at Macmillan for having faith in this project and for being so encouraging throughout its various stages. We would also like to thank those students in literary theory courses who responded in various ways to both Richard Jefferies' short story and to drafts of many of the essays contained in this collection, all of which came to be revised as a result of their questions, queries and insights. Finally we would like to thank King's School, Canterbury, and the librarians responsible for the Walpole Collection in King's School Library, for kind permission to publish 'Snowed Up' for the first time.

Julian Wolfreys and William Baker
Perth and DeKalb

Overture

Introduction

JULIAN WOLFREYS AND WILLIAM BAKER

(NOT JUST) ANOTHER TEXTBOOK ABOUT LITERARY THEORY?

Literary Theories: a Case Study in Critical Performance. Perhaps a couple of things strike you about the title of this collection. Why, for instance, is there the insistence on 'theories' rather than 'theory'? And why the phrase 'critical performance' instead of the more conventional, more commonplace 'critical practice' (which, had it been there, would have signalled some kind of pairing or opposite to the equally absent 'theory')? You see precisely what is absent, yet still partially readable, from the title is another title, which might be something like *Literary Theory: a Case Study in Critical Practice.* Such a title today expresses the conventional, the expected, the predictable; almost, we would say, after so many years of 'theory', the generic, which title might usefully express the following: first (the absent title would imply), there is *theory*, a model or programme separate from the act, the *practice*, of reading literature. Once you have learned the particular set of rules of the theory, once you have come to terms with its key concepts, ways of thinking, then you can go away and use those tools on a literary text of your choice. The implication is that you can, in short, practice theory as the secondary gesture or supplement to the 'primary' activity of understanding and learning 'theory'.

Well, so much for what's not in the title. And equally, we can say, what is not in this book either. Before we go any further,

3

we want you to be aware that this, therefore, will not have been *just* a manual of 'literary theory'. It is that, of course, inasmuch as this is still a pedagogical aid to the introduction of theories in performance; but the essays in this collection are not interested only in teaching you how to produce the perfect feminist or psychoanalytic reading; they are also interested in something potentially more fascinating: which is, showing how a text can be read so as to spark off many different insights and connections in the reader's mind in an interactive and generative, often unpredictable, fashion. The teaching – and learning – processes hopefully will emerge from the acts of reading and writing. We believe 'showing' rather than 'telling' a more effective teaching method, and we hope you will find it so too.

However, this does not explain the 'why' of the title's idiosyncrasies, the double 'why' of 'why theor*ies*'? and 'why *performance*?' The term 'theory' implies in its all-encompassing singularity a certain homogeneity. Despite the apparent disparity between approaches to literary texts on the part of scholars of different theoretical persuasions, the disparity between, let us say, a feminist and a structuralist reading (such as you will find in the first two sections of this book), all such readings are still predicated on a 'theoretical' approach to literature, as distinct, one supposes, from an 'untheoretical' approach. Instead of just getting on with reading, merely picking up a novel, play, poem, short story, and reading any of these, the theoretical reading comes to the text with a range of theoretical – theoretical because developed apparently separately from and outside of the reading and interpretation of literature – suppositions and premises in order to test these out on the seemingly innocent text. Hence the phrase 'literary theory', which acts as a form of objectified pigeonholing, however neutral the application of that term may be.

However, we feel that, at best, the phrase 'literary theory' is no longer serviceable because it is too homogeneous. At worst it becomes an Aunt Sally, something too easily identifiable for negative critique; hence, also, our rejection of the phrase. As these essays demonstrate in their rejection of the pigeon-hole, there is probably no act of academic reading today which is not already theorized in some manner, that is to say, not already informed by some discipline, body of thought, field, discourse, which is conventionally assumed to be extraneous to literary study, and extraneous to literature itself (what do psychoanalysis, feminism, Marxism, linguistics, have to do with literature? It's not our intention to answer that this question here, but you might want to think about another question: what *is* literature?[1]).

The editors and essayists in this collection reject the simple notion of all 'theory' being similar, and part of a general 'onslaught' on literature and literary value, historically determinable as part of the growth of literary studies during the last quarter-century. As we hope to demonstrate, the term 'literary theory' cannot adequately explain or determine how one reads or the means by which one interprets the literary text. At the same time, we also hope that, as a student perhaps coming to theoretical approaches with little previous experience of such methodologies, you will encounter the positive aspect of diversity in reading, in interpreting, without feeling that you are being asked to commit to some theoretical party line, or otherwise being coerced into following one; you should notice that, while there is diversity, there are also amongst the essays certain shared assumptions, as well as differences of opinion, even disagreements, concerning both methods of interpretation and the reading offered by those methods of interpretation. Often we may well be in contradiction with one another.

As a comparison, look at the readings by Mark Currie (Part I: 'Formalist Concerns') and Jessica Maynard (Part II: 'Political and Ideological Accounts') of Richard Jefferies' short story 'Snowed Up' (included in this volume, following this introduction): the former reads the story as valorizing culture over nature, in a gesture of structural inversion, while the latter reads the story as imposing the natural, yet symbolic phenomenon of the snowstorm onto culture as a conservative gesture and critique on the part of the author. Where such contradiction exists there can be *no one literary theory*, in the double sense that one model has any greater truth claim than another, and that several approaches can be gathered together, under titles such as *Practising Theory* or *Beginning Theory*. There are, however, *literary theories*, models of thought, structures of discourse, which can overlap or contrast with one another; processes which can even incorporate, or be contaminated by, ways of thinking common to theoretical discourses not their own. Let's look at one brief example.

BINARY OPPOSITIONS

So far, in this introduction we have been discussing the reasons for the title of this book. In order to explain this in relation to the essays and some of the reasons why they were written, we have been looking critically at the function of the terms *theory* and *practice*. *Theory/practice* constitutes an example of what a number of the critics term a binary opposition. You'll notice in this collection, for example, the common and quite frequent reference in many of the essays to the binary oppositions, pairings of concepts, images, ideas, figures of speech, which play an important part in the short story 'Snowed Up'. Such pairings have a history of theorization, extending back to Aristotle's *Metaphysics*, but it is Ferdinand de Saussure, the Swiss linguist (see Julian Cowley's essay in 'Formalist Concerns'), whose work in the early years of this century with such binarisms in speech (night/day, black/white, good/bad) and their relative semantic values, prior to his death in the First World War, which has subsequently come to inform the more self-aware theoretical approaches to literary criticism (that is to say, those literary-critical methodologies which are happy to admit that they are theoretical in the first place, and not disavow the theoretical impulses in their acts of reading; as you probably know quite well, what was called New Criticism never proposed an overtly theoretical model for its interpretive acts). Here we see how structural linguistics, the name given to Saussure's linguistic model, comes from a discourse outside literary criticism.

With regard to binary oppositions, and other binary pairings, when you read this collection, you will observe that the readers gathered here have not brought to their acts of reading such binarisms or pairings, but have observed these at work *in* the primary text. What all of the readers have done, in their various ways, and with their various theories in mind, is to observe how the numerous figurative and conceptual pairings and oppositions in 'Snowed Up' function within both plot and narrative. They observe also how Richard Jefferies draws the use of such binarisms from general cultural assumptions outside the field of literature, so that the semantic effect of the pairings is to replicate a cultural condition or assumption, creating a sense for the reader of verisimilitude, whereby the literary text appears to approximate the 'real world'. From common observation on the

part of those critics here who do have recourse to binary oppositions, what emerges across the essays is a sense of the complex, multi-layered patterning which structures and overdetermines
the story from various perspectives; you will, we hope and believe, see how, in different ways, the binaries operate or perform in the act of reading in order to make the narrative move
along, and make sense; in short, how the narrative structure is
articulated by such paired figures.

OVERFLOWING 'THEORY', OVERFLOWING THEORIES: CONNECTIONS AND DISJUNCTIONS

In the structuralist, narratological, psychoanalytic, feminist, and
Marxist accounts of 'Snowed Up' there occur references to binary oppositions and structures. Thus from this one detail of
the readings, it can be seen that no one 'theory' is isolated or
self-sufficient. Critical, theorized writing and reading already
overflows, exceeds the homogeneity of the term theory. Each
theory is, already, *theories*, plural within itself, as to the discourses which compose it. Ruth Robbins's feminism (the essay
in the 'Entr'acte' of this collection) and Jessica Maynard's Marxism
(in Section II) are not discrete disciplines, sealed off from other
forms of thought, as their use of binarisms shows. Similarly, Jill
Barker's psychoanalytic reading ('Formalist Concerns') nods in
the direction of feminist ideology. Furthermore, to refer to
Robbins's and Maynard's chapters once again, both writers show
how there is neither only one feminism, nor only a single Marxism, the former moving between considerations of images of
women to poststructuralist considerations, while the latter begins by defining the concept of the dialectic – a binary structure
of sorts – moving on to incorporate more recent developments
in Marxist cultural thinking. Both Maynard and Robbins acknowledge in their interpretations a history of competing and
conflicting discourses – and *theories* – within their respective
fields, Marxism and feminism; fields or theories which are, and
have been, in *practice*, in *performance*, for as long as there have
been attempts to articulate the theory of such political thought.
    Similarly, Julian Cowley's and Mark Currie's essays, both in
the first section, 'Formalist Concerns', implicitly acknowledge

the overlap between their relative structural and narratological positions. Cowley traces the development of structuralism across various disciplines from linguistics to anthropology as he brings the insights of these discourses into play in passing in his reading of 'Snowed Up', while also alluding briefly to where certain points in the reading might be taken beyond the limits of structuralism. Currie incorporates the history of narratology into his reading, acknowledging Russian formalism and the work of Jacques Derrida as intrinsic and necessary to his reading. Importantly, he also locates his reading as occurring beyond the quasi-scientific structure of conventional narratology as that had developed out of structuralism. As you will see, neither critic rests on a single theory, but relies on a range of theoretical models developed out of tensions within their respective paradigms. And from this approach what the reader becomes aware of is that the text is not some neatly unified object, but is marked to its very heart by numerous contradictions, tensions, inconsistencies, gaps in the logic. Each of the critics writing on 'Snowed Up' work to show us such gaps, such *aporia*, as the very condition of narrative itself.

Jill Barker's and John Brannigan's essays (Sections I and II respectively) are particularly convincing in demonstrating how the aporia of the narrative foreground the gaps, the silences, the elisions which occur in our culture, whether within the microculture of the family or the macro-culture of society. Again, like the other critics already mentioned, both Barker and Brannigan show us certain connections between their own theoretical assumptions and other theories such as structuralism, feminism and Marxism. Importantly, they also perform the internal historical differences of their particular discourses as they develop their readings. Barker pursues a Lacanian–psychoanalytic reading of 'Snowed Up' which acknowledges its debt, both to Freud and psychoanalytical clinical practice, and to Saussure and structuralist linguistics. John Brannigan, on the other hand, offers an overview through his reading of the development of (largely American) New Historicism, which has its roots in Marxism, the structural and poststructural genealogical theories of Michel Foucault, along with the intersection with and divergence from its British counterpart, Cultural Materialism.

To reiterate the point once more: there is, then, no such thing as theory. There are only theories at work even within what might be (mis)taken for a supposedly unified discourse. And what this of course points to is something which all the contributors gathered here would agree on, despite their theoretical, ideological, and philosophical differences, is that the development of theories is never completed, never finished. We can never close the book on literary theories; there is no final model upon which the reader can rest, assuming that model to be the truth. There is no absolutely definable feminism, any more than there is *a* Marxism or *a* New Historicism. This suggests that there may be a spirit of feminism, a spirit of Marxism, and that this is what we have to respond to in our readings; it is this spirit to which we must be responsive to and for which we must have a responsibility, *as theorized readers today*. Another name for this spirit might be hybridity. All theories are marked by contamination and hybridity, from one to the other, and throughout their historical and cultural development. As Julian Wolfreys' chapter suggests, there may even be a need to abandon eventually the terms 'theory' and 'theories' in favour of reading and thinking, but with a radically different understanding of what these words now mean. And this is suggested if only so as to move beyond the idea or desire of finding, defining, a fixed programme, a paradigm or structure which excludes other discourses and remains constant, offering the supposed truth of the text through the application of that fixed theoretical programme. One of the aims of this collection which has emerged, *en passant*, is to move beyond a fixed conception of 'theory', much as Terry Eagleton had argued, ten years before the writing of this collection, that, as academics, we needed to move beyond the confines of a limited and limiting definition of 'literature' (1983, 194–218). What the essays gathered here recognize is that a single conception of any single theory cannot work effectively in the interpretation of literature, because literature itself cannot be so simply and unproblematically defined. Each of the essays, instead of foregrounding theory, insists on the ongoing process of interpretation of – reading and thinking about – Richard Jefferies' short story, 'Snowed Up'. The writers collected here do not allow theory to dominate their acts, their performances, of reading; instead their performative readings make possible the emergence of 'theoretical', 'ideological', 'aesthetic', 'philosophical' and 'political' issues.

THE QUESTION OF CRITICAL PERFORMANCE

Which brings us back to the title, and to the term 'performance'. As we said earlier in this introduction, we rejected the
term practice'. We did so for various reasons; not least because
(1) we wanted to avoid the connotations of this being merely a
manual, a here's-how-to-do theory text; and (2) we wished to
avoid the traditional theory/practice binary. As these two points
might imply, we wanted to jettison the idea that theory was
something which implied a competence achieved by practice.
Practising a theory or theoretical reading 'habit' implies that
you can achieve a certain level of professionalism and sophistication. This may be true, but, once again, this has the danger
of returning you to a very safe activity, whereby, without ever
really becoming engaged in the issues at stake in, say, feminism
in a meaningful way, you merely go through the institutional,
academic exercise of honing your reading skills and ticking off
the texts: 'that's *Jane Eyre*, *Hamlet*, and *The Turn of the Screw*
done, now I'll do – [or 'undo' if you're 'doing' 'deconstruction']
– John Donne ['John Donne', you might say, 'undone']'.[2]

Furthermore the idea of 'practice' somehow carries with it
the implicit notion of theory as being somehow finished, as we
have already suggested; there is no further room or need for
development or change, or for new forms to arise, for new com-
binations or interactions between emergent theories. Theory is
dead; all that remains is practice or, to put it another way,
practice is the remains of theory. 'Performance', on the other
hand, suggests an act of reading which is ongoing, now, *today*,
as part of a continual process, attuned to the tensions, developments, changes within the arena of performance, and aware of
the needs of its audience. Performance does not claim to be
definitive, absolute, totalizing in its reading or interpretation,
its translation of the text. The performance of a reading suggests
that other performances are yet to happen, while the performance carries within it, and acknowledges, the traces of past performances, previous theoretical models, critical interpretations;
certainly all of the critics here are aware of, and acknowledge,
those places out of which their critical voices have emerged; no
one writing here pretends to be stating first principles.

The critical performances contained herein work with their
chosen aspects of their respective applied theories, providing

stimulating and illuminating interpretations, in order to provoke the reader into considering 'Snowed Up' from different perspectives, and to reflect on, and possibly revise, her or his own reading habits; by implication, this means that the reader will, we hope, begin to consider other texts from different perspectives, searching out new ways of translating familiar texts into exciting forms; to read boldly in ways s/he has never read before. And, finally, with the term 'performance' still in mind, we have used this slightly unconventional term as a means to break down the separation between theory and practice, even as each of the critics here has already suspended the separate frames of reference, in order to instrumentalize theories in the acts of reading, and in order to offer insights into theoretical arguments from the positions of interpretation and close reading. None of the readings here offers a total picture of a single theory; such a goal is both undesirable and impossible; however, each reading offers a partial performance of both theories and text, performing for the reader a series of versions of Richard Jefferies' *multiply overdetermined story*. (Critics use the term 'overdetermined' to indicate a text which can easily be interpreted from numerous perspectives, and which contains within in it in a highly visible manner the signs of a range of discourses, topics, issues and themes. An overdetermined text is, furthermore, not ostensibly resistant to a form of interpretation.) Each reading is as open to interpretation as is Jefferies' story itself. Even as Edie writes her diary from day to day giving the reader partial glimpses of her world, so the essays also offer the reader partial glimpses, partial performances, of Edie's snowstorm.

THEORIES READ RICHARD JEFFERIES

This collection of essays is divided up into sections, organized around an extension of the performative metaphor, hence the use of the terms 'Overture' to describe this introduction, Richard Jefferies' short story and a brief biography of Jefferies, followed by a note on the discovery of the story's manuscript, 'Entr'acte', which has the feminist essay, and 'Encore' for the final essay. After the 'Overture', the first three essays of the first section are directed largely towards formalist concerns, such as the patterning of the narrative, its structures and movements, and so on. However, these are not the only issues, nor can the critics concentrate solely on these, as though this were merely some academic exercise. The second section, coming after the 'Entr'acte', deals with the ideological and political issues which the story mediates, and it is particularly in the essays of John Brannigan and Jessica Maynard that we see the importance of acknowledging the contexts of literature, both the contexts of the period within which the story was produced and the contexts within which it is received. Between these two sections, the formalist and the political, is the feminist essay, the positioning of which is explained below in the brief discussion of Ruth Robbins's contribution. Finally, the collection closes with a lengthy analysis of various figures, images and tropes of the story which is influenced by the types of close analyses pursued by Jacques Derrida, of which more below. Its purpose is to suggest ways in which the student might read so as to move beyond the simply defined theoretical paradigm, and to escape the programme of any 'theoretical reading'. In doing so, it looks back at the function of various theoretical models used in previous essays.

FORMALIST CONCERNS

This section begins with Julian Cowley's structuralist reading of 'Snowed Up'. We have already discussed some of the implications of this and other essays in this collection in the context of theoretical interpretations, but we want to develop some of these points further in concluding this introduction to the project of reading 'Snowed Up'. Julian Cowley's condensed, allusive essay, which catches the tone of the structuralist work of Roland Barthes to which it alludes in both its brevity and spare, pseudo-scientific tone, is typical not only of Barthes but also of much early structuralist analysis. The aridity and allusion of Cowley's analysis mimics precisely the timbre of structuralist criticism; even as that analysis introduces and brings out the 'binary' oppositions of semiotic meanings which generate meaning and shows how communication is a major sphere of narrative action, it also demonstrates – through its own brevity and aridity – the limits of such criticism and directs the student forward to what will come after. This essay at once shows us the importance of structuralism to criticism today and the very reasons why criticism and 'literary theory' has subsequently moved on. The movement onward, the focus on structure and formal relationships, are all picked up in Mark Currie's essay. Narratology, Currie argues, is not merely an anachronistic theoretical mode and relation of structuralism, but is today, beyond its structuralist origins, intrinsic to 'new critical developments from deconstruction and various new historicisms' (the validity of this statement is certainly borne out by all the subsequent readings of 'Snowed Up' in this book which, however politicized and relevant to 'real lives', rely upon a narratologically inspired interpretation of many elements of the text). In doing so he focuses on, amongst other things, the moral lesson delivered by the editorial voice, something to which Julian Cowley directs us, even though the limits of structuralism do not allow him to pursue such an interpretation. Currie's analysis leads him to suggest that many of the text's rhetorical devices undermine the moral project of the text. And, as stated above, Currie leaves behind structuralism's desire for scientific objectivity and, in the face of the very unscientific strategies of literary rhetoric, performs for the reader the various structured subversions within the narrative which work against the grain of what Currie takes to be the ostensible aim of the narrative, which is to impart a moral message.

Questions of ostensible aims and subversion of those aims are important to Jill Barker's largely Lacanian reading of 'Snowed Up', although it might be said that her essay, reading as it were the unconscious of the narrative, is cynical of the possibility of unproblematic subversion and searches for signs of containment within patriarchal structures, as those very structures are themselves problematized by Edie's emergent sexuality (which is, itself, encoded in various allusive ways). In drawing on Lacan's revision of Freud through a Saussurean lens and the psychoanalytically influenced work of Julia Kristeva, Jill Barker focuses on what she discerns as the three principal themes of 'Snowed Up': (1) Edie's relationship to the symbolic structure of the Law of the Father as played out in the interplay between herself and her father, whose function, for Barker, is as a synecdochic figure for patriarchal social structures; (2) the relationship between Edie and the symbolic significance of the snow, which, through the narrative, transforms the real world into what Barker calls a 'signifying structure' (terminology which the reader will note is clearly drawn from structuralist reading practices); (3) the important manifestation of desire in language. All three themes, Barker argues, are connected to absence, to lack, as expressed through Edie's language. Issues of the gaze, sexuality and theories of the feminine are also given elucidation, as is the tension between 'girlhood' and 'womanhood' (we suggest that the reader compare the different ways in which Robbins and Barker deal with the subject of Edie's adolescence as a way of understanding both the connections and differences between theoretical positions).

ENTR'ACTE

Between the 'formalist concerns' of Cowley, Currie and Barker and the next section comes a feminist analysis of 'Snowed Up'. The tension described by Jill Barker in the last section between 'girlhood' and 'womanhood' within the context of the late Victorian period surfaces again towards the end of Ruth Robbins's essay, which conveys the importance of feminist critique, while also interrogating from a feminist perspective the nature/culture binary, so important in the patriarchal definition and containment of the 'feminine'. Robbins's essay is placed between the formalist and political sections of the book, at the margins or limits of both, in order to show how feminism cannot – and should not – be pinned down to one particular camp, but how its liminal activities, reading along the limits of the literary, and speaking often at the limits of conventional political and philosophical discourses, maintains its performative and changing conditions of articulation. Feminism is never merely an aesthetic, evaluative, academic exercise; it is also profoundly political, and it demonstrates this through the analysis of the ways in which, to quote from Terry Eagleton, 'gender and sexuality [and their representation] are central themes in literature and other sorts of discourse, and that any critical account which suppresses them is seriously defective' (1983, 209). Indeed this is something which Barker's psychoanalytic reading gestures towards but never fully develops. Furthermore, Robbins makes plain at the outset that 'feminism' as a mode of critique draws on the insights of structuralism, psychoanalysis, Marxism, and deconstruction. In doing so, she emphasizes that Edie is constructed in Man's image – in this case, Richard Jefferies' image – of woman, and, as such, is available to a feminist critique. Alongside this aesthetic–ideological interrogation, Robbins seeks to comprehend the culture which forms Edie, and the ways in which Edie either conforms to or subverts cultural assumptions about and expectations of women. Her purpose in pursuing such a reading is to suggest, as she puts it, 'motivations and methods for bringing about change'. In this essay you can see how, while there are connections and bridges between formalist and ideological issues, there may also be discernible irreconcilable gaps.

POLITICAL AND IDEOLOGICAL ACCOUNTS

The motivation to bring about cultural change is shared by Marxism. Like Ruth Robbins, Jessica Maynard discusses the nature/culture binarism with a view to comprehending the culture which constructs Edie's society, this time with direct reference to Jefferies' own writing on both London and agriculture. In looking at the ways in which Jefferies' story presents a technologically advanced society under threat, Maynard exposes the conservative project behind such an apocalyptic vision. Developing her reading from exposition of Marx and, later, Pierre Macherey, Maynard's essay illuminates the exposition by producing a reading of certain of the contexts of the narrative as they are embedded in, mediated by, and, ultimately criticized and rejected through the narrative of 'Snowed Up'. In doing so, she exposes the 'illogicality' of Jefferies' ideology as manifested in its critique of technology and its desire to terminate modernity. The political, scientific, and economic contexts of nineteenth-century culture come under attack by Jefferies' reversionist agrarianism, which attempts to naturalize the vision of the city of London. John Brannigan's New Historicist reading also touches on such contexts as it traces Jefferies' use of natural phenomena to bring about social disruption, and as it delineates its departures from Marxism early on by defining the importance of Michel Foucault's notions of power and discourse. From this it proceeds through its reading of the issues of power and discursive structures in 'Snowed Up' to draw out the internal differences between New Historicism and Cultural Materialism. In New Historicist fashion, Brannigan maps out three kinds of subversion in the text: (1) Edie's rejection of her father's chosen suitors for her hand, in favour of a forbidden suitor of her own choice; (2) the threat posed to the dominant male, patriarchal order by female desire which is connected explicitly to questions of power and economics; (3) the threat of the masses and potential mob rule in the face of social collapse. Through a reading of these figures of subversion Brannigan demonstrates how the narrative's expressions of potential subversion are ultimately contained. 'Snowed Up' is thus read in this essay for the contending power struggles and competing ideologies which are enacted in the narrative, the snow being interpreted as merely the excuse for the possibility of threats to state power. Brannigan concludes his essay by asking the reader to consider how a literary text is related to the social order out of which it emerges, and how we as readers can change our ways of thinking about the relationship between literature, history, and politics.

ENCORE

This section is called 'Encore', not merely as a continuation of the performative metaphor, but also because implied in the term is the suggestion that we always need to return again to the text, to read it again. Julian Wolfreys' contribution to the collection attempts to demonstrate how critical analysis must constantly return to its material, again and again, coming to terms with the material it translates, on the terms of that material, rather than imposing some methodology onto a particular form or narrative. In doing so it asks the reader to take a responsibility for even the most minute and seemingly insignificant of details in a narrative as a way of reading. The essay rejects the idea of a theoretical mode called deconstruction as being an interpretation of the work of Jacques Derrida or 'what Jacques Derrida does'. Instead, Wolfreys, in discussing the place of the 'literary' in Derrida's work, shows how certain of Derrida's thematic interests can be understood through a reading of 'Snowed Up', thereby introducing the reader to Derrida in the act of reading Richard Jefferies. Conversely, he shows in his reading how attention to detail in a 'Derridean' manner produces interesting insights into the articulation of the narrative structure, its literary and cultural assumptions. The reader should pay close attention to a certain 'joke' on Wolfreys' part, this being in the form of the lengthy footnote which provides an exposition of what 'deconstruction' is taken to be conventionally. In subordinating this supposedly primary material to a secondary position of a passing annotation, Wolfreys 'performs' a quasi-Derridean gesture of the kind typically taken to be 'Deconstructive'. Ultimately the purpose of this essay is to direct the student away from formulaic adherence to any camp or school of critical thought.

•

We hope, and believe, that if you are interested in the ways in which literary theories perform their acts of reading you will find that these essays illuminate, enlighten, puzzle, challenge and even, on occasions, goad. They attempt to do so in the hope that you will find new and exciting possibilities for rethinking the functions of literary criticism, to see in such activity, such play, the possibility for change in the ways we think about literature itself and, by extension, other topics. These essays demand active rather than passive readers, readers who question, instead of readers who acquiesce; the writers of these essays write in the positive affirmative spirit of critical, continuous enquiry which is carried out with 'energy, urgency and enthusiasm' (Eagleton 1983, 216). In doing so, they hope – as do we, the editors of this heterogeneous collection – that you will also be infected by such a spirit, rather than by merely seeking what others have suggested is 'Great Literature'. Richard Jefferies' stories and novels have never been considered as being of 'major importance' in the literary canon; yet, as the readings of this long neglected short story suggest through the very act of energetic and enthusiastic engagement, should someone else's unquestioned judgement of what constitutes greatness be the key to what we read and the reasons why we read it? Even the most 'minor' of texts is richly veined by the traces of our past and present cultures and beliefs. Often, such minor texts can provide fruitful sources for questioning why we read, what we read, how we read. And if we can come to question such issues, we can, through the interrogation of the relationship between literature, culture and history (as John Brannigan puts it), begin to formulate questions which seek more fundamental forms of cultural and social change.

NOTES

1. Terry Eagleton provides what is still one of the most interesting, and challenging, assessments of and answers to that question in the opening and closing chapters of his *Literary Theory: an Introduction* (1983, 1–17, 194–218). Most of the critics in this collection belong to the first generation to read Eagleton's book as undergraduates, and while many of them would not agree wholeheartedly with Eagleton's assumptions and conclusions, most have a general sympathy with Eagleton's overall project.

2. This pun – John Donne, undone – is borrowed, with apologies, from the title of Thomas Docherty's excellent book of the same name, *John Donne, undone* (London: Methuen, 1986). No criticism of Docherty's book or methodology is implied here; we've merely purloined the pun for analogous purposes.

The following is a previously unpublished short story by Richard Jefferies. There are in the manuscript illegible (or missing) words and phrases, which we have not attempted to restore, as it is undecidable, in at least one case, whether the author omitted particular words deliberately, at the end of the diary entry. It may be that Jefferies' writing has become difficult to read with time; or it may be that he chose to imitate the possible failings of Edie's handwriting. In the case of omitted words, this again is open to interpretation, and may be a mark of Jefferies' experimentation, a signal for future publication that omissions should be kept as being a sign of greater 'veracity' or 'verisimilitude', in keeping with Edie's diary. With regard to punctuation, there are some ambiguities, which we have let stand as found in the manuscript. There is no way of knowing from any available source whether Jefferies lacked consistency during the writing of this story (perhaps for reasons of health) or whether the inconsistencies are deliberate on Jefferies' part, as a means of imitating Edie's writing style in the diary form, with whatever inconsistencies may have occurred there. There is, to our knowledge, no other version of this particular manuscript. [*The Editors*]

['Edie's Avalanche: Snowed Up'[1]] 'Snowed Up: A Mistletoe Story'

RICHARD JEFFERIES

January 2nd. Papa has just given me such a splendid set of furs, I never saw anything so beautiful. I do believe they must have cost three hundred pounds. I must make a note of it, but I shall never be a good diarist, my last entry I see was a month ago. Oh dear whenever shall I reduce this giddy head of mine to

19

something like order. It was old Mr., I mean the very reverend, at least I'm not sure about his title but he is canon or something at the Cathedral who persuaded me to begin keeping a diary – he said it would help me to classify my ideas, and bring my mind into shape. Of course he put it in much grander words than that.

I shall wear the jacket to the theatre tonight, Lord Bilberton escorts me, perhaps it is not *de règle*,² but I *must* wear it, it is so pretty and so warm, and new, and I can take it off. How *can* people keep their new things a month before they try them on?

Aurelles will be mad if he sees me there with 'pantaloon' as he calls his lordship. Why are guardsmen always so nice and why have they never got ten thousand a year like Mr. Alderman Thrigg, who I believe has been lending paper money, and now I think of it I shouldn't wonder if these furs were bought with some of it. However I can't bother myself about that – a poor little girl like me has so much to think of. I wish papa would let us go to Nice as we used to instead of staying in this horrid Berkeley Square. Why – there's Lieut. Aurelles riding by again: why *does* he *always* ride by just at this time? I do believe he knows I am up here in my room overlooking the square.

I feel so wicked. I've kissed my hand to him: but I'm certain he could not see me – you can't see in at a window at that distance off, now *can* you? He is so tall and strong and noble-looking, such a contrast to wizened little Bilberton, and stout Alderman Thrigg.

A poor girl is just like a shuttlecock or a tennis ball with all these gentlemen tossing her about one to the other. It *is* laughable when I think of it to see fat Mr Thrigg jump up and open the door for me, and Lord Bilberton screwing up his face into a smile of approval (though he hates the Alderman) and Lieut. Aurelles scowling at them both, and trying oh, so hard to play chess – which he does not understand – with papa; and all just because. Well, I suppose I *am* pretty. I think papa wants to play chess with me as the queen. Lord Bilberton has immense influence with the Ministry, and papa wants to be an Ambassador, and Alderman Thrigg has mountains of gold which he made by selling green peas in the City somewhere, and papa's estate is encumbered. If guardsmen would only manage to be rich; but I'm not going to be sold exactly. We shall see!

Jan. 3rd. Phillip, I mean Mr Aurelles, did see me, and smiled, – perhaps he saw me kiss my hand too. He is a *dear* man – he is a kind of Newfoundland dog of a man. There – I shall be a poetess some day. When we came out of the theatre it was so still and quiet in the streets, almost like death itself – the snow had come down, and the carriage wheels made no noise at all. Poor Lord Bilberton – I can't call him 'Charley' as he wants me to, such an *old* thing as that: he shivered and shook, and now today he has sent round to say he'll try and come to dinner but the snow has given him such a cold. Why it is beautiful! I wish I was snowballing Aurelles. I never get any fun now I'm a woman. I'm nineteen you know. Papa wants me in the study – that's certain to be something disagreeable.

How hateful it is of gentlemen when they come to the point as they call it! We girls never care about such nonsense. It spoils life, I'm sure it does and I reflect a great deal, this always coming to the point.

They have both done it. I hate them both, ugly, old – There I've no patience with such people! Lord Bilberton spoke about it yesterday, and Mr Thrigg early this morning. Why didn't they ask *me* first, I call it an insult. I shan't marry either of them, and papa and I have had a desperate quarrel. I won't, and besides I don't see why I should; there is no hurry, and if I did I should run away with – with Mr Aurelles or *somebody*, and – and – I could cry, but I am so cross.

Papa said in his nasty cynical way that I might have which I liked, it made no difference to him. Cool! As if it made no difference to me. He said the ancient name of Audeley was in danger of disgrace – bankruptcy, or something, and either he must get a good appointment under Government, or his mortgages must be paid off. His dear Edie – me of course – would not let our house tumble down, that's not how he put it but I can't remember the fine words. And our luxuries, and horses and carriages, and the towers in the country, and I must be a heroine like Edith my namesake two hundred years ago. And he hoped I had not entangled myself with a penniless soldier –. *That* was just what I wanted.

Didn't I fly at him! Entangle myself! I wanted something to quarrel with him about. So I rushed away and left him. Why can't papa see how handsome Aurelles is?

I do hate this wearisome snow. It keeps coming down so quiet and calm, and cold, it mocks at me – it does not care a bit about *my* misery. I hope though Aurelles won't look in this evening – it would be rather awkward. I must send him a line and tell him to wait a day or two till the air is more settled in here.

Jan. 4th. I shall soon have nothing to do but keep this diary, for it's impossible to go out in this horrid snow. I've got a fire in my bedroom tonight, and am writing cosily before I retire as the books say. It's very jolly and snug here – if one only had *somebody* to chat with. I wonder if I had *somebody* here every evening I should get tired of him! I can just fancy him curled up on this rug at my feet (he raves about my little feet and little paws, and littleness altogether, and wicked black eyes and and –

but no matter). He would be on that rug like a great dog, and make love to me *so nicely* I do believe *forever*.

Lord Bilberton sleeps here tonight. I wonder how he could face the weather to get here with his poor shivering ancient body. He says Piccadilly is quite impassable with the snow, and Curzon St blocked up, and his carriage could not get through it. I believe he was carried here on a man's shoulders. I daresay he is discussing me now downstairs with papa. But I *won't*, no I won't, and if I do I'll run away.

Jan. 5th. This is snow is really something awful. Aurelles can't ride by every afternoon. Lord Bilberton can't go home. He says with his wretched attempts at gallantry that the snow is his best friend and he should like to be imprisoned forever with me – pah! Papa is fidgety and cross, for he could not get his *Morning Post* this morning, and no letters came. It will be fun if we really do get snowed up.

Alderman Thrigg has got here! He has scrambled through and over the snow and he is bigger than Falstaff was. Such a spectacle as he presented I never saw before – my hand shakes now with laughter. 'Ah' said he, 'you need not laugh Miss Audeley, I assure you it is a very serious matter. But never mind I've got here – I shall perish in company with an angel! You are the North Star – magnetic attraction you know' – and there he broke down fairly for want of poetical language and left his absurd similes unfinished.

But if it is all true that he says it really is a serious matter. No on could possibly have believed it till it happened. Thrigg has kept a memorandum of the depth of the snow. The day before yesterday it was 21 inches deep in Cornhill (some stupid place in the East I think). All the trains were delayed. The Scotch express never reached town at all, and there's no news of them, for it seems a rough wind has blown down the telegraph poles and snapped the wires. There were crowds at the station all day – waiting for the trains. The Flying Dutchman from Exeter was seven hours late: they had to dig a passage through the drifts twice – one at Bath, and again between Reading and Didcot. Yesterday it never came in at all and Thrigg says he believes it stopped on the [ ] below Bristol. That's why papa has not heard from the steward at The Towers.

It was 33 inches deep yesterday in Faringdon St., and Thrigg is quite sure that no trains will be able to get in tomorrow: because of the deep drifts – though thousands of men are at work digging. But as fast as they clear it away it fills up again. I do wish Phillip would call – I wish I had not written him that note. I shan't be able to sleep for thinking of the snow.

I never saw anything like it. It has never ceased since we came home from the theatre. Papa in his nasty way says it serves us right for attempting to reach the North Pole – its a judgment. Lord Bilberton, who sits huddled up on the sofa with three carriage-rugs wrapped round him, is half silly with fright. One minute he chatters and grins and the next asks for a prayer book. To marry such a coward – pah! not for ten coronets.

Jan. 6th. Alderman Thrigg is in despair – he declares he shall be ruined. All his vegetables coming to London from fifty different places are snowed up on the way. He is a kind of gigantic greengrocer I think – very low. Still the snow comes down steadily. There is no wind today: and it falls all the thicker and faster.

All business in the City they say is at a standstill – the traffic is stopped, and the streets buried three or four feet deep. The milkman has not been for ever so long, nor the baker, nor the postman, nor anybody else; we have had to send for everything, and the prices are going up rapidly. A pint of milk the footman managed to get for tea cost half a crown! Tomorrow the shop-people said they should not have any for 'love or money'.

After all Mr Thrigg is not so silly as Lord Bilberton. He can talk sensibly enough except when he tries to pay me stupid compliments. He seems to understand the position better than either papa, or anybody else. He says all the provisions people eat in London are brought in daily – the meat and everything else, his darling cabbages and onions included. (Fancy marrying a man who sold *onions*!) If the railway service be blocked for one week like this, all the stores will be exhausted – for they do not keep great quantities now like they used to in Joseph's time in Egypt. At least I think that was what he said. Then he burst out and looked as if he were going to cry – because he might have made his fortune (as if he were not rich enough already) at such a crisis if he could only have got his onions and potatoes in. We are all to be starved in fact.

Jan. 10th. I do believe we *shall* be starved. What do you think – we can't get a joint of meat for tomorrow's dinner! The footman and the coachman have just returned from a foraging expedition, and there's not a pound of meat to be bought – its all sold and eaten. The last leg of mutton was bought for ten pounds; and people offered thirty pounds for another in vain. Wherever *can* Phillip be?

Jan. 14th. Snowing still – nothing but snow. Troubles are coming faster and faster. All the servants have left us, except my maid Ruth Pardon. They said they could not live on flour and water, and there was nothing else in the house.

Such fun! The Alderman has been helping me in the kitchen. Bilberton is helpless. Papa who is an invalid sits and smokes and sips his port, and says he's *quite* comfortable, and shan't stir a foot.

The fire was gone out in the kitchen, and I was trying to light it, when Mr Thrigg waddled in and down he dropped on his knees. I thought he was going to pop the question instead of which he began blowing the fire up with his mouth. He puffed away till we got a good blaze, and then begged my pardon, and took off coat, and went to fetch some coals from the cellar – he said he could not work without taking his coat off. 'It's habit you know Miss Audeley. It's the memory of them old times. Ah!' and the creature actually sighed. But I think there is some good in him. At all events he showed me how to make a pudding.

I hadn't the least idea. He rolled out the dough like – like a cook, and patted it with his great fat white fingers (they are always scrupulously clean) till his diamond ring was covered with flour. He said it would be as hard as a brick for want of something – fat I think. Then he searched the kitchen, and the larder. 'You see' said he 'Miss Audeley in this 'ere crisis the first thing to do is to take stock' by which he meant to ascertain our resources. We found three apples, a lemon, some spice, about a pound of tea, – the sugar was gone; and that was all. The coal cellar was nearly empty; there was only just enough flour to complete the Alderman's dumpling (I always thought the only thing Aldermen ate was turtle soup). The beer barrels were out – the servants having nothing to do had emptied them, and the brewer could not come round to his dray.

Meanwhile the dumpling or pudding was boiling away. 'Oh dear' sighed the Alderman sitting down and panting 'After all the feasts I have been to – all the Lord Mayor's dinners, and to come to a hard dumpling! Dear me – if we only had some potatoes or cabbage or anything, and there's heaps in my warehouses – at least if the poor people have not sacked them.'

I could not help laughing though I was really hungry, and becoming anxious about Phillip; but at dinnertime it was no laughing matter. The dumpling was so hard one *could* not masticate it; and at last papa in a towering rage kicked it downstairs like a football and returned to his cigar and port.

Poor Bilberton was as cadaverous as a ghost. Mr Thrigg was very thoughtful. Presently he started up 'I'll try' he said 'I'm old and not so strong as I used to be but I'll try and bring something from my warehouses.' But when I went to let him out we could not open the door – the snow had drifted against it so high. Not to be daunted however, he got out of the first floor window and dropped onto the heap of snow. To my horror he sank up to his shoulders, and could not move. He puffed and struggled but the more he tried the worse it was, till I really feared he would be suffocated in the snow which kept drifting along.

Papa came up and they got the bellrope but he and Bilberton and I all pulled and pulled and pulled, but it was no use; poor Thrigg was so heavy. There he stuck. It was growing dark now (of course the gas had not been lit for days in the streets – luckily we always used lamps and had a can of oil left) – poor Thrigg was chilled to the bone. Papa shut the window, and laughed at him.

'Ow – ow – ow!' cried the miserable Alderman shivering, and stretching out his hand to me. 'Don't Miss Audeley – don't leave me here in the dark! Ow – ow – ow! I'm perishing with cold! Please Miss – Miss – Miss Audeley!!'

It served him right for daring to ask papa to marry me; but I couldn't see him left like that. So I put on my fur jacket and wrapped myself up well, and sat at that window in the cold room shivering, till it became dark, when I brought a lamp so that he might see a light at all events.

'Miss Audeley – Miss Audeley – ow – ow – ow!' I opened the window a little way.

'Do please throw me a bottle of port wine or I shall die with cold.'

I threw it to him as well as I could, but then he had no corkscrew, so I handed him the poker with which he knocked the neck off. I suppose the wine revived him a little for he began to say that he suffered for me – it was his devotion to me that had brought him into that horrible –

'Devotion' cried a voice I knew well, and there was Phillip in the darkness, he had been guided he told me afterwards by my lamp at the window.

I couldn't help myself I was so glad. 'Oh you dear fellow' I shouted. 'Do come in – make haste – don't step on the Alderman' – He came to the window sideways – it seems the Alderman had stepped into a place where the snow had only just drifted up, and and it was hard all round. 'So you've been forcing yourself on Miss Audeley Sir, have you' said Phillip, putting his foot on Thrigg's shoulder, and giving him a push deeper in the snow. There was a smothered 'ow! ow! ow!'

I begged and prayed Phillip to help him out, and at last he did pull him halfway up, but the Alderman was staunch; to every demand of Phillip's that he would cease to ask my hand he replied he would die first. So Phillip pushed him down again and I grew terribly frightened. I threatened to call the police if Phillip didn't help him out but he only laughed and said that there were none within miles and miles. However he pulled the Alderman up half way.

'Do please say what he wants' I cried. 'You are mistaken Mr Thrigg. I could never have you though you do make such beautiful dumplings. All my heart is Phillip's.'

The Alderman uttered a groan, but gave the promise, and Phillip hauled him in at the window. Thrigg shook himself, and went down to the kitchen fire. Phillip slipped his arm – no never mind. 'And all your heart is mine dearest' he said.

'No that it's not sir' I replied and boxed his ears. I sat by Lord Bilberton on the sofa, and talked so sweetly to him. Phillip scowled at me. Papa smoked and smoked and smoked, and sipped his port. The Alderman walked in the kitchen. About eleven o'clock papa had a fearful attack of the gout brought on by the wine and Phillip had to carry him to bed. We had no supper at all.

Presently Thrigg came up. I suppose he thought it over, and being a sensible man in the main saw how absurd it was of him to want to marry a mere slip of a child like me. He offered his hand to Phillip in a manly way, and they became fast friends from that moment. Then I altered my tactics – I addressed myself to Mr Thrigg, and I believe I soon made up to him for his burial in the snow. If we had not been so hungry, we should have been jolly enough. Some one spoke of the dumpling, and poor Phillip was so sharp set that he actually hunted about, but the rats had eaten it. We could hear them all over the house – they came up the sewer no doubt, and were made bold by starvation and cold.

Phillip told us of what had occurred out of doors. At first he said that people were merry over the snow, and played at pelting each other in crowds. Then when provisions disappeared, and all business was stopped, they seemed to grow despondent, and moped about. After a while the roughs began to plunder the houses (lucky for us they had not come yet to Berkeley Square). His regiment was called out to put down the rioting, and there were some fearful scenes in the city: but at last the snow grew so deep the horses could not charge, sinking in up to the saddle girths, and the roughs had their turn. Besides which the soldiers had no food, and very soon the troop melted away. Phillip was thirty-six hours making his way from Knightsbridge to our house. He could not get along – the drifts were so high he had to climb every step of the road.

Just before we went to bed we could hear the east wind raving again, and as we had [ ] last knob of coal every one spoke with dread of the [ ]. But I did not fear much now Phillip was with us.

Jan. 15th. 'My fingers are so numb I can hardly write: but I must do something to pass away the miserable time while Phillip is out foraging for provisions. Papa is in bed helpless. Bilberton is in bed helpless. The Alderman caught such a violent cold he too is in bed helpless, or nearly. Phillip and I are left alone – for the maid is so frightened and she is nobody. We – or rather he has broken up nearly all our chairs for fuel and has begun upon the tables. We have not tasted meat or vegetables or bread I don't know how long: except the cat – the gentlemen dined on my Persian cat. I *could* not touch it. It is terrible while Phillip is hunting for a little flour. I have twice heard the gangs of roughs go by tonight swearing most fearfully. We dare not show a light.

Jan. 17th. I am *quite* sure if papa and the Alderman do not have a little meat or soup they will die. Yet there is not a snap left in all London. Phillip has risked his life to find some ever so many times. Papa is so weak he can scarcely speak. I do believe I cried two hours last night on Phillip's shoulder. And he is fearfully thin and gaunt. What has become or will become of the poor people no one can tell. And all through a little snow – the despised snow – so fine and impalpable, yet strong enough to completely conquer our civilization. No trains can run. No ships can come up the river. No food, no light, no help. All through the weak, feeble despised flakes of snow!

Jan. 18th. Phillip has gone upon the last forlorn hope. He has previously visited every warehouse the Alderman could remember till this morning. Thrigg suddenly thought of a small grocers and green grocers shop just the other side of St. Paul's or somewhere out there, where it seems he was born. It is such a little out of the way place, it is possible there may be something up there. If not papa must die. An awful period of waiting for us.

Jan. 19th. Phillip came back about six this morning after being out all night – he was so exhausted he fell down on the floor and it was an hour before he came to himself. Fortunately although we had no food we had plenty of wine and brandy and the brandy revived him. He brought us eight tins of preserved Australian beef, and a small bag of potatoes: and how he dragged them along I can't think. If it had not been dark they would have robbed and perhaps killed him.

Oh, what a feast we had this evening – the Alderman is still eating. Phillip is asleep on the sofa. How dreadfully worn and wearied he looks: yes, he has *all* my heart. He had such a journey: the state of London is something appalling. He had to make a long detour to reach the place he wished to find. The bitter east wind drives the hard frozen snow along so swiftly that it cuts the face – it struck him like the pellets from a shotgun. The draught through the narrow portals of Temple Bar kept them clear of drift but so savagely and fiercely did the frozen grains of snow drive in his face there that he could not get by. The people are mad – at least those left are. They could not light bonfires in the huts for the wind, so they set houses on fire, and stood near to warm themselves. Some prophesied about the end of the world – but I can't write these horrid things. The bonded warehouses and spirit stores are full of drunken men who have broken in. I shudder for the poor women and children.

Coming back he heard or saw that in Trafalgar Square there was a drift against the National Gallery quite eighteen feet deep. The entrance to the Haymarket was blocked up. The wind having a clean sweep along the Thames embankment kept it clear, but the Houses of Parliament formed an obstacle against which it accumulated in immense heaps. There is a report that an iceberg is aground in the Thames. I believe Phillip was half dazed with fatigue and wandered about on his return hardly knowing where he went.

Jan. 22nd. We had such a terrible alarm last night – three or four of the roughs found us out. Thrigg says they must have smelt our cooking, by the bye, we had to chop our beautiful walnut table that used to stand in the drawing-room for fuel. Phillip had a revolver fortunately (how nice it is to have a soldier by one's side!) and he fired till they went away. But this morning about three o'clock the rats came up and ran over our beds, we all rushed about in *deshabille* and I thought we should have been gnawed to pieces, but thoughtful Phil had foreseen this attack for sometime, and opened a great tin of pepper which he flung over them. This held them at bay, but we can hear them all over the place – the sound of their sharp teeth makes me shudder at this minute.

Today papa got up for the first time and so did the Alderman. Papa thanked Phil in the great proud way he can employ when he is in his good moods, and said that we all owed our lives to him. The Alderman is always praising him. "Better than gold" he says "better than gold, courage is beyond banknotes in value." Poor Bilberton began to feel that he has cut a sorry figure, and is perpetually snuffling with his nose – a nasty habit he has whenever he is annoyed. As for little me I have lost all my spirits – Phil says I am as quiet as a dormouse – I'm afraid to look at myself in the glass, I am so pale and thin. Fancy having two invalids at once to look after, and see that they don't get into mischief – the fat Alderman and papa.

There is hope for us at last – a thick fog has come on, and the Alderman who knows everything is sure it means a thaw. However *did* this fearful storm of snow happen – no one can think: unless the Gulf Stream changed its course for a time. Certainly the houses are beginning to drip – I can hear the drops falling now. Papa says people will think this storm most extraordinary, but its nothing at all to the convulsions of nature which the geologists have shown to have once taken place.

Jan. 24th. The sun at last! The fog still lingers though: and the streets and Berkeley Square are in such a state I can't describe it – one vast ocean of slush.

Jan. 25th. We have seen a hansom cab! Positively. We regarded it as a phenomenon: something like the olive branches brought into the Ark showing that the dry land had reappeared. Mr Thrigg is closeted with papa, what for I can't imagine.

Well I'm sure, I am to be a commodity bought and sold like the Alderman's onions. He has bought me – for Phil. He has just handed me over to Phil as he would a basket of vegetables! 'Better than gold' he repeated again. 'Better than gold Mr Audeley: this is the man for your daughter Sir.' They never stopped to ask me first and even Phillip seems to take it as a matter of course that I shan't object. On the whole as a means of escaping Lord Bilberton perhaps I may as well agree. So the snow was not such a bad thing for – for Phillip. The Alderman showers his gold on Phil and me, and we are to be married in May – if ever May comes any more.

There's such a noise in the streets now – people are running about once more almost as if nothing had happened. If the sky was to fall they would forget it in ten minutes on the Stock Exchange. That's what Phil says. Certainly *I* shan't forget it. It has sobered me. I mean to settle down and be a good girl, and make Phil a first rate wife! That is if I live, my limbs are chilled to the marrow. I don't think I shall live so as to give a surprise. Mr Thrigg pays Phil's debts [   ].

The Diary ends here. It's quite possible that a lady's fright may have exaggerated matters; but it is also pretty certain that if a fall of snow four feet deep occurred in London and remained on the ground – being supplied by fresh falls – for only one week, the great city of London depending as it does upon stores brought in by rail day after day, would find itself in a very awkward position.

Richard Jefferies
Author of 'A Midnight Skate', etc.

NOTES

1. Alternative titles in the manuscript.

2. It is not *de règle*: it is not the rule, it is not customary (Fr.).

A Biography of Jefferies and a Note on the Manuscript

RICHARD JEFFERIES: A BRIEF BIOGRAPHY

David Blomfield

Richard Jefferies had a short life – 38 years – just long enough for his contemporaries to recognize him as a gifted chronicler of rural life, and too short a time for him to achieve what he most desired, recognition as a novelist of the first rank.[1] He died in penury, agonizing over the fate of his wife and children, yet ironically his family was to be well provided for from the sales of books of which neither he nor his admirers had any great hopes, an autobiographical work that was judged scarcely publishable in its time, and two children's books that even he seems to have underestimated.

Jefferies described himself as the son of a 'gentleman farmer'. This description – though misleading in that the Jefferies were hardly landed gentry – was at least partly appropriate: his father's forty-acre farm, at Coate in Wiltshire, traded consistently at a 'gentlemanly' loss.

What money there was came mostly from Jefferies' grandfather, who had been a successful printer in London, before returning to run the family bakery business in Swindon. It was he who had first acquired the farm at Coate, then handed it over to be run by his son for some thirty-four years.

Though his grandfather was said to be a man of great learning, and his father certainly had a formal classical education, Jefferies' own education was decidedly sketchy. This was partly due to his unsettled upbringing. From the age of four until he was nine – apparently because his mother found it hard to cope with more than one child at a time – he was sent to stay with her childless sister, Ellen Harrild, in Sydenham. Here he apparently attended a preparatory school. When he returned to live at Coate – the Harrilds taking on his younger sister in his place – he was sent to a succession of local schools, where he was accorded a certain respect as the son of a landowner, but received no more than a very elementary education.

Despite this somewhat disturbed childhood – not helped by the death of his eldest sister in a road accident – Jefferies seems to have evidenced no signs of resentment or reaction against his family. Indeed, apart from an understandable tension between him and his father when he was later making little progress in what seemed an unprofitable career, he seems to have been a concerned, and even devoted son. He also retained close ties with his aunt, who on her side, and to the benefit of posterity, conscientiously kept his affectionate letters.

Even his earliest letters illustrate Jefferies' clear determination to become a writer. He would practise descriptive writing, concentrating on the rural scenes that later would make his name. Interestingly, among these is a description of the use of the family home for prayer meetings. There was no church in Coate at the time. Later he writes that his father has contributed the land and £10 for building a church, and that he has also helped the Methodist meeting room over the road. So his upbringing was conventionally Christian, though there is little evidence that he was churchgoer later in life, and his wife's description of a death-bed repentance has been questioned by some of his biographers.

Jefferies' family life might have been generally conventional, but he did attempt one youthful break for freedom. At the age of sixteen, he and a cousin decided to walk to Moscow. In the event they got no further than Picardy, changed direction and tried to go to New York via Liverpool. At this point money ran out, and Jefferies returned home. It is not known what provoked this expedition, but he might have been inspired by family example: we know that his father had journeyed in America as a youth, and Jefferies' younger brother would settle there later. Whatever the reason, it was to prove a unique and uncharacteristic adventure. From then on Jefferies was notably un-interested in life overseas, and very critical of the few holidays he took abroad.

Far more important were two events in the following year. First he fell ill. There are no detailed descriptions of the illness, but it was presumably the first outbreak of the disease that would dog him throughout his life. It is now clear that this was tubercu-losis, though it was never specifically identified as such. Very little was known about it until the 1880s and no appropriate treatment was available. Fortunately, this first attack was mild and brief, and only delayed very briefly the other big event of that year, Jefferies' entry into the world of journalism.

It was as a journalist that Jefferies was to learn his trade as a writer, yet he was apparently far from being a satisfactory re-porter. Over the next few years, he worked for a number of West Country papers, but gained a reputation for covering only those events that interested him rather than those the editors told him to cover. Unsurprisingly, he was considered unreliable, yet he was not unemployable. He was decidedly good at work-ing up series of articles, especially on local and family history. As a result, his first substantial work was all in this area. He toyed with the idea of publishing these articles in book form, but only one was published, and that had to be heavily subsi-dized by himself and the family concerned.

His ambitions however were to make a mark on the national rather than the local scene – especially as his father was evi-dently sceptical of his ability to earn a living from his pen. With this in mind he began to write letters to *The Times*, presenting himself as an expert on agricultural economy, and arguing that public concern over farm workers' wages was largely misplaced. At this time his political sympathies were clearly with the Tories, and the letters not only brought him commissions from London papers, but also the opportunity to approach Disraeli with an idea for a book on 'Fortune and success in life'. Disraeli's reply was no more than diplomatically polite, but Jefferies was shrewd enough to use it as an endorsement when approaching publishers and editors. (For a comparatively quiet and unsophisticated man, Jefferies was always remarkably uninhibited in selling his talents and work to others.)

Though nothing came of either Disraeli's 'endorsement', nor of the book on fortune, it is clear that the letters to *The Times* of 1872 and 1873 were a turning-point in his career. They not only drew him to the attention of the national press, but they also gave him a role to play. He became an authority on agricultural economy. Though far from an expert in the subject, he was well equipped to play the role. His education may have been sketchy, but the most valuable legacy of his childhood was a love of the countryside, along with a knowledge of how a farm should (or perhaps should not) be run. Now this was to supply the subject matter not only for hundreds of articles on agricultural economics and rural life, but also to inform almost all his novels and his two children's books.

From 1866 to 1872, though suspected of having fathered an illegitimate child, he seems to have had little time for social life. In 1873, however, with income from a steady stream of commissioned articles in national magazines, and with the publication of a book on reporting, he could afford to marry. His choice was Jessie Bawden, a close neighbour. At first they lived with his parents at Coate, but by 1876 they had had a child and moved to Swindon. Meanwhile he would stay at times with his aunt at Sydenham to keep in contact with the magazines for which he wrote and the book publishers for whom he wished to write.

By this time he had only three books published – Reporting, one on local history and a novel, The Scarlet Shawl, which he had to subsidize himself. Although at this stage he accepted that his novels were 'too original and bold', he determined that he would not continue to pay for publication. With more courage than conviction, he continued to submit works of fiction to publishers throughout London. Initially all were rejected, but diplomatically – the publishers knew that Jefferies was beginning to make a name for himself as writer of rural non-fiction, and might soon be offering them something on which they might be able to make some money.

Jefferies did have one small success with fiction at this time. In October 1876, he persuaded the New Monthly Magazine to serialize The Rise of Maximin; Emperor of the Occident in 17 parts. Otherwise he had to be content with magazine publication of the occasional short story. Here too there were disappointments, notably in November 1876 when London Society wrote to say that 'we cannot use the Snow story you kindly sent'. This seems to be the one extant reference to 'Snowed Up'.

There is no record that Jefferies tried to place it elsewhere.

In 1877 the Jefferies moved to Surbiton, and he embarked on the most successful decade of his writing career. Here, in suburban Surrey, he wrote article after article, first on agricultural economy and then on rural life in Wiltshire. Not only did he have an inexhaustible fund of memories of his childhood in Coate, but he also was an exceptionally assiduous collector of material from newspapers and other books, which he stored in his notebooks. Hard-working, conscientious, and a fluent and stylish writer, he was a gift to magazines such as *The Livestock Journal, Landscape and Labour*, and especially the *Pall Mall Gazette*, for whom he wrote several series of articles on country life. These in turn were then published in book form by Smith, Elder who at that time owned the magazine: *The Gamekeeper at Home* (1878), *Wildlife in a Southern County* (1879) and *The Amateur Poacher* (1879) and *Hodge and his Masters* (1880).

Despite the number of articles he was now writing, and despite suffering a prolonged battle with fistula – an inflammation adjacent to the anus, now recognized as generally tubercular in origin – Jefferies was throughout this time also writing fiction. His persistence resulted in much of this being published, but none of it received the critical support he earned with his rural non-fiction. Yet among the titles were *Word Music*, and *Bevis*, his two children's books that would outsell all his other books after his death, and foreshadowed Kenneth Grahame's *Wind in the Willows*. He also wrote an autobiographical book, *The Story of my Heart*. After being rejected by several publishers this was eventually published by Longman. Charles Longman was an admirer of Jefferies, and tried for years to get him to write a book on shooting. Jefferies somehow could never get down to it. Sadly sales of the autobiography were a disaster. Still, Longman got his reward. After Jefferies' death it became, along with *Bevis*, Jefferies' best-selling book.

Jefferies never fully recovered from his illness in 1881. From then his notebooks are punctuated with references' to medicines and his lack of energy. In search of a more healthy climate, the family moved first to Brighton in 1882, then to Eltham, then to Crowborough, and finally to Goring in 1886. Even so, he remained extraordinarily productive until the last two years. There were the usual articles, and several books. During this period of ill health, Jefferies published *After London; or, Wild England*

(April 1885), possibly his most important novel (certainly one of the few still in print[2]). It provides a vision of a country submerged into barbarism with its capital in a state of economic, social and cultural collapse. Although there are few notebook entries on Jefferies' part concerning *After London*, we can see that it is at least tangentially related to 'Snowed Up', with their shared themes of great natural phenomena and a vision of a post-apocalyptic London.

Although a strange novel – Jefferies' strangest, John Fowles calls it[3] – it is by no means a cultural or literary anomaly. Jefferies is just one of a number of writers during the latter part of the century who promulgates anti-Darwinian discourses and theories of social degeneration with dire consequences, and whose narratives serve as a conservative caveat in the face of technological advance and change in both social life and contemporary discourses such as Darwin's, which were taken as either implicit or explicit challenges to the established order.[4] Amongst the writers who responded to the traces of degeneration were Hardy, Gissing, Conan Doyle, and, into the twentieth century, Conrad, Wells, Forster and Woolf.[5] Most immediately related to the Jefferies of *After London*, 'Snowed Up' and 'The Great Snow' are Edward Bulwer Lytton's *The Coming Race*, William Morris's *News from Nowhere* and Samuel Butler's *Erewhon*, as John Fowles points out in his introduction to Jefferies' novel.

Of course, with serious health problems Jefferies' pace of work could not be maintained, and with the loss of productivity came a frightening loss of income. Because of the increasing cost of medical care, as Jefferies became increasingly disabled by his disease, the family was eventually in danger of going bankrupt. Friends rallied around, among them C. P. Scott of the *Manchester Guardian*. (Jefferies seems to have turned Liberal in his last years.) A fund was set up, and The Royal Literary Fund offered £100. Jefferies, though shocked at his own rapid deterioration, resented dependence on charity. Still, he knew he had to accept it for the sake of his family. The only compensation was that at least it was recognition that his life had not been wasted, and when he died on 16 August 1887, it was in the knowledge that he had made his mark in his chosen career.

'SNOWED UP': A NOTE ON THE MANUSCRIPT AND ITS DISCOVERY

William Baker

Richard Jefferies's story, alternatively titled 'Snowed Up: A Mistletoe Story' and 'Edie's Avalanche' was part of the collection of Sir Hugh Walpole,[6] which Walpole gave to King's School, Canterbury, where it was discovered. Although there is no note of provenance with the Jefferies manuscript, it is likely that Walpole purchased it amongst his acquisitions of particularly interesting manuscripts at Sotheby's, or from the distinguished London bookseller's, Maggs, during the 1920s or early 1930s.[7] It has, since Walpole's generous donation, remained in the Walpole collection at King's School.

Although seemingly anomalous at first glance, 'Snowed Up' does not exist in isolation amongst Jefferies' output, as some of the essays below make clear through reference to Jefferies' post-apocalyptic *After London*, and other published works by Jefferies, particularly the short story 'The Great Snow'. Also, there is, in the British Library, 'untitled leaves of a manuscript numbered 4–20 written on rectos with text beginning "... snow, and much difficulty was experienced in locomotion"'.[8] Hugoe Matthews and Phyllis Treitel write of another manuscript, '[a] separate untitled MS ... which shares the same theme and common passages of text was published as 'The Great Snow' ... in *The Field* (22 Mar 1947) ... a hard-edged piece of descriptive writing with the devastation intensified and magnified by placing it in London ... commentators have seen this as an important link in the genesis of *After London*'.[9] This untitled manuscript, held by the British Library, was written in 1876, and, with 'Snowed Up: A Mistletoe Story' (also written in the same year), deals with the heavy snowfall of 1874. As Matthews and Treitel suggest, the ramifications for London being hit by natural disaster were clearly on Jefferies' mind, and serve to indicate possible origins for *After London*. Jefferies' concern with the possible social consequences of natural disaster is also explored below by Jessica Maynard, where she connects the disaster of a snowed-up London with Jefferies' grim prophesies concerning agricultural destruction and waste. As David Blomfield discusses briefly above, apocalyptic visions and social degeneration were common themes in the fiction of the 1880s and 1890s.

What is immediately curious though is the fact that the two pieces were not published in Jefferies' lifetime, and only one was subsequently published, 60 years after Jefferies' death. It is likely, however, that Jefferies did try, at least on one occasion, to have 'Snowed Up' published in *London Society*, a monthly magazine which had published other pieces by Jefferies, and was to publish 'A Midnight Skate' in December 1876. The evidence of Jefferies' submission – and rejection – comes in the form of a letter from J. Hogg, editor of *London Society*, who wrote the following to Richard Jefferies on 18 November 1876: 'I find we cannot use the "Snow" Story which you kindly sent.'[10] This is all we know of 'Snowed Up'. Its publication in this collection is its first time in print.

NOTES

1. For a full account of Jefferies' life and output, see Hugoe Matthews and Phyllis Treitel, *The Forward Life of Richard Jefferies. A Chronological Study* (Oxford: Petton Books, 1994), referred to hereafter as *FLRJ*.

2. Richard Jefferies, *After London, or Wild England* (1885), intoduced by John Fowles (Oxford: Oxford University Press, 1980). Interestingly, and as support for the claim that Jefferies' mind was running along similar lines, this edition of the novel includes, as an appendix, the other short story which deals with apocalypse, entitled 'The Great Snow' (243–8). This piece is more conventionally presented than 'Snowed Up', it having a documentary quality and much darker tone than Jefferies' other snow story.

3. Fowles, introduction, *After London* (vii–xxi), vii.

4. On Jefferies' fear of Darwinist determinism, see Jessica Maynard's chapter below.

5. On this theme see, for example, William Greenslade, *Degeneration, Culture and the Novel* (Cambridge: Cambridge University Press, 1994). Greenslade gives only passing reference to Jefferies, and this in the context of his rural writing (204).

6. Sir Hugh Walpole (1884–1941), born in New Zealand, came to England in 1889 and was educated at King's School, Canterbury, and Emmanuel College, Cambridge. As a novelist, he is most remembered for his *Herries Chronicle*, comprising *Rogue Herries* (1930), *Judith Paris* (1931), *The Fortress* (1932) and *Vanessa* (1933).

7. For more information on Walpole's collection and other interesting purchases of this time see P. H. Muir, 'Sir Hugh Walpole', in *Book Collector*, 4 (1955), 217–18; P. H. Muir, *Book Collector*, 5 (1956), 38–47; Rupert Hart Davis, *Hugh Walpole: A Biography* (London: Macmillan, 1952).

8. George Miller and Hugoe Matthews, *Richard Jefferies: A Bibliographical Study* (Aldershot: Scolar Press, 1993), D13.7.

9. *FLRJ*, 79–80.

10. J. Hogg, letter held in British Library, quoted in *FLRJ*, 79.

PART 1 FORMALIST CONCERNS

1

'Snowed Up': A Structuralist Reading

JULIAN COWLEY

'I've got a fire in my bedroom tonight, and am writing cosily before I retire as the books say' (21). Edie's diary entry for 'Jan. 4th' alludes to conventions of literary expression, to phrases that characterize the writing of fiction. The reference to what 'the books say' affirms the diary's factuality; it too is written, yet it is distinct from those completed works of imagination. Here we may see the writer writing, in a particular place, at a specific time. What could be more real?

It is the end of the day, when diaries are usually composed; it is 'Jan.', not 'Dec.' or 'Feb.'; and it is the 4th, rather than the 3rd, or the 5th. But no year is given, to ground our reading in history, and it is prudent to ask what historical authenticity, what reality is actually conveyed by the specified date. Experience may tell us that in January, in England, snow may well fall, so there is a credible relationship between the action of this story, centred on heavy precipitation, and the time of its setting. Yet it is surely essentially the case that 'Jan. 4th' acquires meaning *only* in relation to other dates, from which it is distinct, within our calendar system for indicating the passage of time.

Let us turn to that fire, keeping Edie warm as she writes. We are tacitly invited to envisage it, to imagine its comforting glow. The invitation is issued not only by Edie, but by Richard Jefferies, the author of her writing. The fire is an example of those descriptive details which add flesh to the bare bones of storytelling, and convince us that here is a substantial world. Often such details have less apparent significance than this source of heat in a story of isolating snowdrifts. The fire, then, fulfils a double function: it contributes to a set of thematic oppositions of warmth and coldness; and it adds to the solidity of the world we project as we read 'Snowed Up'. The French critic, Roland Barthes, noted how such descriptive details (to his end the more superfluous the better) deliver 'the reality effect' (Barthes 1982, 11–18). As readers, our sense of 'concrete reality' resides largely in such particulars of concocted, fictional worlds.

Our perception of concrete detail relies, Barthes suggests, upon 'the *direct* collusion of a referent and a signifier' (1982, 16). In other words, the verbal registration, whether written or spoken, of 'a fire' (signifier) leads us directly to an actual, physical fire (referent). For Barthes, a structuralist reader, immersed in the structural linguistics of Ferdinand de Saussure, 'this is what might be called the *referential illusion*' (1982, 16).

Saussure, whose theory of language provides the basis for the wide range of practices known as structuralism, denied words this seemingly natural referential status. In his *Course in General Linguistics* (1916), he proposed a model in which the verbal or graphic *sign* (for example, a word written or printed on paper), unites a phonic *signifier* (for example, the sound of a word when uttered), and a *signified* (a concept). In our case, the printed word 'fire' fuses the sound made when it is read aloud, or mentally pronounced during silent reading, and a generalized, conceptual understanding of 'fire'. The referent is excluded from this model; we have lost direct access to that actual mound of burning coals, throwing out its palpable heat. Structuralism surrenders 'the referential illusion'.

Saussure, in effect, rejected the common-sense notion that the structure of language imitates the structure of things in the world. Instead, he conceived it as a self-contained system, generating meaning according to internal relationships of difference. In the *Course*, he explains this conception by analogy to the game of chess, where 'the respective value of the pieces depends on their position on the chessboard just as each linguistic term derives its value from its opposition to all other terms'. Chess is possible because of 'the set of rules that exists before a game begins and persists after each move' (Saussure 1981, 88). Language similarly has its constant principles that underlie all meaningful instances of language use. At the same time, however, the values of meanings of the words also depend on, and emerge out of, their relationships with other words, other phrases, and so on. In Saussure's view, then, while invariant rules are the basis for variant utterances, the act of signification is essentially arbitrary.

In Barthes's analysis, descriptive details in a text do not form a bridge to the world of things, rather they signify the 'category of the real'. Structuralist approaches regard the text as a literary system, and aim to clarify how that system produces meaning. The structuralist reader attends to sets of differences within a work, or works, and identifies a structure for consideration – this might be, for instance, genre, narrative, or character. Attending to descriptive detail, Barthes sought to show how the ostensibly incidental belongs integrally to the literary system, and may be encompassed within structuralist analysis more familiarly handling, 'separating out and systematizing the main articulations of narrative' (1982, 11).

In his influential essay, 'Introduction to the Structural Analysis of Narratives', Barthes leaves no doubt as to where the emphasis falls in his study of tales and telling:

> Narrative does not show, does not imitate; the passion which may excite us in reading a novel is not that of a 'vision' (in actual fact, we do not 'see' anything). Rather it is that of meaning, that of a higher order of relation which also has its emotions, its hopes, its dangers, its triumphs. 'What takes place' in a narrative is from the referential (reality) point of view literally *nothing*; 'what happens' is language alone, the adventure of language, the unceasing celebration of its coming. (1977, 124)

It is stating the obvious, perhaps, but it goes against deeply engrained habits of reading to point out that the fire in Edie's bedroom is a linguistic phenomenon. So, indeed, is the bedroom. And so too, alas, is Edie. Even the diary, emerging before our eyes, is just an illusory entity, a linguistic knot in the web of Jefferies' storytelling. Why stop there? Richard Jefferies . . . what do those words signify . . . ?

We have jettisoned the projected world with which we began. Now let us turn to the structuralist adventure of *how* 'Snowed Up' comes to have meaning. Given that the tale is written in diary form, the organization of time, the nature of temporal relationships within it, suggests itself as a good point of departure.

The Russian Formalists stressed an important distinction between *fabula* and *sjuzet* (these terms broadly corresponding to 'story' and 'plot'), and investigated ways in which a chronological sequence of events might be modified or distorted in an act of plotting. Viktor Shklovsky's study of Sterne's *Tristram Shandy* is a classic of such analysis. Formalist work stimulated a considerable amount of subsequent structuralist investigation.

Gérard Genette made a notable contribution with *Narrative Discourse* (1980). Genette is particularly concerned here with the time of narration, and distinguishes three broad areas of classification: *order*, *duration*, and *frequency*. An analysis attending to 'order' would remark how the sequence in which events occurred stands in relation to the sequence of their narration. So, we might note how the gift of furs made by Edie's Papa is temporally subsequent to the act of persuasion which prompted Edie to keep a diary, yet those elements appear in inverse order in the telling. From this inversion, aspects of what we may read as Edie's temperament emerge. The role of recipient suits her well; it is her excitement at the gift that is registered in the opening lines. But the diary is a chore; she finds it laborious, and so, uncongenial. Reference to the reason for its composition effects a cooling of the warmth of her initial excitement. We might say that in a textual system based on the opposition of production and consumption, Edie is located toward the latter pole. That location is established in this initial instance of narrative order, and is corroborated by later instances within the tale.

Duration relates to the pace of narration. In a written account, a decade or a century might be dealt with in a few lines, while pages might be dedicated to a momentary occurrence, or to the experience of a few minutes. Such distortion is particularly characteristic of Modernist narratives, such as Virginia Woolf's *To the Lighthouse* (1927). In Jefferies' tale, it is evident that the diary entries are not of uniform length: 'Jan. 15th' is considerably shorter than 'Jan. 14th'. In this case the relative brevity of the later entry is rationalised internally: 'My fingers are so numbed I can hardly write . . .' (26). Here duration may be read as a measure of coldness, within the meaning system that proceeds from the opposition of coldness and warmth.

The length of the entry for 'Jan. 14th' also reflects the fact that the preceding entry is dated 'Jan. 10th'. A period longer

than a day has elapsed; there is catching-up to do. But the missing days produce meaning of another kind. They testify to Edie's
unreliability, to her lack of dedication to the task of writing.
This characterological evidence supports the overt testimony of
the confession: '. . . I shall never be a good diarist, my last entry
I see was a month ago. Oh dear whenever shall I reduce this
giddy head of mine to something like order' (19–20). In a textual system differentiating order and disorder, Edie veers toward
the pole of disorder. The practice of writing is presented, on the
other hand, as an agency for order. She remarks how the clergyman who advised her to keep a diary 'said it would help me to
classify my ideas, and bring my mind into shape' (20). Those
missing dates, then, register lapses into disorder.

In the light of this structure of meaning, our reading of the
'Jan. 14th' entry may be suggestively developed. It begins: 'Snowing
still – nothing but snow. Troubles are coming faster and faster'
(23). The accumulation of snow signals greater disorder, and as
a corollary the pace of troubles arriving is increased. This substantial entry may be regarded as an assertion of order against
the advent of chaos, an attempt to establish shape amid form-
lessness. To identify another system of opposition, the diary is
an accretion of the blackness of print, against the white nothing-
ness of snow, beyond the walls of the house. The terms of this
opposition are developed further within the house, in the servants'
declaration that they could not live on (white) flour and water,
and Alderman Thrigg's descent to the cellar in search of (black)
coals, with their promise of life-sustaining warmth.

Genette's third term is 'frequency', where a single event may
repeatedly be recounted in a narrative, or, alternatively, a repeated action may receive a single mention. A variant of this
notion of frequency, featuring prominently in 'Snowed Up', is
the regularity of Edie's reference to her suitors. This repeated
reference establishes a set of relationships between her character, the nature of the suitors (according to her perception), and
the situation in which she is a prize to be won, a commodity to
be purchased, or a gift to be bestowed by her father. I do not
seek to emulate here the complexity and sophistication with which
Genette reads texts. Rather, I have drawn on his terms to illustrate
the kinds of structural category that can be utilised in a structuralist
reading. The way I have used them demonstrates that numerous
systems to generate meaning are present simultaneously within

any text. So, a verbal matrix may further the story and develop character, at the same time. This is scarcely a revelation, but structuralists such as Genette, Barthes, and the Bulgarian theorist, Tzvetan Todorov, have produced subtle, rigorous and stimulating models for analysing the internal operations of that matrix.

In explaining how linguistics may provide the foundational paradigm for a structural analysis of narrative, Barthes points out that 'linguistics stops at the sentence, the last unit which it considers to fall within its scope' (1977, 82). Structuralism posits a homology, a corresponding formal organization between the sentence and the structure of more extended signifying systems, such as the textual narrative. In short, Barthes declares that 'a narrative is a long sentence', although it cannot be reduced to 'the simple sum of its sentences' (1977, 84). Just as a linguist can identify the particular order that constitutes a sentence, and can analyse how that order produces meaning, so a structuralist reader can attend to the arrangement of narrative elements, and to the generation of meaning through that ordering. It is evident that structural analysis can elucidate the combination of elements involved in a narrative's unfolding along its horizontal axis (in structuralist terminology, derived from Saussure, the syntagmatic axis).

Barthes takes pains to point out that 'to understand a narrative is not merely to follow the unfolding of the story, it is also to recognize its construction in "storeys", to project the horizontal concatenations of the narrative "thread" on to an implicitly vertical axis' (1977, 87). Reading is not just a matter of moving from one word to the next, but crucially involves movement across levels of meaning. The vertical (paradigmatic) axis is vital to the generation of meaning, which is never simply the culmination of a simple, horizontal thrust.

I have suggested that a number of binary oppositions are set up on the vertical axis of 'Snowed Up': warmth/coldness, order/disorder, blackness/whiteness. Others may readily be added: wealth/poverty, fatness/thinness, age/youth, mobility/immobility, and so on. The meaning of Edie, of her diary, and of the events it records may be seen to arise from these minor meaning systems; in keeping with Saussure's teachings, it proceeds from internal differentiation, rather than through reference to external events or circumstances.

We need, then to recognize 'storeys' within our story, but it is important not to confuse these with depth, of the kind familiarly associated with character defined as a discrete entity, with a psychological dimension. Structuralism approaches characters not as distinct individuals, but as components of a system, or in terms of relationships. In analysing narratives we are not confronted with flesh-and-blood beings; rather, as Barthes points out, we are faced with 'paper beings' (1977, 111). Indeed, it is appropriate to structuralist reading to drop the notion of 'beings', and to examine characters as participants. They participate in what Barthes calls 'a sphere of actions'. This is to be understood not in terms of 'trifling acts', but of major narrative articulations such as desire, communication, or struggle (1977, 107).

This notion of spheres of actions is indebted to work performed, during the 1920s, by the formalist Vladimir Propp. He took a sizeable sample of Russian folk-tales, and set out to isolate their common features, to discover the invariant model underlying the variations constituting a diverse, yet identifiably related, range of stories. Propp identified thirty one 'functions' within the invariant model, with 'function' conceived as 'an act of a character, defined from the point of view of its significance for the course of the action' (Scholes 1974, 62). These functions are not tied to particular characters, yet they form the fundamental components of the tales; they are limited in number, and while not all occur in every tale, the sequence of their appearance is unchanging. This disclosure provided a vital, pioneering example for later structuralist study of narrative.

In addition to functions, Propp identified seven 'spheres of action' within the folk-tales. These are basically roles performed in the realisation of each and every narrative. In Propp's case they are: villain; donor; helper; princess and father; dispatcher; hero; and false hero (Scholes 1974, 65). Importantly, role was not of necessity identical with one specific character; a character might take more than one role; one role might be performed by more than one character. As with the structuralists, a certain level of abstraction is crucial to identification of the basic terms of analysis.

It would be possible to apply Propp's spheres of action to 'Snowed Up', but he appears here as a precursor to Barthes, and what follows will look more broadly at how Jefferies' characters participate in communication, as one of the major spheres of action (in Barthes's sense) of the story. It will soon become apparent that a number of the minor meaning systems referred to already can be subsumed within this sphere.

Communication assumes a message, a sender and a receiver. It also requires a medium to bridge the gap and convey the message, and a capacity, shared by both the interested parties, to understand what the message says. At the end of 'Snowed Up', an editorial voice enters, having tacitly framed Edie's narra-- tive from the start, to draw a lesson from it. This act of overt communication provides a new focus for local instances of meaning generated throughout the tale. The conclusion highlights how snow, rendering the railway immobile, constituting a major break- down between sender and receiver (in this case of goods), fore- grounds a recurrent structural configuration of the story. It is notable that the editor takes for granted a shared interpretative competence with his reader, a kind of understanding that is distinctly male-gendered; Edie may have exaggerated things, but the editor and reader, more detachedly the donor and receiver of 'Snowed Up', may communicate none the less as reasonable beings. Structuralism alerts us to the fact that the editor and his projected reader are in fact produced by the text, rather than producers of it; the addresser and his assumed addressee are poles of a relationship established within, not beyond the liter- ary system. As Barthes puts it, 'the signs of the narrator are immanent to the narrative' (1977, 111).

Edie, as diarist, is, in a sense, both sender and receiver, al- though an implied reader can be detected in the text, who is other than its 'author'. The message may be read as the need for order as opposed to her habitual disorder, with the black print, as mentioned before, accumulating sense against the blan- ket of snow that conceals information under uniform whiteness. More pressingly, perhaps, the message is affirmation of a sub- ject position for Edie, engaged as an 'I' in the act of writing, in opposition to the object role in which she is cast throughout the story – notably, as a prize to be won, or a gift to be be- stowed. Indeed, while being realized in the text as both sender and receiver, it can equally be argued that Edie is the message, in that she is regularly conceived as this object of exchange between her father and her suitors.

The category 'communication' clearly accommodates that of 'exchange', which we might differentiate as having a more overtly material basis. It also draws into its sphere the classification 'desire', which often figures as the dynamic or motive force evoked in the communicative act. For example, the diary opens with reference to a set of furs, Edie being the recipient, her father the donor. It is a gift, yet the furs are clearly given in expectation of a reciprocal giving; for example, of love, or allegiance, or obedience. The object of Edie's desire, the furs, once attained, enhances her sense of a self that might be perceived as the *actual* object of desire. This leads us into complex areas of psychoanalytic reading, so let us return to the significations of material exchange that generate a structure of meaning in 'Snowed Up'.

Papa, being a law-abiding citizen, aware of the economic rules governing exchange in capitalist society, has paid a substantial amount of money for the furs. Edie speculates that some of that money might have been borrowed from Alderman Thrigg, her suitor who, she believes, 'has been lending paper money' (20). The Alderman 'has mountains of gold which he made by selling green peas' (20). In our structuralist analysis, the gold and peas do not refer to actual gold and peas; rather they signify a communicative action, where seller and purchaser assume the roles of sender and receiver, and the coins and the vegetables are messages sent through the medium of commercial transaction. The Alderman signifies 'wealth' on the text's paradigmatic axis, while 'poverty' (its binary opposite) is signified by Lieutenant Aurelles, a penniless soldier.

Thrigg and Lord Bilberton make a formal approach to Edie's Papa, as rivals asking him to give her away as their bride. Thrigg's wealth is the obvious token of exchange in his negotiation, while Bilberton 'has immense influence with the Ministry' which might enable Papa to become an Ambassador. Again, wealth and poverty are the terms within which meaning arises, as Papa fears bankruptcy unless a good deal might be struck using Edie as coin to buy social advantage. It is appropriate to note here that Claude Lévi-Strauss, a prominent champion of structuralist methodologies, used just this equation of woman and money (with language as a shared third term) in his extensive anthropological writing on systems of kinship and marriage regulations.

The 'formal' and the 'informal' provide another pair of terms constituting our sphere of communication. Edie, referring to the soldier, her favoured suitor, has to correct herself, rather coyly, when informality sneaks in to expose her desire: 'Phillip, I mean Mr Aurelles, did see me, and smiled, – perhaps he saw me kiss

my hand too' (20). This transgressive, non-verbal act of communication between lovers is set in opposition to the con-
tractual approach to marriage assumed by the other suitors. Yet
while Phillip must still be distanced as Mr. Aurelles, Lord
Bilberton's efforts to establish informal contact with Edie are
rebuffed: 'I can't call him "Charley" as he wants me to, such an
old thing as that' (20–1).

Age is a key factor in the story's communicative relationships:
Edie and Aurelles are young; Thrigg, Papa and Lord Bilberton
are old. Philip's youth and good looks clearly differentiate him
from the other men. They also serve to constitute him as 'hero',
who (in accordance with Propp's scheme) might be seen as engaged in a form of quest to win the hand of the tale's 'princess'. In other words, he is mobile or dynamic, in contrast to
the immobility or stasis of the older men. That immobility is
graphically rendered when Alderman Thrigg, weighed down by
his bulk, gets stuck in a drift, until rescued by the Lieutenant.
Aurelles's energy can be read as a model of communicative efficiency, of the effective delivery of the message, in contrast to
the inefficiency of the older competitors. His competence in action is rewarded when he is granted permission to marry Edie.

Early in the story Aurelles is seen to fall short when he assumes the formal approach to courtship. He is presented playing chess with Papa, but Edie tells us that he does not understand
the game (20). I remarked earlier that the editor who concludes
'Snowed Up' assumes in his reader a shared level of competence
in the game of interpretation. Here the chess-game highlights a
lack of equivalence between the father's competence and that of
the suitor. Underlying Saussure's linguistic theory is a tripartite
distinction between *langage*, which 'includes the entire human
potential for speech', *langue*, which is 'the language-system which
each of us uses to generate discourse that is intelligible to others',
and *parole* , the 'individual utterance' (Scholes 1974, 14). In
this context, we might say that *langage* is analogous to the human
capacity for playing games, *langue* to the rules of chess, and
parole to a particular game, or to moves within it. Not understanding the rules of chess, Aurelles is deprived of the capacity
to participate meaningfully. By analogy, he is excluded, on account of his social inferiority (gauged in terms of wealth), from
the communication game that would allow him to speak directly with Papa, and consequently his message to the father of

the 'princess' has to be transmitted as action, as accomplishment of the heroic deed.

Edie declares: 'I think papa wants to play chess with me as the queen.' There are sets of rules which locate her as a character, and determine her relationships with other characters. Another analogy occurs to her: 'A poor girl is just like a shuttlecock or a tennis ball with all these gentlemen tossing her about one to the other' (20). Here, as elsewhere in the story, the adjective 'poor' is used ambivalently, inviting sympathy, but also registering powerlessness, as in the binary opposition of wealth and poverty. The racquet games mentioned may be read as models of a communicative situation in which sender and receiver roles are assumed alternately by both players, with the ball or shuttlecock a message, with very limited informational input, caught up in a self-referring feedback loop.[1]

Against such formal games, Edie suggests another kind of play: 'I wish I was snowballing Aurelles' (21). The snowball replaces the tennis ball in an informal and far less closely regulated game; one, accordingly, identified with children rather than adults. Within the binary terms 'age' and 'youth', Edie is held in an uneasy tension, and in this case we can see how her subjectivity is formed in an ongoing oscillation between maturity and immaturity. These terms combine the age/youth distinction with that of formality and informality. Snowballing signifies pleasure of an ostensibly childish kind. It contrasts sharply with the obligation Edie faces, of seeing her father in his study: 'that's certain to be something disagreeable' (21).

Barthes has observed that 'many narratives ... set two adversaries in conflict over some stake'. He goes on to say that this is 'all the more interesting in that it relates narrative to the structures of certain (very modern) games in which two equal opponents try to gain possession of an object put into circulation by a referee'. And he adds that 'there is nothing surprising in this if one is willing to allow that a game, being a language, depends upon the same symbolic structure as is to be found in language and narrative'. He concludes, with a flourish, that 'a game too is a sentence' (Barthes 1977, 108–9). This bold assertion might seem to push structuralism's claims rather too far, but it does help to draw together certain of the narrative components that form 'Snowed Up'.

Immediately after displaying relish at the prospect of snowballing,

Edie compounds her disgruntlement at the prospect of a meeting
with her father with the outburst: 'How hateful it is of gentlemen
when they will come to the point as they call it! We girls never
care about such nonsense. It spoils life, I'm sure it does and I
reflect a great deal, this always coming to the point' (21). The
language of men, then, is directed towards specific goals, and
ideally it follows a straight line to reach the culminating point.
In Barthes's terms, the participant in the game strives 'to gain
possession of an object'. Snowballing is not purposeful in this
way; although she cites Aurelles as her target, Edie is suggesting
a less straightforward pursuit of her goal. In her game, the prize
is not won directly but seduced through more devious means.
Her writing, similarly, while serving the overt goal of order, is
in reality an erratic performance, full of digressions and diversions.

Coming to the point is presented as the gentleman's way, and
the means for it is a set of conventions that produces the gentleman's agreement. Edie sides instead with nonsense, being a 'girl'
and so excluded from such an agreement. Casting this position
in a positive light, she declares, 'I shall be a poetess some day'
(20). Art, conceived as acts of imagination, is set up in opposition to the workaday factuality of men doing business. Coming
to the point might appear an efficient communicative act, but it
may also be perceived as the extinction of desire. Desire, once
satisfied, ceases to exist, and Edie, seeking location on the side
of pleasure rather than that of non-pleasure, favours the hero's
quest over the business deal. The tale supports this inclination,
for, as I have said, Phillip's actions achieve results which the
direct address of the men of social power does not.

The dashing hero is elevated above the man of commerce in
Edie's esteem: '(Fancy marrying a man who sold *onions*!)'(23).
None the less Thrigg is 'not so silly as Lord Bilberton' (23). The
Alderman communicates well enough, and demonstrates a high
level of competence in interpreting the situation in which the
characters find themselves: 'He can talk sensibly enough except
when he tries to pay me stupid compliments. He seems to understand the position better than either papa, or anybody else' (23).
Note that the *payment* of compliments is not successful; the
anticipated purchase is not completed. Comparably, Thrigg's re-
sourcefulness is channelled into the making of a dumpling, which,
while it might resemble a large, rather grubby snowball, brings not
pleasure but disappointment, as it proves inedible. A major part

of the problem is that this older man does not share the code in which Edie's messages are sent. Their resources for comprehension might overlap, but they are by no means identical. Aurelles, on the other hand, similarly powerless in economic and institutional terms, shares far more with the young woman.

But thus to align Edie and Aurelles is too simple. The aspiration towards being a poetess arises from a striking simile in which the soldier is compared to a Newfoundland dog. Suddenly the questing hero is cast as a dumb yet loyal companion: 'I can just fancy him curled up on this rug at my feet (he raves about my little feet and little paws, and littleness altogether, and wicked black eyes and and – but no matter). He would be on that rug like a great dog, and make love to me *so nicely* I do believe *forever*' (21–2). Evidently, Aurelles frames her as a lapdog. Both aim for positions of dominance within the relationship, and so assign the other to positions of subordination. The opposition of littleness and greatness obviously adds to this tension.

The rescue that Aurelles performs involves dragging himself through the snow in classic Newfoundland-dog fashion. Still, the gift of Edie Audeley is granted to him, along with presents of money from the grateful Thrigg. I have mentioned that in Propp's model of the spheres of action in narrative, a single role could be executed by more than one character. This is well illustrated here, for both Mr Audeley and Alderman Thrigg constitute the donor at this point in Edie's narrative. Marriage will follow, but the canine comparisons suggest that the relationship will not be unalloyed harmony; rather it will involve struggles for power concordant with other relational structures produced in the story.

At the end of Edie's account, 'people are rushing about once more almost as if nothing had happened' (29). The scene of animation shows a resumption of normality in the sphere of communication. Earlier the breakdown is presented in terms of failing technologies: 'All the trains were delayed. The Scotch express never reached town at all, and there's no news of them, for it seems a rough wind has blown down the telegraph poles and snapped the wires. There were crowds at the station all day – waiting for the trains' (22). Immobility and silence come together with the fall of snow. The thaw brings rushing crowds, and 'such a noise in the streets' (29).

Crowds have not always appeared so benign in this narrative.

At the height of the crisis they appear as an unruly and dangerous mob, whose significance springs not only from the familiar
opposition of order and disorder, but also from the differentiation of 'us' and 'them' which points to distinctions of class within
English society, and to the relationships existing between the
classes. To pursue that issue would draw us into political or
ideological analysis, of the kind exemplified by Marxist criticism.[2]

In this treatment of 'Snowed Up', I have been conscious of
preserving, where convenient, the referential illusion, attributing
thoughts and feelings to the 'paper beings', before restoring a
critical distance, so as to isolate and identify the components of
the integrated systems that generate the story's meaning. Structuralism has been criticized for being too abstract, technical,
and consequently lifeless. This view has been encouraged by a
proclivity to highly specialized vocabulary, or, to put it more
negatively, technical jargon. I have purposefully avoided such
terminology, but it should be said that the vocabularies developed by critics such as Genette and Todorov have served a useful function in compelling reflection upon what has often been
taken for granted, or simply ignored, in literary study.

Structuralism has also been criticized for its exclusion of the
historical dimension of its object of study. There is some justification for this view. In his comparison of language and chess,
Saussure stressed that 'in chess, each move is absolutely distinct
from the preceding and the subsequent equilibrium. The change
effected belongs to neither state: only states matter' (Saussure
1981, 89). An analytical practice derived from this may provide
insights into relationships at a given moment in time (synchronic
analysis), but it will neglect matters of development or evolution (diachronic analysis). In this chapter, I have not sought to
produce a rigorous structuralist reading of Jefferies' story, but
to explain some of the basic assumptions of the approach, while
indicating how it can furnish tools for literary analysis, focusing the reader's attention on aspects of the text which might
otherwise have remained concealed.

I have paid particular attention to the area of communication, in part because, as Barthes remarked, 'narrative as object
is the point of a communication: there is a donor of the narrative and a peceiver of the narrative' (1977, 109). Each of us, as
we read it, becomes the receiver of 'Snowed Up'; common sense
dictates that Richard Jefferies is its donor. But early on I sug-

gested that we might question why the author's name should be exempt from our revised understanding of signification. For the structuralist reader, the play of signs (or *semiosis*, from the Greek word for sign) is endless. Heated debate has been generated by Barthes's essay 'The Death of the Author', where he provocatively states: 'To give a text an Author is to impose a limit on that text, to furnish it with a final signified, to close the writing' (Barthes 1977, 147). We have accepted that Edie is a product of her fictional diary, rather than its producer; should we take this further step and declare Richard Jefferies a product of the text which concludes with his name? Is it possible to uphold our rejection of the 'referential illusion' without taking this step and embracing unequivocally the endlessness of *semiosis*?

In the *Course*, Saussure suggested that while language is the most important of our systems of signs, it is one among many that constitute our social world. He proposed 'a science that studies the life of signs within society' (Saussure 1987, 16), which he called *semiology*. The anthropological work of Lévi-Strauss was important in developing this science, also known as *semiotics*, but it was with Barthes that it reached its apogee. Fashion, food, shopping, wrestling; he took the whole gamut of social practices and read them as signs. In doing so, his overriding concern was to remove the gloss of the 'natural' from our social environment, an environment arrived at inexorably through historical processes. This naturalization, in effect, unquestioning acceptance of the world as we find it, was the focus for a series of studies he called *Mythologies*. Such semiological investigation goes a long way to meet the charge that structuralism neglects history. It can also teach us that to read practices as signs does not in fact dematerialize those practices; the world does not dissolve just because we take language to be the key to reading it. So Richard Jefferies remains the donor; for 'Richard Jefferies' authored Edie's story, even if we dispel the referential illusion of the Author. And so the snow begins to melt, and we may admit the noise once more. . . .

NOTES

1. The badminton analogy was later used, comparably but with more trenchant effect, by Henry James in *What Maisie Knew* (1897),

where it casts light upon the situation of a child caught between divorced parents.

2. For an example of this kind of analysis, see Jessica Maynard's Marxist interpretation and John Brannigan's New Historicist reading in this collection. From another political perspective, that of feminism, see also Ruth Robbins's chapter, below.

2

Snow Me Again:
A Poststructuralist
Narratology of 'Snowed Up'

MARK CURRIE

Narratology is not usually seen as a poststructuralist critical approach. It is perceived as a structuralist enterprise, a phenomenon of the 1960s, when systematic and scientific approaches to the analysis of narrative were still in fashion. Now, of course, the authority of scientific method is considerably diminished in criticism after two decades of assault from poststructuralist theory and renewed interest in politics and history. Narratology undoubtedly flourished in criticism which was committed to formalist close reading, which put aside sociological and historical questions in order to focus on the text itself, on the technical operations of a narrative. Structuralist narratology developed an impressive terminology for the description of technique, analysing narratives in the way that a linguist would analyse a sentence; a rigorously analytical language sure to offend any critic still concerned with pre-critical issues like characters, literary value or emotional response.

This perception of narratology as a timely but now outmoded science is an extremely reductive version of recent intellectual history. I would see the evolution of narratology as a more incremental process, not an evolution leading towards anything in particular, but an increasing stockpile of available critical terms and models which can be and are adapted to non-formalist critical approaches. Those who speak of the death of narratology usually work with a model of the linear displacement of one critical paradigm by another, but neither the rise nor the fall of narratology could be adequately historicized in this way. Structuralist narratology could not have advanced the study of narrative in the spectacular way that it did if it had not been for its formalist progenitors in the European and Anglo-American traditions. Notably, the study of narrative point of view in American New Criticism, the critiques of realism in Russian Formalism or the analysis of speech and thought presentation in British stylistics were all places in which the systematic analysis of narrative was advanced either before or alongside structuralist approaches. It is also true to say that the most rigorous analytical concepts of structuralist narratology did not really impact on university literary studies until much later, and here I am thinking of certain key publications which synthesized narratological method for the Anglo-American tradition; works such as Leech and Short's *Style in Fiction* (1981) and Shlomith Rimmon-Kenan's *Narrative Fiction* (1983). Whatever revolutionary moment structuralist narratology may have inhabited in its heyday in the 1960s, the impact of narratological method was certainly greater in literary studies at large in the 1980s, when it was operating alongside new critical developments from deconstruction and various new historicisms, cultural materialism and rejuvenated Marxisms (see John Brannigan and Jessica Maynard, below). Rather than a model of linear displacement, it would be more realistic to see the new criticisms of the 1980s and 1990s as approaches which were enabled and resourced by narratology; in short, as the products and not the successors of narratology.

It wouldn't be possible to reflect the influence of narratology in contemporary criticism here, but it is worthwhile identifying some of the poststructuralist tenets that have given narratology a new emphasis, tenets which are at work in the reading presented here. One important change in emphasis is in the account poststructuralist theory offers of the relationship between a critical discourse and its literary object. The conviction of most early structuralist readings was that the object–text had inherent structural properties which could be described with scientific objectivity by the reading (see Julian Cowley's chapter, above).

The poststructuralist tends to work from the view that the object–text can be construed in an almost infinite number of ways, none of which is more faithful to the text itself than any other. In other words, where the structuralist was concerned with *structure*, the poststructuralist is concerned with *structuration*, or the ways in which the text is constructed by criticism. This change goes hand in hand with the idea that a critical work should not maintain any pretence to objectivity, but must become more honest about its own role in projecting structure on to the literary work: that the reading must be reflexive and self-conscious of its own textuality, its own values and its own motivations (in order to compare precisely the two kinds of reading being described here, compare and contrast the reading of Julian Cowley with that of Julian Wolfreys). This is not to say that the critic is absolutely unconstrained by the text in hand, but that very often the reading will not co-operate with the text, or will attempt to find in the text unconscious and unintended meanings which go against the grain of what common sense would tell us the text means. Perhaps the most pertinent difference between structuralism and poststructuralism is in the attitude to the binary opposition as the basis of meaning or a structural principle for narrative. Structuralist linguists perhaps overstated the importance of the binary opposition as a meaning generating unit, while narratologists were sometimes obsessive about the structural role of opposites in narrative. The poststructuralist critic often shares this obsession but tends to view the opposition as an unstable basis for meaning and as a place where values and hidden ideologies are inscribed. As this reading will illustrate, the poststructuralist narratologist sees the binary opposition above all as a hierarchy, or as a kind of violence, rather than an innocent dyad, often as the source of aporia or doubt, rather than the stable basis of intelligibility. From this point of view, narratives which seemed to yield familiar and unproblematic meanings have been rendered more complex and indeterminate in meaning by the poststructuralist critic.

'Snowed Up' is constructed around a very familiar narrative proposition: a young woman in the marriage market rejects the rich, fat, and ugly suitors approved by her father in favour of someone more lean and handsome. It is also constructed as a fable teaching us that courage is 'better than gold', so that as the penniless Phillip wins out over Bilberton and Thrigg, the value of gold as a credential for marriage is questioned. The story has to remove obstacles to Edie's union with Phillip by subverting the system of values which, at the start of the story, make him less eligible than his wealthy competitors, namely the whole structure of urban bourgeois life and its commercial basis. The narrative function of snow is that it momentarily displaces the commercial basis of marriage with a system of values which derive more directly from nature, where courage and strength are at a premium.

Fables of this kind do not often remain in control of their moral message, in that there are aspects of the narrative which seem to work against its apparent moral aims. An obvious place to begin in this case is at the end, where Phillip and Edie are showered with gold by Alderman Thrigg in a gratuitous act of happy resolution. But the dichotomy for Edie on which the story turns – ugly-but-rich vs. handsome-but-poor – is destroyed by this ending. If Phillip is to have any value beyond being a good man to have around in a snowstorm, his qualities must some-how be applicable to life after the thaw. Showering him with money is not a way of endorsing courage over gold, but of trans-lating one system of values into the other, acknowledging that the only way to confirm the value of courage is through its exchange value with gold, thereby using the values which are the object of the narrative's critique as the standard by which the supposedly superior value of courage is measured. From Edie's point of view, the gold ensures that she will not have to live the consequences of her preference. She has the best of both worlds, but this ending destroys the opposition which formed the narra-tive's basic proposition.

A traditional narratology of the fable would usually collect aspects of narrative technique which were part of the rhetoric of the moral lesson; in so doing it would marshal evidence for the co-operation of narrative technique and moral aims. My critical stance here is that, like the ending of the story, many of the text's rhetorical devices work against its moral project to the point where it cannot be claimed to have a morally coherent position at all. To demonstrate this, I will first analyse aspects of the narrative which work in the service of some moral project and then examine those which subvert it.

Most narratives, in the first or third person, are written after the event. They look back on the events they describe from a position of teleological retrospect, that is, they know which as-pects of the story are of significance in the light of their outcome. Even when a narrator pretends to be telling it as it happened, withholding subsequent events, the narrative speech act is structurally retrospective, written from beyond the end of the plot sequence. The perspective of a diary is different. Each entry is retrospective, but written without knowledge of the next entry. The speech act is not unified in time; like any narrative it relates events bit by bit, but knowing them only in this fractured chronological perspective. One simple effect of this is a state of suspense as to whether Edie herself survives the snowstorm, a question which would not arise in a conventional first-person narrative where the narrator must survive events in order to recount them. A more significant effect is what is sometimes called retrospective irony, where we realize the significance of some aspect of the narrative only in the light of an outcome of which we were ignorant on first reading. Edie, for example, hates the snow through most of her ordeal. The positive function of snow in revealing Phillip's courage is apparent only in retrospect, so that her periodic moans about the weather acquire ironic force for a second reading. This is a tested didactic technique, preventing ironies from working against Edie until her narrative is complete. It is part of a general strategy of the diary to yoke a reader to Edie's evolving perspective, positioning the reader as a fellow traveller through events, keeping the distance between her perspective and ours to a minimum along with ironies that might come between us. It is often part of the rhetoric of a fable that perspective on the significance of events comes only at the last moment, as revelation.

The diary form yokes the reader to Edie's perspective by excluding any external viewpoint from which events are known or judgements made. There is of course one exception, in the quasi-authorial comment which ends the narrative. There are two obvious functions of this intervention. (1) It seems to miss the point altogether of Edie's journey through the snowstorm, resisting any moral summary in favour of a bland assessment of the diary as a meteorological record. On the assumption that an author should never preach, this is a way of distancing the author from the moral project of the story. It is an author manipulating a reader into thinking that no manipulation has occurred, that our judgements have been in direct response to Edie and not narratologically controlled. (2) It provides a sexist contrast between the giddy exaggerations of a lady's 'fright' and the sobriety of an authorial voice. The abstracted, rational language, the hint of scientific assessment and the understated hypothesis that London would 'find itself in a very awkward position' (29), are all signs of narrative objectivity and reliability which contrast with Edie's scatty unreliability. Both functions of this intervention help to confirm the impression of unmediated access to Edie's inner thoughts and aim to disclaim her fictionality.

I will return to the question of Edie's disclaimed fictionality shortly. For the moment I want to dwell on the importance of Edie's unreliability as a narrator. The pseudo-author who ends the narrative is not the only man in the story who contrasts with Edie's unreliable perspective. The diary is framed by that contrast. Unlike the closing paragraph, the opening one yields the insight from Edie's perspective:

> It was old Mr., I mean the very reverend, at least I'm not sure about his title but he is canon or something at the Cathedral who persuaded me to begin keeping a diary – he said it would help me to classify my ideas, and bring my mind into shape. Of course he put it in much grander words than that. (20)

In the background, presiding over the diary's inception is a patriarch upholding the values of mental classification and shape, a religious man who sees Edie's diary as discipline for her giddy head. Within the fable we are therefore offered two alternative ways of looking at Edie's diary: (1) as a way of giving shape to disordered thoughts, and (2) as an historical or meteorological documentary. Here the text is articulating different possibilities of reading, both of which effectively ignore the moral aspect of her dichotomy and locate the value of the text elsewhere. But the unreliability of Edie's account of events is highlighted by both of these perspectives. In the case of the opening paragraph, Edie's unreliability is signalled immediately by her inability to report basic information about the title of old Mr somebody at the Cathedral; her unreliability as a narrator obscures even the report of his perspective on her unreliability, so that the grand words which evangelized her on behalf of classification and order are lost, imaginable only through the failed memory of her reported speech.

Why frame Edie's story in these declarations of her unreliability? I have already suggested an answer to this question: that it is part of the moral rhetoric of the story to distance the author

from Edie's narrative, and that part of this strategy is to auth-
enticate the diary as Edie's own discourse, free from authorial
control. This distance ensures that readers will respond to Edie
as a psychological entity, as if eavesdropping on some private
discourse. This way our response to Edie as a character will
entail response to the moral project of the story without assign-
ing the manipulation of that response to an author other than
Edie. The absence of teleological retrospect in the diary form
assists in the creation of this authentic impression since its function
is not only to produce a more strictly chronological sequencing
but to make that sequence a chronology of psychological states.
Because our only access to events is through Edie's perspective,
and because that perspective is not unified but constantly changing
in response to events, the experience of reading the diary is of
journeying through a variety of frames of mind. Though we are
structurally yoked to Edie, without much external perspective
or additional information, our judgement of Edie's psychology
is nevertheless likely to change from the beginning of the story
to the end. At the start, our sympathy for Edie is at its lowest,
where the unreliability of her self-commentary is most obvious.
When Edie declares that 'a poor little girl like me has so much
to think of' (20), or describes Berkeley Square as 'this horrid
Berkeley Square' (20), our judgement of her as a person is unlikely to be positive. The idea that she is poor, burdened or
deprived is not consistent with surrounding information about
the presents she receives, the triviality of her concerns or the
privilege of her lifestyle. There is a glaring lack of self-knowledge here which opens up a gap between her self-portrayal and
our response to her. But after the snow, in which we watch the
destruction of Edie's spoilt bourgeois expectations, this gap begins to close. We chart her psychological change through the
disappearance of alienating self-judgement and the dwindling of
this kind of ironic incongruity which encourages us to judge her
harshly. We accompany Edie in her passage from giddy youth
to a more sober maturity, and the passage is mapped by her
diminishing unreliability as a narrator.

But this kind of response depends on a certain credulity in
Edie as a psychological entity, and in the authenticity of the
diary as non-fiction. When we think of Edie's narration, as recent narratology is inclined to do, from a position of critical
distance as an authorial or textual strategy, these questions of

psychological change and self-knowledge are transformed. Edie's narrative is in a sense embedded in an authorial discourse which is pretending to be absent, which disguises its strategies in the illusion of Edie's authenticity as a character. The author must disclaim Edie's fictionality in order for the moral project of the story to be effective. I want to argue that it is not only by adopting a stance of critical distance that one encounters the issues of authorial strategy, or that one unmasks the rhetorical strategy of the narrative. The text itself goes some way towards pointing these narratological issues out, at one level presenting Edie as a character whose fictionality is disclaimed, and at another highlighting her artificiality as a text, whose fictionality is declared. That is to say that critical distance is not only distance between a critic and the fiction, but that it is also internal, that the narrative adopts distance from itself, narrates its own narratology, and develops a critical function in relation to itself.

Moments in a fiction when a narrative seems to adopt distance from itself, when it becomes self-referential or talks about itself, have been termed 'metanarrative signs'. Gerald Prince, for example, has argued that metanarrative signs are not only features of contemporary experimental novels (metafictions) which take self-referentiality to extremes but are an inherent feature of all narratives. Prince sees these metanarrative signs as moments where a narrative refers to its own constitution, as glosses on its own underlying codes and conventions.

Metanarrative signs in 'Snowed Up' are in abundance, perhaps because the diary form is inherently self-referential. It is the idiom of self-consciousness, an apparently readerless self-rumination in which it is conventional to contemplate the act of self-analysis as writing. Edie begins in this spirit, declaring in the first paragraph that 'I shall never be a good diarist' (19) and explaining, as I have discussed, the motives for the diary as a way of reducing 'this giddy head of mine to something like order' (19–20). Moments of explicit self-reference like this punctuate the narrative: 'I shall soon have nothing to do but keep this diary' (21), Edie declares on 4 January in a moment of self-reference which suggests that writing might take over from living altogether. The humour of this comment lies in the giddy logic it conveys: if Edie were to stop living except to write her diary, the diary would no longer be referential except to itself; she would be keeping a diary about keeping a diary. If a diary is a form of self-consciousness anyway, this comment suggests an unstoppable logical regress in which the diary would have to adopt a self-conscious attitude to its own self-consciousness, the writing being endlessly about itself. Giddy perhaps, but a profound articulation of a poststructuralist precept.

Various other metanarrative signs of a less explicit kind can be found in Edie's discourse. Edie, for example, has a keen sense of herself as a writer which emerges as a self-consciousness about her turn of phrase and quality of expression. After describing Phillip as a Newfoundland dog of a man (20), her self-evaluation is a reminder of the fact that she is writing, as well as being one of those moments when her self-assessment and our assessment of her are far apart: 'There – I shall be a poetess some day' (20). She is also critical of Alderman Thrigg's 'want of poetical language' (22) and the 'absurd similes' (22) with which he woos her, despite faltering herself in moments when a simile is required: 'He rolled out the dough like – like a cook' (24). These are ways of highlighting Edie's inability as a writer and constitute part of the metanarrative. A similar function is performed by references to the writing situation itself, as when we are informed 'My fingers are so numb I can hardly write: but I must do something to pass away the miserable time' (26); or, 'I've got a fire in my bedroom tonight, and am writing cosily before I retire as the books say' (21). References like this to the act of writing are themselves metanarrative, and in the second example the effect is compounded by the reference to books and to a familiar metanarrative cliché. This vague intertextual reference of course reminds us that Edie too is in a book, that she too is artificial, and therefore functions in the same way as her father's more specific linkage of Edie with a fictional character which she reports to us in indirect free speech: 'I must be a heroine like Edith my namesake two hundred years ago' (21).

References to other books are established metanarrative devices which assert the fictionality of the discourse at hand even if, at another level, they can be considered as ways of establishing the reality of a character by contrast: Edie might be saying that she is *like* a heroine as a way of asserting the reality of her existence, but the fact that she *is* a heroine is an irony which highlights her fictionality. The same function could be attributed to the theatre in the narrative: 'When we came out of the theatre it was so still and quiet in the streets, almost like death

itself' (20). Like books, theatre could be said to have conditioned Edie's imagination and her sense of the dramatic possibilities of a diary, a link strengthened by her prescience of the
connection between snow and death. At any rate, as she leaves
the theatre and encounters the deathly atmosphere of the snow
for the first time she is walking from one work of art into another,
or one plane of representation to another. Like books, the theatre
can therefore function simultaneously as a way of authenticating the bourgeois reality being represented, and as a way of
highlighting the artificiality and fictionality of Edie's discourse.
This metanarrative device is very reminiscent of the way in which
Henry James uses books in *The Turn of the Screw*, where his
governess repeatedly puts down a Gothic novel and walks immediately into some supernatural apparition, the fictionality of
which is thus signalled in advance as part of the systematic confusion of the reliability and unreliability of the narrator, and of
art and reality in the tale.

'Snowed Up' also makes use of a metanarrative device which
is not a momentary signal but a structural feature of the narrative: it creates a surrogate author who, within the terms of the
fiction, is a dramatized storyteller apparently responsible for the
substance and style of the narration. Any narrative voice might
be seen as an authorial surrogate in the sense that the author's
own rhetorical control is hidden behind the adopted voice. All
narratives have this aspect of ventriloquism. But when the narrator is dramatized as the subject of, or participant in, his or
her own story, or when the process of creation, oration or writing of the story is dramatized (as opposed to the 'authorial'
self-effacing voice of the third-person omniscient narrator), the
metanarrative effect is more explicit. Edie is a surrogate author
because the writing is hers, and the act of ventriloquism of the
external author is hidden behind the authentication of her diary,
his lips apparently sealed. Again the metanarrative effect here is
a kind of irony, that within the fiction we have a figure who is
an analogue for the author, so that as we see Edie grappling
with her narrative the effect is simultaneously to hide and highlight the external author, where any gain in realism of the diary
form is subverted by the illusion-breaking effect of the analogy
between internal and external author.

It is very obvious that, aside from this latest and more structural metanarrative aspect, metanarrative signs occur more fre-

quently in the early stages of 'Snowed Up', and disappear altogether towards the end. If Edie seems preoccupied at first with the fact that she is writing her diary it is a preoccupation that soon yields to a less self-conscious record of events. There is a sense in which Edie's journey through the narrative is a journey from self-reference to reference. I have mentioned that Edie's journey, aside from its moral dimension, is a process of maturation, from giddiness to sobriety, so that it would be reasonable to assume that the self-consciousness of Edie's metanarrative signs are associated with her giddiness and immaturity as a writer. If we add to this the contrast made in the closing authorial intrusion between 'a lady's fright' (29) and authorial balance, this journey is also the narrative of a narrator in the process of becoming more like the hidden author who represents the values of objectivity and transparency in writing, and whose self-revelation at the end completes Edie's quest. Ultimately this is the way that the analogy between Edie and the real author works, the distance between them decreasing steadily as the narrative progresses.

Consider the representation of speech in Edie's narrative. Several times at the start, Edie declares with metanarrative unreliability that she cannot remember the exact words of the speech she is reporting: 'Of course he put it in much grander words than that' (20), she reports on 2 January; and the next day, reporting her father's arguments about marriage, her memory for speech is no better: 'that's not how he put it but I can't remember the fine words' (21). This is not a problem that the omniscient narrator would ever have. The powers of recall of an omniscient narrator are of course unrealistic, making no attempt to represent the human possibilities of knowledge, memory or access to other minds. These memory failures can be seen then as authenticating signs which represent actual problems of recall in the process of narrating, and which belong categorically to the rhetoric of the dramatized, unreliable narrator. Yet Edie improves in her ability to represent speech accurately as she progresses, to the point of unrealism, reproducing in this paragraph the timing and faltering of the Alderman's speech with a more naturalistic precision:

> 'Ow – ow – ow!' cried the miserable Alderman shivering, and stretching out his hand to me. 'Don't Miss Audeley – don't leave me here in the dark! Ow – ow – ow! I'm perishing with cold! Please Miss – Miss – Miss Audeley!!' (25)

Is Edie just exercising poetic licence here in the moment of highest drama? Perhaps, but this is just one of the ways that Edie's self-consciousness recedes and yields to narrative convention. As Edie refers less to her own act of writing, her representation of the snowstorm becomes more lucid, more transparent, more objective, less giddy. A paradox emerges from this movement; that the narrative becomes more realistic in its transparency to events and characters, but less realistic as a first-person narration. It is as if there is a subtle, seamless transition from one narrative voice (the first-person narration which foregrounds Edie's personality as a writer) to another (the third-person convention of the more self-effacing narrator). This can be summarized as a two-sided process: a decrease in subjective realism and an increase in objective realism.

One last point about the recession of metanarrative signs which no poststructuralist could ignore is that the self-references which abound at the outset of the narrative are conversational in character, and as they disappear, the contrasting values come to the foreground. At the opening Edie is talking on paper, in the best conventions of epistolary poetry or novels which adopt the tension of speech and writing as a rhetorical ploy. As someone who has been directed for the first time towards diary-writing as a form of personal development, it is plausible that her style should be conversational, and that it should become less so in the courses of the narrative through practice. One of the most important features of the story, then, is that as Edie journeys through the moral structure of her narrative, she also acquires ability as a writer and leaves behind the immature chattiness of her early entries. Thus, moral understanding is not only Edie's only destination. That understanding comes with other positive values like writing, and this association is consistent with the authorial self-revelation as a form of closure for the narrative. The interest here for a poststructuralist critic is double: it makes the writing of the story self-referential in the sense that it is partly a story about writing, about the acquisition of writing skills, a story which narrates its own constitution; and it articulates a familiar theme taken from Jacques Derrida's philosophy, which claims that speech has consistently been seen as having some metaphysical priority over writing in fiction and philosophy (see Julian Wolfreys' chapter, below), but that texts which advance this priority contain counter-suggestions that the hierarchy of speech and writing is in fact the other way around. I don't wish to do any more than refer to this theme for the moment, and to point out that if Edie has changed for the better by the end of the narrative, part of her improvement lies in the fulfilment of the churchman's hopes in the opening paragraph which so clearly endorse the value of disciplined writing over formless conversationality. It is also worth pointing to J. Hillis Miller's analysis of Joseph Conrad's *Heart of Darkness* as a comparable example and clear articulation of the importance of the speech/writing problem to poststructuralist narratology (see bibliography for details).

Edie's journey, or her narrative process, begin to look much more complex than that of a moral fable when these different dimensions of her journey are identified. It would be useful to summarize the various associated ways of construing the process as follows:

From	To
Singledom	Marriage
Poverty	Wealth
Giddiness	Order
Youth	Experience
Narrator	Author
Female	Male
Subjectivity	Objectivity
Conversation	Writing
Nature	Culture

Reading from left to right in this table will provide alternative interpretations of the narrative process and its oppositional structure, while reading from top to bottom of either column is to construct a connotative chain in which the positive or negative values of the story are associated with each other and can enter into substitution with each other. Whereas a structuralist narratology would see these oppositions as the basic meaning-generating units of the story, poststructuralist narratology tends towards seeing these not as innocent oppositions but as hierarchical ones in which the values of the story are inscribed. In this case, the deconstruction of the story consists in a demonstration that the text is not simply a coherent valorization of the second term over the first, but that the text advances counter-positions which unsettle the hierarchical oppositions on which it seems to depend.

The last opposition in the table above – nature/culture – has not yet figured substantially in the discussion, but has an important role in the oppositional structure of the narrative (see also Ruth Robbins's and Jessica Maynard's essays, below). Assuming that the impact of the snowstorm on urban life represents the power of nature and the fragility of commercial and social conditions in the city, and that any positive transformation of attitudes undergone by Edie and the other actants in the narrative are brought about by means of this natural intervention into culture, the function of snow in the narrative appears uncomplicated. It works as a warning that urban bourgeois values are subject to some transcendent authority, that the values upon which Edie's marriage is being decided at the start of the narrative are narrowly materialistic, that city life is dependent on nature for its stability, or that culture is within nature. From this assumption, most of the narrated events belong to a scheme which asserts the superiority of nature over culture. Commerce is brought to a standstill, inflation – the dread enemy of economic stability – rears its head, social order collapses as gangs of 'roughs' roam the streets (27). As the obtrusive reference to the story of Noah's Ark at the end of the narrative makes explicit, the snow represents the wrath of God, provoked by moral bankruptcy, followed by the restoration of order. Symbolic events also seem to co-operate in this scheme, such as the episode in which Thrigg is buried to his shoulders in the snow, powerless despite his wealth and because of his weight against the might of nature, and forced to retract his claim to Edie's hand. This is a kind of symbolic recognition of the corrupt basis of his interest in Edie, and the turning-point of the power relation between Thrigg and Phillip: the point at which commercial values concede to natural forces.

With the reference to Noah's story as a clue we might expect a more straightforward pastoral attitude than the one that 'Snowed Up' articulates through Edie, invoking as it does the Adamic myth of a fall from nature, into a state of corruption to which the flood is a corrective. This is the Christian version of the pastoral sensibility which idealizes nature as an Edenic state of innocence, and which views subsequent culture as a lapse into corruption. The basis of the Adamic myth is that nature comes first – that nature has temporal as well as conceptual priority over culture – just as, for example, in the book of Genesis, Adam then Eve can be read as Adam over Eve. In 'Snowed Up' this introduces a fundamental tension into the narrative structure, since it imports this temporal priority as conceptual priority into a narrative which, as a fable, structures itself around the assumption that the telos (endpoint) and not the origin of the journey is where the positive values of the story are to be found. Two schemes contradict each other, one which sees temporal progress as a process of deterioration, the other which sees progress as an ascent into civilized values and culture.

An example of this crossed structure at work in the narrative would be the associative links it advances between youth, innocence and nature. We expect the association of these terms to be unproblematic in the best convention of pastoral literature where nature is a state of innocence before the fall, an ideal state to which we would seek to return: it is the youth of culture. Pastoral narratives often make use of this associative link by yoking their protagonists to the temporal scheme of the fall. Wordsworth's *The Prelude*, for example, presents the speaker's return to nature as the same step as a return to childhood. Dickens can chart David Copperfield's loss of innocence as a departure from the rural setting of his childhood, so that the process of exposing him to corruption functions as part of the moral contrast of country and city.

In 'Snowed Up' nature is not innocent and innocence is not the positive value of the story. There is a kind of anti-pastoral scheme at work which valorizes culture over nature even if nature is seen as the more powerful force, as the transcendent realm which contains urban life and upon which all civilized values depend. Thus, as Edie loses her innocence she does not descend into corruption but ascends to civilization, and her progress is not linked to any pastoral sense of loss. Nor do we witness any gushy idealization of nature as the positive pole in the moral contrast with the city or the corruptions of capitalism. References to life outside London tend to confine themselves to economic perspectives, such as the agricultural source of Thrigg's fortune or her father's ownership of The Towers, the country house which is under threat from his imminent bankruptcy and which Edie can save by marrying money. Edie might, as her name suggests, represent Eden at some mythic level but her narrative does not represent nature as paradise regained.

Derrida argues in *Of Grammatology* that the relationship of writing to speech is one of supplementarity, that speech has a temporal priority over writing which has established a sense of its conceptual priority. He argues also that this hierarchy has a paradoxical logic: that writing is seen as a secondary and derived representation of speech, yet that the possibility of writing is prior to speech and can be seen as its origin: that a possibility produces that to which it is said to be added on. This logic of supplementarity replaces the temporal, linear account of speech and writing, or of nature and culture, with a conceptual circle. If the logic of supplementarity claims that speech is always already writing, or that nature is always already culture, 'Snowed Up' certainly adheres to this logic. Thus, when Edie begins her diary in conversational style before acquiring a more mature approach to writing, there is clearly a paradox involved. Edie's conversation is talking on paper. It is the pretence of conversationality in writing. I have argued that metanarrative signs in 'Snowed Up' function both as authenticating devices and as reminders of the authorial presence of the story by creating an analogy between Edie and the real author. These might now be seen as ways in which the text deconstructs its own opposition of conversation and writing, reminding us that her conversation is always already a form of writing and that her narrative is authorially controlled from the start.

If this can be seen as part of the general interaction of culture and nature in the narrative, the idea that there is a Derridean logic of supplementarity at work can be supported at other levels of the text, such as imagery. There are two prominent examples of this. The first is the constant personification of snow: 'I do hate this wearisome snow. It keeps coming down so quiet and calm, and cold, it mocks at me – it does not care a bit about *my* misery' (21). This personification gives the snow what A. J. Greimas would have called an *actantial function*. Greimas identified various abstract roles that characters in narratives could play, principally those of hero, villain and helper. In this example, Edie casts snow as villain, working against her wishes. The snow prevents Phillip from riding by Edie's window, it imprisons her with the suitors she wishes to reject, and at times takes on the image of an invading army 'strong enough to completely conquer our civilization' (27). The personification of snow invites the reader to view it as an actant quite explicitly, as an ally to Bilberton for example: 'He says with his wretched attempts at gallantry that the snow is his best friend and he should like to be imprisoned forever with me' (22). But when the whole narrative is taken into account, the actual actantial function of snow is that of helper, not villain, helping Edie to fulfil her wishes and bringing happy resolution to her problem. On a second reading, the perspective on snow as helper ironically undermines those moments in which snow is cast as villain. The experience is similar to that of rereading *Pride and Prejudice* in the knowledge of Darcy's ultimate suitability for Elizabeth, a knowledge which undermines her early judgements, but which could not be exposed as wrong at the time without sacrificing the close relationship between reader and heroine on which the didactic project of the story relies.

The second example of this kind of imagery which disrupts plotted oppositions can be found in the first sentence: 'Papa has just given me a splendid set of furs, I never saw anything so beautiful. I do believe they must have cost three hundred pounds' (19). In terms of the relationship between nature and culture, the furs have an ambiguous position. On one hand the fur coat is clearly a commodity representing bourgeois, urban values. Its beauty for Edie seems to lie mainly in its expense. It is, as she suspects later, part of the transaction of her marriage, paid for with the Alderman's money. It is also an item of fine clothing which Edie can wear to the theatre, and so is associated with culture and civilization. But the image is two-sided, showing foreknowledge of the natural catastrophe to come, and associating Edie with a more bestial level of survival that she will have to adopt. The image of Edie in a fur coat is also linked with the imagery which she uses to express her affection for Phillip, that 'Newfoundland dog of a man':

> I can just fancy him curled up on this rug at my feet (he raves about my little feet and little paws, and littleness altogether, and wicked black eyes and and – but no matter). He would be on that rug like a great dog, and make love to me *so nicely* I do believe *forever*. (21–2)

If Edie imagines herself with Phillip in this sexually charged moment as animals, she implies a contrast between this natural level of bestiality and the cultural restraints represented by her father which dictate that sex is not the proper basis for marriage. Like metanarrative signs and the function of snow, this double-edged image imports a perspective from some future point in the narrative as a kind of irony, as a meaning which can only be perceived in retrospect in a first reading, or on rereading. The first sentence of the story then contains the possibility which is to come, evoking the conceptual circle rather than the linear priority in the relation of culture and nature, and implying from the start the co-implication of nature and commerce.

Fables have two important rhetorical strategies upon which the coherence of their moral message depends. The first is authorial absence, since the slightest scent of authorial manipulation will destroy the impression of freely reached moral judgements on the part of the reader. The second is linearity, which ensures that perspectives reached at the end of the story do not overly alienate us or divert us from the steady evolution of the lesson. In 'Snowed Up' the first of these strategies is undermined by metanarrative signs which foreground the relationship between narrator and author while the second is undermined by a certain way of reading which finds in the text a logic of supplementarity working against the way in which a temporal sequence assigns value to oppositions. Neither of these subversions of rhetorical strategy should be seen as descriptions of the way that reading occurs. A text cannot control the readership in this way as if that readership were an homogeneous entity. These subversions are not, as many deconstructionists have claimed, things that the text does to itself. They represent the interests of a poststructuralist approach to narratology, an approach which aims not to suppress evidence which seems to confuse the moral message of a fable, but to highlight that evidence as a way of sustaining contradictions, and as a way of resisting the reduction of the narrative to some successfully communicated morality. The reading may also correspond to some actual experience of a reader. In my case it helped to articulate a feeling of doubt in the first reading at the moment of closure and revelation which could only be analysed on rereading. Snow me again. I didn't catch your drift.

3

Does Edie Count?: A Psychoanalytic Perspective on 'Snowed Up'

JILL BARKER

INTRODUCTION

Within a literary context, psychoanalysis is that mode of criticism based on the insights of Sigmund Freud and on the reinterpretation of those insights by Jacques Lacan, Julia Kristeva, and a constellation of important lesser stars, too numerous to name. This is not the place to embark on a full exposition of the principles of psychoanalytic theory: that has been done most efficiently elsewhere.[1] As my reading of 'Snowed Up' progresses, I will show how various psychoanalytic concepts permit us new insights into the text. The set of clinical praxes dealing with people's psychological problems, and subject to development, diversification and controversy, is not obviously related to the needs of literary critics. Although the aim of the analyst is therapeutic, the critic has no patient, and can achieve no 'cure'. Frequently, as a result, the analyst's goal is not ours, though both deal with words: the discourse of a subject, whether living or fictional, through which desire is expressed. A literary critic aims for a greater understanding of a written work: success for us is to see the text sparkling and new, like a familiar landscape viewed at an unaccustomed time of day, and transformed by the insight that a new point of view brings to it.[2]

What is there in literature for the psychoanalytic literary critic to analyse? Where do we locate the subject, the owner of the text's psychic structures? Early psychoanalytic critics discussed the author or the characters in a story. To answer these questions in a postmodernist context, it is necessary to know that Freud's original perceptions about the psyche have been altered through the contribution of later thinkers into a redefinition of the subject as linguistic: people are not just producers of language, but are themselves constructed by the linguistic structures within which they function. If we treat the text itself as subject, we can read it as containing and facilitating the expression of desires, just as a person undergoing psychoanalysis expresses needs by narrating the past.

The power of psychoanalytic criticism is that it takes *texts* seriously, as opposed to their cultural context, or the biographies of their authors. For the psychoanalytic literary critic the events of the narrative can be read as symptoms; they are at one and the same time 'real' within the narrative, and metaphoric of a psychic structure. Eagleton puts this point elegantly in his *Literary Theory*:

> by attending to what may seem like evasions, ambivalences and points of intensity in the narrative – words which do not get spoken, words which are spoken with unusual frequency, doublings and slidings of language – [literary criticism] can begin to probe through the layers of secondary revision and expose something of the 'sub-text' which, like an unconscious wish, the work both conceals and reveals. It can attend, in other words, not only to what the text says, but to how it *works*. (Eagleton, 182)

Because a text is read as giving access to profound psychic structures in the same way that a psychoanalyst reads the discourse of a patient, the critic traces the paths that desire follows through an obscure and variable code of significant symbols and metaphors. This mode of criticism gives us a method by which we can open a text out to complex metaphoric readings. Furthermore, as Eagleton points out, 'by reinterpreting Freudianism in terms of language, a pre-eminently social activity, Lacan permits us to explore the relations between the unconscious and human society' (173). Whichever school of psychoanalytic thought one favours, it is important to see that the fundamental themes and structures of loss, desire, numerology and language are inextricably bound up with one another.

The patterns begin to fall into place. This story of a young woman and a snowstorm is an invitation to the psychoanalytic critic, since it is overtly a narrative of transition: the growth of individuals into a better understanding of themselves, of their sexuality and of their place in a wider world.[3] The learning process and the achievement of adult socialization are exactly what psychoanalysis deals with. Even more to the point, we have here a protagonist explicitly constructed in her own wilfulness: who walks, talks and above all *writes* desire. It is relevant that those desires are established in a variety of crucial relationships to the paternalistic structure in which she lives. The narrative thus locks Edie into two large, related symbolic structures: the first is a complex interplay of subjections and resistances to her F/father (and the shorthand term 'Father' includes the patriarchal social structure, created, as we have seen, through denial); the second is submission to the snowfall, with all its practical effects and metaphoric significances.

At a single stroke, then, this story exposes three enormous psychoanalytic themes: firstly, Edie's clash with social expectations suggests the Law of the Father, together with its imposition – on/acceptance – by the subject; secondly, in the snow we see the imaginative transformation of the physical world into a signifying structure; and finally, with Edie's own description of her needs, we see the movement of desire in language. Though this chapter will deal with each of those themes in turn it will become clear that they interlock at many points.

It is no coincidence that each of these three themes returns us to the issue of lack, for it is absence (perceived as loss) that generates desire, and absence too that generates language.[4] Lacan's contribution to our understanding of human psychology involves a refocusing of Freud. Where Freud dealt with the construction of the subject through its lacks and desires, Lacan elaborates the moments when that construction is an essentially linguistic act. Language institutes loss, but it is also both a response to loss, and an attempt to seize power over loss.[5] It is the foregrounding of language-as-subject that makes the literary text a legitimate object of analysis in its own right. This is why Peter Brooks can say that 'Psychoanalytic criticism can and should be textual and rhetorical' (1987, 2). That fraternal connection between desire and language is what insists that desire track its quarry through language, as a series of ever-receding and ever-seductive goals. Just as the object of desire recedes through language always aimed for but never acquired, time unrolls in front of Edie's diary, a discourse always in the present, yet always resumed and revising itself up to the moment of satisfaction: that sense of closure at the end of the story which fictional narrative purports to offer, and which, as a stasis beyond which the narrative does not proceed, is equivalent to death.

THE NON/M DU PÈRE (THE LAW OF THE FATHER)

The position of the subject in relation to the Law of the Father is of particular interest in the discussion of desire, but also necessary to the tale of Edie's movement from rebellion to conformity. 'Subject' is a key term for these discussions, being used to describe the source of the more or less coherent set of perceptions, responses and utterances that we normally associate with an individual.[6] It was not until Freudianism was put together with structuralist and poststructuralist theories of language that a sophisticated psychoanalytic theory of the construction of the subject in language was made explicit. Using the term 'subject' recognizes that the person who says 'I', and who claims to be unified, independent and consistent through time is in fact shifting and variable, contingent on circumstances and, most importantly, constructed by the signifying codes within which he/she functions. The subject of a sentence in the sense of the 'I' who says 'I am' with such confidence, is also the *subject of* (in the sense of 'the one who submits to') defining external forces, in particular language structures, social hierarchies and economic pressures.

All desire is the desire of the Other, says Lacan, and his remark contains at least three available meanings: (1) that our desires are identical with those of the Other, because it is the desire of the Other that has prevented us from having our primary want; (2) that we desire what we are *supposed* to desire; (3) that what we desire is a mask (a veil) behind which the Other places itself. 'Otherness' and 'the other' are terms in widespread, commonplace critical use, often functioning as apparently non-technical terms, or at least ones whose theoretical background is uniform and widely accepted. Such an assumption is deceptive. For psychoanalysis, 'otherness' involves either an external, coveted condition (an object of desire), or an external structuring set of constraints through which the 'self' is defined. It is in this context that we can consider how Edie's desire relates to her surrounding circumstances.[7] Edie is apparently embedded in a multi-faceted patriarchal structure, which most obviously consists of family and social expectations, and financial constraints. At another level, the structures of language and of the passage of time are crucial to Edie's positioning of herself. Our first impression is that her goals are entirely to do with negotiating exactly how she is to move from the position of daughter to that of wife (positions which are not wholly dissimilar in her world, and which are entirely to do with power relationships between Edie and men). It seems that her goals are to be realised *through* her father: he provides the furs, and beyond that the whole lifestyle within which Edie functions, but which she also resists. All her activities within this area of paternal sponsorship consist of more or less public ways of making contact with men, and of assessing each one's potential as a partner. She chats to clergymen at church; she is escorted to the theatre; and when directing her own activities, she focuses on handsome and well-bred but penniless army officers. The fact that, for Edie to approve of a man, he must pass muster as a sexually desirable object, while her father's criteria are wealth and status, should not obscure the totality with which Edie's desires are congruent with patriarchal expectations. The question is not whether she will marry or not, but whom she will marry, and under what circumstances. Are we, therefore, approaching a text in which the Name of the Father has been invoked, and Edie has already entered into maturity, defined as an understanding of the Symbolic order? The narrative appears to show us a powerful father and a relatively helpless and unaware child, whose girlish rebellions are doomed to tragedy. Deciding whether this is a reasonable interpretation of the situation or not depends on how one reads Edie's rebelliousness. One needs to make a clear distinction between the small 'f' father and the capital 'F' Father of the *Law of the Father*. The former is a character with a named relationship towards Edie; the latter term refers to a structure whereby a desiring 'person' is denied satisfaction, and in accepting that denial and sublimating[8] it or transforming it, enters into a capacity to use those very structures and find them enabling. There are times when Edie's father is the source of the Law of the Father in her life, and times when his position in the structure is quite different. In this story, the Father may usually be equated with those forces which establish rules, the social conventions, and the Symbolic order.

The discourse of the diary overtly constructs Edie as rebellious in small and large things by insistently placing her sense of her own identity within a context of Symbolic structures. This is revealed if one considers the movement of the sense of self through the opening diary entry, that for 2 January (19–20). After the date, the next word is 'Papa', thus instituting two controlling structures: those of time, and of the father/daughter relationship. Within that relationship, Edie is the recipient of the furs, a gift which she evaluates aesthetically and then in terms of its monetary significance. Edie next claims an incapacity for the task of keeping a diary, advertising herself as disorganized and so a failure: 'I shall never be a good diarist' (19). But there is no sense of regret in her words, no believable feeling of failure. The conventionality of her choice of phrase suggests rather a self-satisfaction, supported by a loving tolerance of her own foibles, made manifest in the remark that follows: 'Oh dear whenever shall I reduce this giddy head of mine to something like order' (19–20). Edie sustains the role of the scatterbrain even in private communication with her diary. She conveys a sense that a 'giddy head' is a perfectly appropriate accessory. With a significant choice of cliché, she suggests to us that imposing order on her mind would be to 'reduce' it. Furthermore, a 'giddy head' attracts male attention, as it stimulates people to seek to help her sort it out. She brings out the tutelary and the paternal in older men, as when the 'canon or something' (20) advises her to keep a diary. Within the complex set of remarks that informs us of these details we find evidence of the quality not just of her mind, but also of her emotional interactions with the world, for in muddling up her mentor's titles and position, she rejects status and worldly description, offering us as incontrovertible facts only 'old' and the Cathedral. She thus name-drops for our benefit the status of the man's dignity, respectability and circumstances, while pretending to deny that she cares about that sort of thing by jumbling up his possible titles. Next in the movement of the first entry comes a succinct summary of what the canon suggested: 'classify my ideas and bring my mind into shape' (20) lays claim to intelligence through her acceptance that she *has* ideas and a mind which are worth organizing, even though currently disorganized by external standards. That sentence undermines her presentation of herself as foolish, if ever we were to believe in it. It points out that she is not so disorganized that she will miss the chance to satirize the orotundities of an elderly gallant: '– he said it would help me to classify my ideas, and bring my mind into shape. Of course he put it in much grander words than that' (20). The 'grander words' can only be pretentious utterances in comparison with the compact, accurate phrases into which Edie has transformed them. The next movement of Edie's thoughts asserts the satisfaction of her own desires ('I must wear it') against social behavioural norms. With the French phrase 'not *de règle*' Edie trivializes social customs, controlling them by alienating them (20). Edie is a deflator of pretension.

Thus Edie is involved in a relationship with social expectations through which she gradually achieves insight – or so it appears – and so can be seen as a 'subject' moving into the Symbolic order.[9]

These first few sentences of the story merit close attention, for they encapsulate the problems of interpretation that the story as a whole offers. In refusing the social custom of keeping new clothes unworn, Edie appears to express a simple wish to wear the furs – a wish that belongs with the infantile expectation that the self and gratification are as one. Her rationalization of this, however, is clear and precise, once one accepts that a restricted linguistic code can perform argument. It involves a careful comment about the custom (alien to us) of keeping new clothes unworn: 'How *can* people keep their new things a month ...' (20) suggests an excess of emotional control in these people. The reason why Edie refuses to conform is based on a sense of the value of her own wishes, and on a perceived illogicality in the custom. Other rebellions cluster thick and fast around the small-scale issue of the furs, revealing it to be at least symptomatic, and probably therefore symbolic, of the wider area of Edie's relationship to authority generally. She objects, as we have seen, to the ordering and classifying of her ideas, and her written style resists the use of an elaborated 'mature' language code. The scene in which she waves to Lieutenant Aurelles shows Edie in rebellion against the paternal definition of an appropriate husband. Edie asserts the indomitable individual will against the powerful forces which would constrain her. Such a humanistic,

individualistic reading has attractions; it is certainly the reading
of herself to which Edie would subscribe. Evidence of this can
be seen later, when she establishes her judgement in contrast to
her father's casual remark: '... it made no difference to him.
Cool! As if it made no difference to me' (21); but the text itself
renders that interpretation problematic. Not only is Edie's ignorance staggering, she boasts that it is; in other words she is very
well aware that naiveté is exactly what society expects of her.
Innocence and winsome skittishness increase her saleability. Not
only does *Edie* enjoy refusing to be organized by the clergyman,
or by the formal structures of written English, *he* enjoys her
refusal. The irony of her knowledge of the attractions of ignorance makes her seem less of a fool, for her style of language use
now strikes us as *chosen*. She is thus the less to be pitied, and
more of a manipulator within the system. Edie recognizes that
power resides in language and writing and she uses these to
control the men who attempt to control her, by refusing them a
voice of their own in her representation of the world. With her
father: 'I wanted something to quarrel with him about. So I
rushed away and left him' (21). Her 'quarrel' involves imposing
silence on him; and the passion of anger is expressed as significant absence. Edie habitually refuses to allow other people's words
to stand. When she reports their speech, she mediates their
language, re-rendering it in a form she declares to be simpler.
Thus, while appearing to demonstrate her own simplicity and
inadequacy, she in fact refuses the claims of others to complexity, and exercises a power to interpret, and restrict meaning.
When she puts the original speakers forward as pompous fools,
urgent to impress and out of control of their own floridities,
she is a clear-sighted critic, the source of truth no less. We are
prevented from judging whether she is right or wrong about
these people, for the original has vanished, overlaid by her gloss.
So we are offered, and even positioned by, a dominant discourse
which glances at the possibility that other discourses might exist,
while overlaying and pre-empting them. Indeed, Edie's self-present-
ation is largely spurious: she calls herself a 'poor little girl' and
a 'poor girl' (meaning 'mere' or 'inadequate'), while revealing
her own sense of control and superiority.[10] The masochistic vision
of herself as a shuttlecock or tennis ball is conventional, and
quickly superseded by the sadistic superiority in which she mocks
the suitors' behaviour, and relishes her power to make them

ridiculous. 'It *is* laughable when I think of it to see fat Mr Thrigg jump up and open the door for me, and Lord Bilberton screwing his face into a smile of approval (though he hates the Alderman) and Lieut. Aurelles scowling at them both, . . .' (20).

We could read the situation as a matchmaking game whose rules appear to be familiar to all concerned. Even Edie's rebellion against the father is contained within that game: she chooses to flirt with Aurelles, a different representative of male authority, and in many ways a more satisfactorily conventional 'real man': young, virile, and committed to the army hierarchy. Edie voluntarily adopts the role of the unruly girl,[11] which is a position of desirable 'otherness' for the 'fathers'; all these elderly men she meets and charms. As a refuser of authority, she offers them the titillation of the marginal, the forbidden, the cheeky child–woman who plays with a refusal to conform. At the same time she is properly youthful and virginal, and functioning in a structure which makes her sexual fate inevitable. Of this they are aware but she (*apparently*; but we may reasonably harbour doubts) is not. I will look more closely at Edie's desires later. Part of her charm for the men lies in her inevitable eventual submission/constraint. Her tiny transgressions are token ones: they take place within a context of utter dependence.

Even at the beginning of the story there is thus one sense in which Edie rebels against the Law of the Father, while in another she acquiesces in it. It is as if two voices compete for dominance. How do we cope with this contradiction? In the past critics found contradictions such as this troubling, and in need of resolution. They referred to the idea of the author's intention, and saw contradictions in texts as the failure by authors to realize their intentions effectively.[12] The psychoanalytic concept that all individuals are 'split' (or 'divided') subjects, and that the split functions within language, enables us to theorize the contradictions, and work with them rather than attempting to achieve a resolution which inevitably denies the validity of one side of the contradiction.

In 'Snowed Up', then, we perceive a 'split subject', the necessary condition of being human according to Lacan. For the moment it is convenient to treat it as Edie's psyche which is split between an energetic claim to infantile gratification, and an identification with the alienating syste... which denies gratification. The subject ('I' figure) demonstrates within its language the very source of that division, the pain with which a renunciation of wholeness and an acceptance of absence has been made. For Edie, the loss and the yearning for wholeness are expressed in her divided narrative of the snowstorm: heavily structured, and claiming that language is transparent to truth; yet also a world of dream-like images and significances. Her writing is thus the code of codes, the Symbolic order *par excellence,* and Freud's 'royal road to the unconscious'. She strives through simplicity of diction and an imitation of spoken forms towards an imagined primal simplicity of psyche: towards the infantile bliss of non-differentiation, of a stable subject. Edie implies criticisms of elaborated linguistic codes, partly by showing how they can be summarized, partly by denying that she can use them. At the same time, however, she yearns towards the complexities offered by metaphoric and other poetic forms. She uses the game of chess rather clumsily as a metaphor for her own condition, and disdains an incapacity with metaphor as laughable: 'and there he broke down fairly for want of poetical language and left his absurd similes unfinished' (22). 'Snowed Up' puts forward exactly that imaginative situation referred to by Julia Kristeva, one in which a narrated crisis images a crisis of the spirit: '[literary] creation . . . proposes a configuration of which the prosodic economy, the dramaturgy of characters and the implicit symbolism are an extremely faithful semiological representation of the subject's battle with symbolic breakdown' (Kristeva 1987, 109–10). Kristeva sees literary creativity as therapeutic, and as a way of disposing of the stresses of our psychic crises by reliving them in a symbolic form. Metaphoric and rhetorical structures (or incoherences) in texts are comparable to structures within dreams, and can be analysed in similar ways and according to similar principles of condensation and displacement.[13]

Edie's subjectivity is ambivalent, but there is a further split within this story, which we can approach by considering how another code is used: that of numbers. Like language, counting and numbers generally are a part of the Symbolic order, generated by acknowledging an external authority, and giving up an oceanic sense of power. It is in relation to the governing structures of the Symbolic that the diary's consciousness of number becomes important. 'January 2nd', the diary begins, with the second day of the first month: the 'one' of the solipsistic subject, and the 'two' of the unbroken infantile dyad. The Law of the Father manifests itself further in the text through the movement of significant numbers. Framed, located by counting, and obsessed with numerical structures, the diary ticks out a fixed number of days; 24 days of writing enclose the 21 days of isolation by the snowfall. Both figures are encompassed by the space of time which the first rebellion described: the month Edie refused to leave between receiving the furs and their first wearing. That time structure images the larger one, of life itself. Edie has tried to restrict paternal interpretations of time: the social reading of her age as conducive to marriage is a constraint she dislikes. Again, she is obliquely interested in the counting of money. We notice her pride in the furs: 'they must have cost three hundred pounds' (19). She wields this counting to give herself pleasure, but not with her father's interpretation of money as capable of buying and selling people.

The sum of £300 introduces a significant tendency of the story to collect groups of three. Edie particularly likes to count up to three, but this is in order to exercise control. Three as we have seen is the number that institutes the symbolic. It is *her* estimate that values the coat at £300; she finds *three* suitors hugely entertaining, and has gone to some lengths to add a third suitor to the two her father has selected. 'It *is* laughable when I think of it to see fat Mr Thrigg jump up and open the door for me, and Lord Bilberton screwing up his face into a smile of approval (though he hates the Alderman) and Lieut. Aurelles scowling at them both, and trying oh, so hard to play chess – which he does not understand – with papa' (20). Yet what is entertaining to her, in spite of her acute observation of their differences, is their essentially undifferentiated comic condition: each is ridiculous in her eyes. Edie stands outside the paternal numbers game: she counts, or refuses to count, in order to control, while the men count with dedication, from within the structure.

The rebellious Edie is eventually contained not by social mores nor by paternal prohibition (including an appeal to her family's history, another patriarchal structure). The narrative puts before her a completely compelling law: the possibility of starvation. Even Edie cannot defy the law of the body, a law invoked and expressed in numerical terms: the inches of snow, the number of days, the quantity of sustenance obtainable. This deadly serious counting is another version of the counting of money and the counting of Edie's age into womanhood. It is as if Edie's refusal to count (in the metaphoric sense of the social interpretation of money, age and so forth) draws down a stringent lesson upon her, in the form of the snowfall, which denies Edie the game of subversive counting she enjoyed. Numbers therefore constitute a symbolic system which Edie, again split, both understands and strives to refuse. The narrative, as a voice separate from Edie's, brings the snow crisis to bear on her. It begins to appear that the snow has several sources – further evidence of division within the narrative.

THE SNOW

A consideration of numbers and of the split subject brings us to the major event of the story. The snowfall is a narrative trigger by which the impasse between Edie and her father can be solved, and as such it is rather a creaky plot device. More significantly for psychoanalytic criticism, it is a complex metaphor for the situation of the subject in the world. Freud taught how to read a patient's discourse, and in particular the semi-fictional obscure and often illogical discourse of dreams, as coded narratives of how the structure of the unconscious mind is conditioned by childhood events. His discoveries form part of a philosophical tradition which sees the subject as entirely constructed by the multiple discourses in which it is embedded, rather than as autonomous and self-determining. There is thus much less distinction between the real and the fictional than we are accustomed to making. The fictions people tell (about) themselves are a kind of truth.

By using the perceptions of Freud and later psychoanalysts about the relationship of language and psychological structures, we can consider a text as if it were the discourse of an unconscious mind, and so arrive at insights into the symbolic structures of a piece of writing. Because the symptomatology of the psychic structure is manifested in physical effects, and in a metaphoric discourse paralleling these effects, the key to the story of the subject's situation involves a literary analysis of the patient's speech *as a metaphoric representation*. The speech of the analysand offers a kind of 'reality' in code; similarly, physical symptoms are also codes (that is, metaphors) for psychic structures. In the case of physical symptoms, the psyche *writes* its desires (and desires will always include frustrations) on the body of the subject. A text, too, can be thought of as a body, on which linguistic features such as plot structure and imagery are inscribed as metaphors of psychological stress. Following from this, the events of a narrative need not be seen with their apparent cause/effect relationships, but rather as if they were events in a dream. Motivated by needs other than those of the plot, the unconscious subjectivity of the text offers us events and images together with emphases which guide our interpretations in psychoanalytically interesting ways. The snow thus does not occur because of weather conditions, nor yet because someone called 'Richard Jefferies' wishes to place Edie's world under threat. Of course each of these readings – the realistic and the narratological – is a possible one among many others and deserving of interest, as the variety of essays in this volume shows. Psychoanalytic criticism should make no claims to arrive at *the* truth. It does, however, arrive at insights which reach in two directions: *back* into the imaginative text under scrutiny, and *outwards* into the text of our lived experience.

Both Edie *and* her father lack emotional nourishment, and with the snowfall that condition becomes global. The image of their need is projected on to the whole world, and again we observe the infantile situation of believing one's own condition to be universal; this is the undifferentiated emotionality of Lacan's pre-Mirror phase, the phase before the Symbolic order. That vagueness – the lack of boundary definition – is present in the text because we cannot be sure about Edie's diary. We have no external cross-reference with which to check her perceptions against facts. This of course is also a feature of psychoanalytic discourse: for many purposes, it is how she perceives the world that matters, not whether or not it is factually precise.[14] In the condition of the newborn child, exposed, cold and starving, the father is frightened but Edie is not. She feels confidence in her own power, expressed through her rather blank prose style as a matter-of-fact acceptance of all events equally. That power is an omnipotence, an oceanic capacity to identify with the snow and to that extent the snow is *Edie's* power over the world: her power to forestall her enforced sexualization, to hold the whole world of society in stasis, to threaten the basis of Mr Thrigg's money and Lord Bilberton's authority by showing social constructs to fail in the face of youthful vigour. Thus the snow reifies Edie's evaluation of masculine worth. The accuracy with which the snow mimics Edie's emotional state makes clear its status as an artefact of a desiring psyche.

As a function of Edie's unconscious, the snow moves the entire world into stasis. By stopping all movement of goods, traffic and money, it images the emotional halt that she craves; the pause in which she will enjoy her sense of power before moving into marriage. It imposes that originary static perfection first contained in the Garden of Eden, to which Edie's name partly refers. Edie says explicitly that marriage will deprive her of the *fun* of the social world. The virginal whiteness of the snow co-operates with Edie's wish to stave off marriage: '... such nonsense. It spoils life, I'm sure it does' (21). For Edie, sexual maturity is a threat. Faced with this threat, the discourse of the diary constructs an anorexic world in which nourishment is denied and 'normal' social relationships abrogated.[15] This focus on the physical rather than the social also involves a refocusing of the sexual drive on to the need for food. (In traditional Freudian terms, the genital phase is regressed to the more infantile oral phase.) That regression is shown to be life-threatening. Substituting food for sex could be seen as a fetishizing process, except that there are even 'foods' that Edie rejects. For all that the snow co-operates with Edie's emotional need to stay a child, it denies her physical needs for nourishment with which to sustain life. In this way, the snow contains exactly the ambivalence that Melanie Klein ascribes to infant images of the maternal breast: Klein suggests that the good breast nourishes, and the bad breast denies nourishment. Furthermore, it has that appearance of all-enveloping whiteness that the breast has for the tiny infant. For Edie, the motherless child, this seems particularly appropriate: the immobilizing snow renders visible her own emotionally malnourished condition. Furthermore, the absence of maternal affection has left her the only woman in the story, and so she is vulnerable to being defined as an object in a masculine world.

It appears that Edie's moving to sexual maturity must involve *becoming* her own mother, by marrying one of the elderly husbands on offer. Unable to do this, Edie plunges into physical starvation as she does into linguistic childishness, with something like joyous welcome. But she is not allowed to escape as easily as that. Externalizing her crisis as the immobilization of an entire city also galvanizes others into action, to see that she and they do not starve. Do they thus provide her with the maternal nurturance that she needs in order to move into adulthood? I will argue when I come to the discussion of desire that the story contains a narrative of how Edie finds a 'mother' in an unlikely place, and discovers that mothering is emotional.

THE MOVEMENT OF DESIRE

Although some mention of desire and lack has already inevitably been made, it is important now to focus on the various loci of desire in the text, on the trajectories it follows, and the destinations it reaches. The desiring subjects that demand most consideration are 'Papa', Edie and Mr Thrigg, and I will discuss them in that order.

Apparently desperate for money and respectability, 'Papa' requires the sacrifice of Edie's identity in order that his own might remain intact. He too seeks stasis, since the acquisition of money through Edie's marriage is intended to cover his financial losses and maintain his continued identity, realised as the houses, estates and lifestyle to which the Audeleys are accustomed.

These wishes mask the (unnamed) father's desire for control over Edie's sexuality. He wants her to marry a version of himself; or rather, a version of the self that he aspires to be. The two suitors, Bilberton and Thrigg, are *his* contemporaries. He pretends that furs given by one of them have in fact come from him. In short, the father suffers from an incestuous confusion over the boundary between himself and a suitable lover for his daughter. He craves the successful suitor's wealth, status and worldly competence. He is also confused about the boundary between himself and his daughter, for he believes that the person who will gain access to her husband's symbolic virility will be himself. If the father's desire is narcissistic (wealth and power for himself), so, too, is the desire that Mr Thrigg eventually reaches, that the young man should win Edie as a prize, for in Aurelles he sees a type of manhood to which he aspires.

'Papa' is not a potent father. Clearly some mismanagement has led to the ruin of the family fortunes, thereby rendering him impotent in the world of men, and effectively dependent on Edie for the restoration of his potency. Defined only by his desire for lost possessions, Edie's father is a threatening late Victorian image of the consequences of failure to cope in a material world. Thus this father can scarcely fill the role of the Father of Lacanian theory, for, nameless and castrated, neither the *Non* nor the *Nom du Père* is available to him. No wonder Edie can manoeuvre with such freedom. When the transforming power of the snow arrives, it is her father who retreats into complete infantilism: 'Papa who is an invalid sits and smokes and sips his port, and says he's *quite* comfortable and shan't stir a foot' (23) (demonstrating both a regression to the oral phase, and loss of mobility). Eventually, his regression moves towards silence: 'Papa is so weak he can scarcely speak' (27). Edie thus moves into a clearly enunciated version of exactly that maternal position *vis-à-vis* her father that the advent of sexual maturity has placed her in from the start of the story. He 'needs' her to provide him with nurturance, in the form of the wherewithal for life. Family relationships are thus seriously deformed, and with an absent (presumably dead) mother, and an infantile, dependent father, it is not surprising that Edie, at the beginning of the story, is apparently incapable of maturing out of her solipsistic desires for pleasure.

Edie's desires are extremely complex, and within this discussion I want to pursue the argument that they are not primarily sexual, once the debris of her conformity to the expectations of society is cleared away. Even in the sought stasis of the snow, desire works on in Edie, and her habitual communications with the outside world are turned inwards, to the private language of the diary. The diary is clearly a function of the snow, since she has never before been capable of keeping one going. We have already considered some of the transformations of Edie's desire. To her, language is problematic for she envisages an adult future in which she will write more poetically. Yet she also sees poetry and a use of metaphor as a failure of sexuality; the older men who use 'fine words' and offer compliments are ridiculous and repulsive in her eyes. Only when Mr Thrigg offers clear, practical information does he become interesting. 'He can talk sensibly enough except when he tries to pay me stupid compliments. He seems to understand the position better than either papa, or anybody else' (23). Edie's linguistic desire therefore is for information couched in clear unadorned terms, and for the power that information brings. Power is what will protect her identity against the rival incursions of her father.

From a sexual point of view, it appears that Edie wants Phillip as a husband. The theory of the drives means that desire may move through *other* aspects of the senses than the most obvious, the genital. Her desires are at least bi-valent: for physical pleasure, and for a sense of control. Both of these are realized in the scopic drive that Edie exercises so much.[16] The scopic drive describes the erotic satisfaction of seeing, of deliberate *looking* at a chosen object of desire.[17] Such desire is not a substitute for genital sexuality, but has a genuinely separate status. Its pursuit is not sublimation. Looking provides Edie with both the apparent passivity proper to a well-bred Victorian woman, and the sense of power that comes from turning her acquaintances into objects of her gaze. Edie uses the visual with intense pleasure, and is absolutely frank about its relationship to her desire to control. The ridiculousness of a situation is for her constituted either visually or verbally. Either case results for Edie in a sense of her own superior awareness. Traditionally theorists consider the male gaze on the female object. Edie upsets this convention: her gaze can be intrusive or collusive. When she looks at the three suitors with her father and cruelly observes their grotesqueries, it is intrusive. Again, when the spectacle of Thrigg stuck in the snow strikes her sympathies for human suffering, and she realises that his life is in danger, her acute joy in the spectacle he creates rivals even those powerful life-and-death emotions. Perhaps Edie is sadistic, but closer to the point is the 'Instinct to Master'. It is significant in this context that the rhetoric of vision informs her discussion of others. She uses 'see' to mean 'understand', in 'Why cannot Papa see how handsome Aurelles is?' (21). Of course, Papa cannot 'see' that Aurelles is handsome in Edie's sense. When she wants to be courted, she projects her scopic concerns, hoping that Aurelles will 'look in' that evening. She thus operates a system in which the *object* of desire reveals the direction of her gaze. When the other suitors gaze at her beauty and covet it, she returns their gaze with hidden pleasure in their look, and adds an intrusive look of her own which debases them as sexual beings.

Scopic control, flexible, varied and subtle, shows her complex capacities for visual eroticism in the early scenes with Aurelles. These are presented on one level as if she desires him sexually, but in the game of role-reversal she turns him into a spectacle: a visual object of desire. It seems to be his beauty she admires, and she engineers the situation where she can observe him. At the same time she offers herself to be gazed at by Aurelles, partly in order to set up a power structure similar to that she exercises over Thrigg and Bilberton, partly as an exchange for her use of him as an object of visual erotic pleasure. Aurelles apparently co-operates in this, controlling his own presentation as object by riding past at predictable times of day, while gazing covertly at the location of the (supposedly invisible) object of his desire. Edie has complete control over how visible she is, while maintaining an illusion of innocence (few readers would believe her disingenuous remark '– you can't see in at a window at that distance off, now *can* you?' [20]). In addition, Edie's desire for Phillip does have the expected content. Her fantasies about their time together show him as a person she can talk to, but also as controllable. In his absence, she transforms him into a gentle Newfoundland dog – emasculated and unthreatening: 'he would be on that rug like a great dog and make love to me *so nicely* I do believe *forever*' (22). This nineteenth-century idea of bliss is one of endless flattering conversation.

Edie has seen herself as content with a deceptively childlike condition: 'I never get any fun now I'm a woman' (21). As long as she remains unmarried she can enjoy her desire to stand on the edge of the game and feel her own power through mockery of their behaviour, and the expression of that mockery through language. Edie's self-creation in language is characteristically polymorphous. As Ruth Robbins will show more fully in the next chapter, it is as if she is trying out a variety of self-images, all of which are partly credible, but none fully so. For example, the claim to have had more fun before she was a woman is not borne out by the evidence. Edie apparently has a great deal of fun, but of a rather solitary kind. She is the real chess player, though this is at first obscured by her ability to mask her sense of dominance and claim to be ultra-feminine through her twittering, almost moronic, certainly banal, prose. The fun of flirtation is partially present at the instant when it occurs, but is completed by the fun of writing about it later and denigrating the person in question. In this way, language is used doubly to gain pleasure. But the ridicule debases the original joy by making it seem a pretence. Furthermore, the solitude and the expressed yearning for old times of childhood, which may refer to a now lost comradeship of the schoolroom, make the pleasures of ridiculing gallantry seem isolated and hollow. Yet the language used has an ebullience which is *almost* irresistible, or would be so if it only seemed a little less artful. For behind the 'arts' of womanliness lies fear. It is exactly this sense of multi-layered emotional ambiguity within language and of an associated confusion about Edie's desire and its goals that makes the story as a whole rich in suggestion, and ultimately opaque to interpretation. Edie in fact seeks the Other of paternal authority in its various forms in order to define herself; always against it, but always contained within the structure that it establishes. She is thus held by a kind of psychic centrifugal force.

I have postponed my brief discussion of Mr Thrigg's desire almost to the last, for it is his transformation that is the key to the conclusion of the story, and to the concluding points in my analysis. Thrigg is involved in both the discourse of nourishment, and in that of sexual desire. He relocates himself within the narrative structure, changing his own values in order to take the place of the absent mother, and by doing so assists the other characters as well to new orientations towards the world. It is Thrigg who begins the story in the position of a sexual being: the monied and powerful man who wishes to marry a beautiful woman. He sees no clash between this aspiration, and the paternal position he occupies as a friend of Edie's father. His first reaction to the snow is that of a profiteer: he sees it as a chance to make a killing on the markets, and bewails the lost opportunity. Thrigg owns warehouses full of food which have been blocked up by the storm, and at first, therefore, he and they seem to be useless. What he *can* offer Edie is information. He treats her seriously, enlightening her ignorance in terms she can fit into her extant cognitive structure '. . . for they do not keep great quantities now like they used to in Joseph's time in Egypt' (23). When this information mode veers back into the masculine world of a consideration of his financial losses, Edie's interest vanishes, as does her capacity to comprehend: 'At least I think that was what he said' (23). And starvation is the consequence on every level. Thrigg, however, is tenacious. He again seeks to nourish Edie, both literally and with information, when he shows her how to make a dumpling. Again he fails: the food, when offered, cannot be eaten. Next, Thrigg attempts to go in search of food, and is stuck in the snow all night. Edie's father takes her place at the window, gazing on Thrigg and laughing at the dehumanized spectacle of the man framed by the window and the snow. At this point Edie adjusts her position with regard to Thrigg. He ceases to be ridiculous to her, and she keeps him company as a fellow human being. A link between them is forged, bonded by the nourishment she provides for him. The light she shines for Thrigg brings to them, as a kind of benison, the heroic Aurelles. The possibility of a caring relationship has been opened up. Thrigg next invokes his own birthplace, where food might yet be found, and at last, from a location that one might call the Name of the Mother, come the reviving potatoes and tins of meat. Finally, Thrigg offers Edie what she has never before received: a genuinely unselfish love which will take her expressed desires seriously, and try to fulfil them. Explicit with that belief in her comes a denial of financial values, and of the commercial world. ' "Better than gold" he says "better than gold, courage is beyond banknotes in value" ' (28). Although Edie's objection is significant: 'They never stopped to ask me first' (29) (I will discuss this below), we know that Thrigg's generosity perfectly answers her earlier wish: 'If guardsmen would only manage to be rich' (20). Significantly, the end of the snow is directly associated with Thrigg: '. . . the Alderman who knows everything is sure it means a thaw' (28).

At the end of the story, he moves from both of those positions into that of the asexual facilitator of other people's sexuality. His money no longer is worshipped for itself (as a fetish, or substitute for sexual satisfaction) nor for the things it can buy (a youthful wife), but as a means for sorting the world into a harmonious order of romantic propriety: youthfulness and courage are the new values.

As part of Edie's surprise ending, however, we find these expectations called into question. When marriage to the Lieutenant is placed before her, Edie reveals the true nature of her desire. She first remarks that the snow has changed her: 'I mean to settle down and be a good girl, and make Phil a first rate wife!' (29) Somehow, coming so soon after 'perhaps I may as well agree', this feels like exactly the same sort of shifting whim that we have heard from her before. It is not clear that Aurelles is the ideal husband for Edie. His virtues are his beauty and his reliability in a crisis; his disadvantages are fecklessness with money (we have heard he has debts) and his impractical susceptibility to a pretty face. Neither his good side nor his defects suggest anything of Edie's lively and satiric turn of mind, nor of her delight in language. She would have to be 'sobered' indeed to make Aurelles a suitable wife. Whether we believe her or not probably depends more on our own desires than on the evidence of the story.

Once Edie can have Aurelles, she is no longer sure that she wants him: a Lacanian gesture indeed. It reveals the desire for Aurelles as a desire for the perverse and the unattainable. With Aurelles incorporated within the structures of allowable desire, the attraction shifts: desire is not directed at any obtainable object at all, however superficially charming it may be. Desire exists in movement, and the satisfaction of desire is death. The movement of desire constitutes language, and its cessation is silence. We suspect that Edie's notion of being 'a good wife' is unlikely to be fulfilled. Edie only apparently learns about female virtue. Her cutting-off is arbitrary, and the imposition of the ending falsifies the endless fluidity of the discourse of fluctuating desire.

Edie's desire, therefore, is *to desire*. Her ideal identity is *to be unachieved*, and the stasis which we thought the snow implied perhaps should be better read as a perpetual state of flirtatious indecision. Put like this, it seems that Edie understands the nature of desire very well, and in the denial of that desire she sees death: 'If May ever comes any more', she muses (29). 'May' is also the verb of possibility, of 'maybe', and Edie casts an unconscious doubt on the idea that the possibility will come true. Edie, after all, never moved into the world of self-preservation (the world of the 'ego instincts'). Life and death belong in the Symbolic for her: she could not bring herself to eat her cat, for example, even though starving. Her thoughts of death are not a function of starvation, but of the thaw: they are a reaction to the denial of desire. She raises the doubt about survival a second time, more explicitly: 'That is if I live . . .' (29). On one level, this sounds like the old, flirtatious, capricious Edie. On another, the phrase holds a grim prophecy.

And the end of the snow, the end of Edie's rebellion, is also the end of her inscription of herself. The diary ceases. Silence ensues, filled by the released male voice of the editor/author. Yet there is a cynical further writing present in the text which tries to inscribe Edie as something other than her representation of herself. She perceives herself as powerful and knowing. We, however, perceive her as a victim – trapped, helpless and ignorant

– but also as something more culpable: frivolous, petty-minded and amoral. The source of this 'writing' of Edie arises out of a conflict between the representations of rebellion: in one breath adorable, challenging and enchanting to the men who observe her. Their observation echoes through her mock-naïve assessment of her own power over them. In another breath the real channels of Edie's desire (lingistic power and the control of visual pleasure) are occluded in order that she might play the safer role of the attractive rebel. Aware individuality is masked by a different and more acceptable form of minor self-assertion, restricted to details such as wearing the furs and arguing over the choice of a husband. Yet the diary never quite permits us even *this* radical conclusion. Edie, the motherless child, the commodity with an exchange value in the commercial world, seems as cold, as frivolous, as emotionally illiterate as a late nineteenth-century male stereotype of womanhood might be. Displaying herself and her story, she is a privileged narrator, but is also the conduit through which another voice inscribes its wit and narrative skill on the page. Desire in the text comes from the doubled voice that makes Edie's artlessness into art. She is manipulated to reveal herself artlessly by an external, intrusive desire which, for want of a better word we call 'Jefferies'. 'Edie' marks the pages of her diary with a narrative which is about the marks made upon snow, and by snow upon people. These are Chinese boxes of excessively clever complexity, in which the disingenuous author of the doll-like Edie seems increasingly sinister. He writes Edie writing the snow and writing desire. The double voices of male desire, and of female desire as written by a man, involve a kind of revenge on Edie in which we as readers co-operate.

It is a force outside Edie which gives her the snow and counts its duration inexorably up to three weeks; which traps three suitors in the house; which causes three trips to be made out into the snow; and which suggests three alternative titles at the head of the story (one of the four phrases is repeated). As in any good fairy-story, the satisfaction of enough groups of three breaks the magic bondage in which the princess is held, and delivers her up to her ideal lover. I like to feel that in Edie's turn towards death and silence, we see an absolute rebellion against the domination of Jefferies' magic spells of the threes of the Symbolic order.

NOTES

1. See in particular Elizabeth Wright, *Psychoanalytic Criticism* (1984), and Terry Eagleton, *Literary Theory* (1983). Full bibliographical details for these and other books are given in the Bibliography.

2. For definitions and explanations of the terminology of psychoanalytic thought, see *The Language of Psychoanalysis*, ed. J. Laplanche and J. B. Pontalis (1988).

3. Freud discovered the nature of the unconscious mind as we now understand it. He realized that processes within the unconscious are made observable in several ways, including physical symptoms, dreams, and such linguistic patterns as repetitions, puns, errors (the 'Freudian slip') and jokes. One might add silences to this list – those things which are implied, but unsaid. Freud further theorized that the unconscious mind contains events and knowledge that we have 'repressed', and that the functioning of the unconscious, whether for good or ill, depends on events of early childhood and on the manner in which each child negotiated those events. The experience of infancy, for example, contained first a sense of oceanic power, followed by the discovery of the possibility of loss. With the knowledge of loss comes a desire for that which was lost, or for some representative of that lost completeness. The most important theorist to re-read Freud was the French psychoanalyst, Jacques Lacan, whose prose is notoriously difficult and playful. Where Freud saw psychic processes as crucially concerned with growth towards a maturity interpreted largely as a contented conformity with social expectations of gender, Lacan's exegesis saw the same psychic processes involved with the entry of the subject into what he labelled the 'Symbolic order'. This is the area in which all systematic structuring, including linguistic representation, takes place. The Symbolic takes its place in Lacan's theory in relation to two other orders: the Imaginary and the Real. Edie's situation principally involves the Symbolic.

4. Freud discusses this in his well-known description of the child's game of 'fort/da'.

5. On Lacan, see Wright (1984) for a clear introduction to Freud's theories, and to Lacan's interpretation of them. For a more detailed introduction to Lacan, see Malcolm Bowie's *Lacan* (1991).

6. The term has already been used in this volume, in Julian Cowley's structuralist reading of the story.

7. Julian Cowley (above) has identified the set of furs as one possible object of Edie's desire.

8. *Sublimation*: 'Process postulated by Freud to account for human

activities which have no apparent connection with sexuality but which are assumed to be motivated by the force of the sexual instinct. The main types of activity described by Freud as sublimated are artistic creation and intellectual inquiry' (Laplanche and Pontalis, 431).

9. The rationale for the movement of the subject into the Symbolic order runs as follows. Unless we accept some restrictions, we cannot differentiate ourselves from our surroundings and so become fully human and aware. Such a distinction can only be made for us by an external force, since while the infant (or for that matter, any person) is in the solipsistic state it cannot initiate a sense of self as distinct from a surrounding not-self. Acquiring a sense of self therefore involves the loss of that blissful oneness of earliest infancy, but in exchange for this burden of separation – of being human – comes a huge compensation in the form of a capacity to make patterns. Patterns conform to rules, and rules (once again) can only exist by virtue of saying 'no' to some possibilities. For many, the most important pattern we make is that of language, which Saussure identified as a binary structure. To the binarisms of linguistic theory, Lacan added the idea of the third term which institutes the opposition between the other two: the Name of the Father, punningly expressed in French as *le Non/m du Père*. For both Freud and Lacan, the first 'no-sayer' in a child's life is the Father (not necessarily the literal father of the child), who denies the child its previous absolute access to gratification. In particular, the Father steps between the infant and the mother. In doing so, he forces the child to leave behind its sense that it and the world together form a complete and undifferentiated whole, and to accept that a third term exists.

10. Ruth Robbins, in her chapter on feminist theory (below), reads this self-description differently.

11. See Joan Rivière, 'Womanliness as Masquerade', *International Journal of Psychoanalysis*, 10: 303–13.

12. Such theories were exploded by W. K. Wimsatt and Monroe Beardsley on the intentional fallacy, in *The Verbal Icon* (1970), and later by Roland Barthes in 'The Death of the Author' (Barthes 1977, 142–9).

13. *Condensation*: 'One of the essential modes of the functioning of the unconscious processes: a sole idea represents several associative chains at whose point of intersection it is located' (Laplanche and Pontalis, 82).

   Displacement: 'The fact that an idea's emphasis, interest or intensity is liable to be detached from it and to pass on to other ideas, which were originally of little intensity but which are related to the first idea by a chain of associations' (Laplanche and Pontalis, 121).

14. This is not to say that her perceptions are true, only that they feel true for her, and this belief is useful in therapeutic circumstances.

15. For a discussion of the relation between eating disorders and psychological maturation, see Kim Chernak, *The Hungry Self* (1986).

16. On the pleasure of looking and scopophilia see Laura Mulvey, 'Visual Pleasure and Narrative Cinema' in *Visual and Other Pleasures* (1989, 14–29).

17. See the discussion in Mulvey.

Entr'acte

4

'Snowed Up: A Mistletoe Story': Feminist Approaches

RUTH ROBBINS

And if you examine literary history, it's the same story. It all refers back to man, to *his* torment, his desire to be (at) the origin. Back to the father. There is an intrinsic bond between the philosophical and the literary (to the extent that it signifies, literature is commanded by the philosophical) and phallocentrism. The philosophical constructs itself starting with the abasement of woman. Subordination of the feminine to the masculine order which appears to be the condition for the functioning of the machine.

Hélène Cixous

INTRODUCTION

It is not possible in the space which I have available to give a comprehensive account of the development of feminist literary theories and their practice.[1] Feminism is a pluralist mode, where many different approaches are available: it seldom seeks to be proscriptive and consequently several very different approaches to literary texts all adopt the label 'feminist'. The placing of this essay in the middle of the present collection signals that feminist literary criticism 'borrows' or appropriates from other theoretical discourses. A feminist critic may choose to concentrate her (or occasionally his) attention on the formal or aesthetic qualities of a text; or she may make the political positioning of the text her central focus. This essay does both, using, for example, some of the assumptions of structuralism, psychoanalysis, deconstruction and Marxism in its analysis of Jefferies's story. But the essay makes no claim that it represents *the* definitive feminist account of the story; indeed, such a claim would simply reinforce the proscriptive and authoritarian readings of some other forms of theory which feminist theories and practices seek to challenge.

There are fierce arguments about the precise nature of feminism, and different versions of feminist theory may sometimes seem to be at odds with each other as well as with the masculist assumptions which they all seek to modify, deconstruct or destroy. But what all versions of feminism share is a double commitment to place women at the centre of critical discourse, and to do so as part of a wider political process, where the women 'outside' the text – in the 'real' world – are engaged with various struggles for equality and revaluation. That is, the sexual politics of the world outside the literary text, and the sexual politics which the text exhibits or disguises are seen in feminist theory as part of a continuum of political action. The analysis of the text is linked to an analysis of the world in which the text was/is produced. My account, for example, deals with Edie's story from a quasi-structuralist perspective; but in doing so, it also insists that the narrative structures are connected in some way to the real world. This strategy shows both how feminism is happy to appropriate other discourses, and how those discourses are in turn modified by their exposure to feminism. That is, feminism makes a political reading through structuralism possible, despite Julian Cowley's suggestion which is that this kind of approach is often perceived as ahistorical and apolitical.

The political commitment in feminist literary theory is a function of the origins of feminism in the twentieth century in the Civil Rights movements which swept the United States during the 1960s. The history of feminism is, however, much longer than such a statement might imply. Mary Wollstonecraft, after all, in her novels and her political treatise, *A Vindication of the Rights of Woman* (1792), had begun the process of analysing and rejecting the social structures by which she perceived that women were undermined in society: how they were increasingly equated with children, how they were under-educated, and how they were refused the right to enter the 'masculine' public domain. In Britain, through much of the nineteenth century, women undertook a series of political campaigns for equal treatment before the law. As early as 1866, the Langham Place group, including women such as Barbara Bodichon, Emily Davies and Elizabeth Garrett, produced a petition asking for the franchise to be extended to women as part of the process of the second Reform Act of 1867. Women's groups were active in the discussions which led to the 1857 Matrimonial Causes Act which made divorce possible (though it remained unlikely) for the first time. And feminist interventions certainly led in part to the repeal, in 1886, of the Contagious Diseases Acts which had legalised the forcible medical examination of female prostitutes. Throughout the period too, women writers, and particularly women novelists, had charted female dissatisfaction with their man-made worlds, both overtly and covertly. Similarly, in the US, in the 1840s, the movement towards female equality was linked to the Abolitionist movement, rather as twentieth-century feminism developed in part from the Civil Rights movements, and as early as 1848, women's suffrage had become an issue for debate and demand.

In other words there is a long tradition of questioning the social position of women, and a long tradition also of taking direct action in order to change that position. But in the 1960s and 1970s this tradition became more activist, and more articulate, in the sense that the discourse it adopted sought to connect several different areas of oppression. For example, the women who supported the Civil Rights movements for black emancipation in the 1960s began to suggest that the arguments for equality between black and white were also arguments which could be applied to the inequality between the sexes. Moreover, just as racial oppression had been shown to have economic effects, so too sexual oppression was shown to have effects beyond the personal suffering of the individual, hence the adoption by feminists of the slogan: 'The Personal *is* Political'.

It is not that the claim for male/female equality is new. Wollstonecraft complained in her posthumously published novel *Maria: or, The Wrongs of Woman* that women are hemmed in by 'the partial laws enacted by men' (Wollstonecraft [1798] 1976, 155). And Charlotte Brontë's Jane Eyre makes a plea which is at once personal and particular, and applicable to the general situation of women:

> It is in vain to say human beings ought to be satisfied with tranquility: they must have action: and they will make it if they cannot find it. . . . Women are supposed to be very calm generally: but women feel just as men feel; they need exercise for their faculties, and a field for their efforts as much as their brothers do: . . . it is narrow-minded in their more privileged fellow creatures to say that they ought to confine themselves to making puddings and knitting stockings . . . or laugh at them if they seek to do more or learn more than custom has pronounced necessary for their sex. (Brontë 1966, 141)

Brontë's character makes a series of important claims in this outburst: women are human beings just like men; they therefore have the same needs as men, and ought, morally speaking, to have the same rights; there should be some kind of equality. Men may be more privileged than women, but they still belong to the same species; they are 'fellow creatures'.

What changed in our own century is that the link between the arguments about equality and direct political action became far more explicit. Following the lead of Simone de Beauvoir in *The Second Sex*, who argued that the concept 'woman' was culturally produced rather than biological, the women's movement began to combine political analysis with cultural analysis in their struggle for equality. If, as Gayle Greene and Coppélia Kahn have argued, 'the inequality of the sexes is neither a biological given nor a divine mandate, but a cultural construct', then it is 'a proper subject of study for any humanistic discourse' (Greene and Kahn 1985, 1).

The study of gender inequality may indeed be a particularly 'proper subject of study' in the analysis of literary texts, since literature at once reflects and participates in the creation of the culture in which it takes place. Literature, that is, may act as a code-giver, a text which gives us examples by which we should live. The Bible, after all, is a literary text which tells its readers how to behave; and in this sense it *forms* the culture in which it is read. But it was also created *out of* a specific culture. It reflects the history of an ancient tribe wandering in the desert.

The writers of the Biblical texts observed the world around them, and implied through their narratives that their own very culturally and historically specific way of life was 'natural' because it was 'God-given'. So the Bible at once shows us something of the history and culture of the society in which it was produced, and creates our culture and history through its dissemination.

It is this dual perspective on the literary text – on how literature both reflects and creates the culture in which it is produced and read – with which feminist literary criticism and theory has been particularly concerned. In its beginnings, with writers such as Mary Ellmann (*Thinking about Women*, 1968) and Kate Millett (*Sexual Politics*, 1970), the method was largely (though not exclusively) to take texts produced by male writers, and subject the attitudes to gender in those texts to intense scrutiny. The women in male-authored texts were 'discovered' to be 'man-made', to have been created in implicit and usually unacknowledged support of an ideology of masculine superiority. These representations of women, according to Mary Ellmann's analysis, conformed to a series of (actually contradictory) stereotypes: women are presented at once as being 'naturally' material and spiritual, formless and confined, for example, as well as exhibiting passivity, instability, irrationality, piety and compliancy. They do not conform to ideals, always inscribed as male-gendered by their male creators, such as firmness, consistency, activity and intellect (Moi 1985, 34).

This procedure of dealing with the images of women produced by men has been described by Elaine Showalter in her 1979 essay 'Towards a Feminist Poetics' as 'feminist critique'; and she argues that it is a useful but limited approach, since its effect finally is to continue focus attention on male-authored texts – to continue to assume, that is, masculine **authority**. She proposes a second phase of feminist criticism, in which the critic will focus her attention on writing *by* women rather than writing *about* women. This involves a process of scholarship, through which 'lost' or ignored texts can be recovered and studied – a task which she undertakes herself in her book *A Literature of Their Own* (1977), and which is also the method which informs Sandra M. Gilbert and Susan Gubar's important study of nineteenth-century writing by women, *The Madwoman in the Attic* (1979). Through this process of textual recovery, it will be possible, Showalter suggests, to construct a *tradition* of women's writing which stands in opposition to, and thereby seeks to modify, the male-defined literary canon. By seeking to understand the mechanisms by which cultures promote gender inequality – by gaining access to a critical language which empowers the female reader and the female writer – the feminist critic seeks political change in the wider sphere, beyond the literary text. (Moi 1985, 75)

Showalter's approach, as Toril Moi has argued, also has its limitations. For one thing, the number of 'recoverable' texts from history is obviously limited: sooner or later the scholar will come up against the fact that there are no more books in the library. Moreover, Showalter implies that texts written by women must be treated differently from those written by men. There is an assumption that representations of women *by* women will somehow be more 'authentic', more real, than those by men. Whilst it is obvious that feminist critics might seek to ask different kinds of textual questions from those which have traditionally been asked by men, if women's writing cannot be subjected to rigorous analysis as men's writing has been, then it may well find itself rejected as a lesser form. Again, as Toril Moi has also suggested, Showalter's approach is dependent on identification both with the female author and her female characters. We are asked to see ourselves in them. This is problematic, since it implies that the female reader/critic has a merely personal relationship with the text, rather than an analytic perspective on what is written (Moi 1985, 75–9). If, as Ellmann's list of stereotypes implies, women are seen by patriarchal culture as dependent on personal relationships, as intuitive and irrational, then Showalter's method risks replacing women in precisely the same position into which patriarchal culture has also traditionally placed them.

Feminist theory has signposted various routes out of this impasse. Particularly in France, with the writings of Luce Irigaray, Hélène Cixous and Julia Kristeva, whose work draws on Lacanian psychoanalysis, and Derridean poststructuralism, there have been various moves to deconstruct the whole arena of binary thought with its implicit hierarchies. Cixous, for example, writes her critiques of texts and society in a form which decisively ignores traditional cultural models of analysis and perspective. Her style implies that criticism is itself creative, and that it cannot be interpreted beyond itself; it resists arguments in (masculine) logical forms, resisting also interpretation and paraphrase.

For precisely these reasons, however, Cixous's route is particularly difficult to imitate or to apply. The complexities of French feminist theories have made them the subject of no small resistance in Anglophone theoretical traditions. None the less, the questions raised by Cixous's approach may well be fruitful inasmuch as they provide clues as to how a contemporary approach to feminist theory and praxis might develop. As I have already suggested, there is not only one feminism, but many, and just as feminist politics implies co-operation rather than proscription – opening up new routes rather than forbidding certain pathways – so too does feminist literary theory. Cixous's approach, with its fusions of creativity and analysis, dramatizes the idea that feminist theory and practice is different from those forms traditionally practised in the (male-dominated) academy.

This possibility of disruption of norms is something that I want to suggest is also true of the character of Edie in Richard Jefferies's short story, 'Snowed Up: A Mistletoe Story'. I say again that I make no claim that my reading of this story is definitive in terms of feminist theory. But it is fed by several different strands of feminist inquiry, which are explained as I proceed. Edie is a man's image of a woman, and may therefore by subjected to the kind of analysis which Showalter calls 'feminist critique'. But there may also be ways in which a masculine version of femininity is not merely a conformist or conservative version; such a version may open up and become subversive of the patriarchy which has created it. My approach will therefore be to interrogate different areas of the text. What unites all my questions is their 'woman-centredness', alongside a sustained double interest in the culture which has formed Edie and the ways in which she conforms to and/or subverts the assumptions of that culture; how, as it were, her interventions in culture, and how our reading of those interventions, might suggest motivations and methods for bringing about change.

EDIE'S LANGUAGE

As a female character in a fiction written by a man, Edie's own writing comes into being at the instigation of a man. It is his assumptions about what 'writing as a woman' might mean which form her. Within the text as well, however, Edie also writes at the instigation of a man. It is 'old Mr., I mean the very reverend, at least I'm not sure about his title but he is canon or something at the Cathedral who persuaded me to begin keeping a diary' (20), Edie tells us. Ironically, the reverend gentleman has suggested to her that writing things down will help her to 'classify [her] ideas, and bring [her] mind into shape' (20). Articulation in diary form, Edie has been told, will give her a sense of perspective, and will help her to know her own mind. But, as her failure to remember who the reverend gentleman is indicates, the ideals of order and classification, which writing apparently implies, are immediately subverted. The diary form, with its chronological imperative, seems to be a manifestation of order; but in the case of Edie's diary, as she suggests herself, she does not write regularly ('I shall never be a good diarist, my last entry I see was a month ago.' [19]). Moreover, even during the crisis which is the basis of the story, there are days when she does not write at all, and her entries are uneven in length and tone. Edie's writing is not ordered, and certainly in its initial stages, the diary demonstrates her inability to separate the trivial from the important.

In a sense this is the point of the story, which – as 'Richard Jefferies'[2] tells us at the end – is about the 'awkwardness' which would descend upon London after a heavy snowfall. London, as a capital of 'civilization' – the very opposite of the randomness of nature – is reduced to a scramble after what are, finally, the essentials of life: warmth, light, food. The aspects of urban living on which a definition of 'civilization' is predicated – a culture which tries to ignore nature's necessities – are destroyed; the normal order of things, the hierarchy of the trivial and the necessary, is overturned.

Even before the snow has precipitated this disaster, however, Edie demonstrates in her own diary her inability to keep 'order'. It is not, as Julian Cowley also notes, that she does not know the 'rules', but rather that she is not in the least bit interested in observing them. She comments, for example, that she is going to wear her new furs to the theatre, even though she knows that it is not 'de règle' (20); the rules are literally a foreign language to her, and she demonstrates her tendency to obey her impulses rather than behaving according to abstract conceptions of what is right. In this representation of her, she is aligned with the aspects of character which are seen to be 'feminine': she chooses impulse over order, pleasure rather than rules; and her focus is on herself, rather than on the world outside herself. She embodies, that is, the feminine quality of passion, not the masculine quality of reason; and this observation is borne out by a close examination of her syntax, vocabulary and emphatic girlish style.

Edie's most usual syntactical construction is the simple sentence. Her sentences tend to be short, and there is very little in the way of subordination as we follow her thought processes through their grammatical structures. Where sentences are long, their length is produced through a process of co-ordination: her ideas tend to be linked only by juxtaposition, punctuation or the (often implied) conjunction 'and'. This style implies a number of things about Edie. First of all, it is a style calculated to mimic the structures of conversation. Her writing appears, that is, to be as spontaneous as speech, with idea tumbling after idea. Such a language is also suggestive of a certain kind of mind. This is clearly not the language of logic, analysis and perspective, the very qualities Edie would need if the diary were to serve the function of producing 'order' in her mind. Take the following example, from very early in the story:

> A poor girl is just like a shuttlecock or a tennis ball with all these gentlemen tossing her about one to the other. It *is* laughable when I think of it to see fat Mr Thrigg jump up and open the door for me, and Lord Bilberton screwing up his face into a smile of approval (though he hates the Alderman) and Lieut. Aurelles scowling at them both, and trying oh, so hard to play chess – which he does not understand – with papa; and all just because. Well, I suppose I *am* pretty. (20)

On the face of it, the simile of the shuttlecock or tennis ball is extremely perceptive on Edie's part, since it precisely describes her situation as an object in a game between men, with no will and no power of her own.[3] But Edie does not develop this simile into an analysis of her situation; she cannot go beyond the description in part because, although she is not a participant in the game, she is an enthusiastic spectator of it. She is both subject and object, gazer and gazed at. The pleasure she takes in the masculine competition for her favours has a serious consequence. It prevents her from being in a position to understand her own situation, and stops her too from being able to see a connection implied in the story (but not seen by Edie herself) between her particular suggestion and the situation of women in general. So, for Edie, at this early point in this story, her insight into her own position as object is interpreted as being merely 'laughable'. The connection between the men's games and her own objectification is one created only from a syntactical juxtaposition of the two ideas. So Edie may know her own position, but she does not fully *realise* it and its consequences. The long sentence, which begins with the laughability of the situation, is built up with the repeated conjunction 'and'. The connection between the parts of the sentence is positional rather than logical. When Edie comes to the point of making a causal connection between the actions of the men, and her own position, it is a connection which is left incomplete; the causal conjunction 'because' is followed by a full stop before it is followed by the reason: 'Well, I suppose I *am* pretty' (20).

Edie is written by a man, but she is supposed to be 'writing as a woman'. Her enthusiasm, her illogicality, her emphasis on self and so on, are all, it is implied, functions of her femininity. Jefferies himself suggests at the end of the story that 'a lady's fright may have exaggerated matters', hinting that an account of such events written by/as a woman must necessarily be treated with some suspicion precisely because the writer is not only female, but also a 'lady', a female whose existence is removed from the real world of masculine work and analysis by virtue of her class as well as her gender. In Edie's version of London in the snow, events cannot be fully known or finally closed. Again she turns to simile to describe her situation as object: 'I am to be a commodity bought and sold like the Alderman's onions. . . . He has just handed me over to Phil as he would a basket of vegetables! . . . They never stopped to ask me first'(29).[4] The simile of the game in the earlier part of the story has been replaced with a simile from the world of commerce. Edie's marriage is to be a purely commercial transaction. Whilst her tone implies that she is indignant at this treatment, she remains unable to place her indignation into a more analytic frame. Her fate under the commercial regime is rather better than it would have been under the rules of the earlier game (Phillip, for example, lacked the strategy to beat her father at chess). At least she has got the preferred suitor; so making a fuss about the process by which this outcome was achieved seems almost pointless – what she wants is the illusion of autonomy, rather than a change in outcome. There remains, none the less, her rather bitter comment that the snow 'was not such a bad thing for – for Phillip' (29). There is no mention of her own feelings.

In the next paragraph, the diary breaks off rather ominously, probably in mid-sentence. The ending is ominous because Edie has suggested that her experiences in the snow have taken their toll on her constitution: '. . . my limbs are chilled to the marrow. I don't think I shall live so as to give a surprise' (29). Her voice falls silent. Her account remains open, the ends are untied. Closure – the finality of a fixed, stable meaning and interpretation – is imposed on the story by a masculine voice, that of 'Richard Jefferies', who tells us that the point behind the tale is not Edie's own ending, but a speculation as to what would happen if London were attacked by snow. It is, he claims, about the larger world of commerce: the 'love story' is merely incidental.

This precisely contradicts Edie's own view of her story. Closure is precisely what she seeks to disrupt, and she suggests, quite early in her diary that this is a function of her gender: 'How hateful it is of gentlemen when they will come to the point, as they call it! We girls never care about such nonsense. It spoils life . . . this always coming to the point' (21). Her interest in life, that is, is not teleological (end-determined). She is interested in the process at least as much as she is interested in the results. Like the princess in the fairy-story,[5] the *process* by which she will be married is more important than the marriage itself; in the story, then, the marriage is postponed, deferred until May, 'if May ever comes any more' (29). Edie's doubts about whether chronology really is inexorable, after the snow, places her marriage into an impossible future, takes it out of time, just as 'once upon a time' and 'happily ever after' in fairy-stories remove their fantastic events from the reality of measurable time (her sense of time, one might say, is feminine). So whilst her marriage to Phillip is part of the larger process of commerce to which Alderman Thrigg belongs, the bargain has not been closed by the end of the story.

There are at least two ways in which the feminist critic might approach the question of Edie's representation. The first arises out of Showalter's 'feminist critique' in which the (female) reader is invited to read the (male-authored) text 'suspiciously'. In this kind of reading, the critic interrogates the text to discover whether Edie's presentation of herself is merely a construction of femininity which is determined by the patriarchal culture in which it is produced, and which is thereby fundamentally inauthentic. One might ask to what extent young women ever really talked like Edie talks; we might compare and contrast representations of women speaking written by women with other examples written by men. In a detailed reading of passages from, say, Samuel Richardson's *Pamela* (1742), an early epistolary novel in which the heroine is also a male-authored woman, writing 'as' a woman, we would perhaps see similarities (a kind of tradition of representation, one might say) between Edie and Pamela. We might contrast these representations with ones written by women, such as Brontë's Lucy Snowe in *Villette*, for example. And additionally, we might also seek 'authentic' diary records, written by women towards the end of the nineteenth century, to see if Edie matches up.

What these points of comparison and contrast would reveal, however, is likely to be inconclusive. Men and women are participants in the same culture, even if there is an inbuilt inequality in their relationships with that culture. If women's roles in a given society are narrow and restrictive, it may well be that women will seek to protest against the social structures in which they exist at the same time as they also internalize those structures, and begin to live by them, despite distrusting them. It seems unlikely that there is an absolute, scientifically observable distinction between the language forms used by men and by women. Moreover, to suggest that Edie is merely the victim of man-made language or of the masculist assumptions of her society seems to me to be dangerously reductive, implying as it does that the role of victim is the only possible space for a woman in a patriarchal culture.

There is another way of reading her position. Edie's language resists the logic of critical metaphrase: that is, her writing does not belong to masculine categories of logic and analysis which permits – or demands – authoritative interpretation. Her language cannot be simply paraphrased; it is not so much what she says as the way she says it which matters in the formation of her character. Just as the meaning of her sentences is unstable because it is so seemingly unstructured, so too is the meaning of Edie herself. I have already implied that as a character within this text she is both subject and object. She is an object of exchange between men in a game that they are playing. What they fail to realize, however, is that she is also a subject – a centre of consciousness in her own right. Just as they interpret and subsume her into their game, she also subsumes and interprets them in the secret, covert text of her diary. As Nelly Furman has suggested, following the anthropologist, Claude Lévi-Strauss, the meaning of (a) woman will be different 'according to whether woman is understood as being person or sign' (Greene and Kahn 1985, 61). Within this text, Edie is clearly both things, a living, fully functioning human being, *and* an object like a shuttlecock or a basket of vegetables which has a value in much the same way as paper money has value, through an agreed convention that it is valuable.

So, another question we might ask is: which is Edie's more important textual function? As subject or object? As person, or as token of cultural exchange?

The text itself clearly signals its intention that Edie's story is merely a fictional example of what happens in a civilized society when the usual rules are disrupted. The intervention by 'Richard Jefferies' at the end of the story suggests that the story is 'really' about larger questions of commerce in the face of a natural disaster: Edie's tale is merely a vehicle which enables these questions to be raised; in which case Edie is what the men in her story think her, an object.

Yet at the same time, the text also carries another, perhaps more subversive message. It charts a progressive breakdown in civilization. At first the trains stop running; inessential services grind to a halt, which causes irritation but is not life-threatening: 'Papa is fidgety and cross, for he could not get his *Morning Post* this morning, and no letters came' (22). Things become increasingly serious as the milkman and the baker cannot get through, and there's no meat left in the city. Just as women usually are in this society, even under normal conditions, the men are trapped in the house where they show themselves to be relatively useless. Men whose social positions Edie is supposed to respect are reduced to objects of her sympathy, or, perhaps, her contempt: eventually the older men even take to their respective beds, where they are described as being 'helpless' (26). She gains a certain liberation from the situation: the illnesses which overtake the older men permit her to enjoy the unchaperoned company of her preferred suitor, Phillip: 'Phillip and I are left alone . . .' (26). In their comparative helplessness, they are not unlike Edie herself, a young woman who has been brought up as an adornment and whose only interests are relatively 'frivolous': Edie is less able than Alderman Thrigg to prepare food, or to light a fire; once the servants have gone they are all, as it were, marooned on a desert island in Berkeley Square, and without the trappings of civilization – the things which give them their status in society – they collapse into a feminized existence. But for Phillip's hunter–gatherer instincts, they would all starve or freeze to death. The trappings of powerful masculinity in the 'civilized' patriarchy of London are thereby exposed as mere veneer. Lord Bilberton's social position, Mr Thrigg's wealth and Edie's father's parental authority all cease to mean anything in these new circumstances. It is the 'uncivilized' abilities of Phillip (a man who in normal circumstances has no power, being merely a debt-ridden guardsman) to forage for food, and to protect the household from the roughs on the streets whose value increases in relative terms. And even Phillip requires the Alderman, acting as his fairy godmother, to produce the capital which makes marriage with Edie possible in the world beyond the snowstorm.

Finally, the reader of the story is more interested in Edie herself than in her specific circumstances. We are intrigued to know whether she is capable of development, and in this sense, whilst Edie is an object to her menfolk, she is a subject to us. Their relative indifference to her implies a criticism of the culture to which they all belong. Once the snow has melted, civilization immediately reasserts itself: 'people are running about once more almost as if nothing had happened. If the sky was to fall they would forget it in ten minutes on the Stock Exchange. That's what Phil says' (29), comments Edie in her diary, showing how even her insights have been resubjected to masculine authority. The interlude during which powerful men have been reduced to the domesticity of women is just that – an interlude, a mere break in the game. Except for the Alderman's almost magical generosity, nothing has changed. And even that generosity is explicable in terms of market forces (gold is exchanged for Edie who secured his life from the snow). Edie's story – and specifically her way of telling it – exposes the limitations of civilization on more than one level: it is not only about what would happen to London if the snow fell, but also about what happens to its institutions, here represented by individual people, if the worst were to happen. At the same time, the story also shows how relatively easy it is for the social system to reassert itself, particularly if the 'victims' of civilization are not in a position to analyse – and thence to seek to change – their situation.

NATURE AND CULTURE

'Is female to male as nature is to culture?' is the titular question of an article by Sherry B. Ortner. Ortner takes a binary opposition which is common in Western cultures, and interrogates the extent to which it is a gendered opposition, in which the privileged term has been assumed by masculinity (Humm 1992, 253–5). It is a question which is also asked, though in a very different way by Hélène Cixous, in her essay 'La Jeune Née' (Marks and de Courtivron 1980, 90 ff; Moi 1985, 104). Cixous proceeds by listing a series of common binaries, following the poststructuralist insights of Jacques Derrida on the function of binary oppositions in Western thinking.[6] Heading her list of binaries with the question: 'Where is she?', what Cixous suggests is that all these oppositions – by which, according to structuralist analyses, meaning is generated – form part of a gendered hierarchy. If one asks 'Where is she?', one discovers that the less valued terms of the opposition is always feminine. The very language that we use is, then, according to Cixous, based on gender inequality, since the feminine half of the binary is always a negative or impotent quality. All binaries therefore return to 'the fundamental 'couple' of male/female' (Moi 1985, 105).

In the mid- to late Victorian period in which Jefferies was writing, as Elaine Showalter (in *Sexual Anarchy*, 1991) has argued, there was a crisis in the definition of gender, and one of the most debated questions was that of the meaning, and proper place of women in society. During the 1880s, for example, there were fierce debates about the level of education which should be available to women, as women began to demand access to the universities (Showalter 1991, 7). It was still assumed, certainly in the case of middle-class women, that marriage was the ideal career, and that husbands and fathers would provide the material needs of their girl children. What was not understood was that the relative positions of the sexes were not 'natural' or God-given, but that they were culturally and historically specific.[7] The definitions of woman contemporary with the story began with the assumption that women were the weaker sex; that they needed to be protected from the harsh worlds of business, commerce and politics, and that they needed education only to the extent that this made it possible for them to make decent mothers. An ideal state of affairs was supposed to be one in which men and women operated in 'Separate Spheres' (the term comes from the 1860s); women worked in the domestic sphere, protected from painful reality outside, but also acting as moral guides to their menfolk, in that they provided for them also a pleasant refuge or respite from their external tasks. In this way, woman's role was to act as the enabler of culture, who made culture possible: but she was not finally a participant in culture.

When Simone de Beauvoir wrote that 'one is not born a woman, one becomes one', she was asking her readers to consider the idea that 'woman' is a cultural construction, rather than a bio-logical one: and the importance of this remark is that it seeks to demonstrate that the ideas about sex roles which any given society may have come to regard as 'natural', are not really so; and, given that they are not 'natural', they may even be changed. Modern feminist theories have taken this original insight and developed it further. If the category 'woman' is not merely a biological fact, but a cultural construction, we must separate out the strands of biology from culture when we speak of them. The agreed convention of feminist theory is that 'female' is used to refer to biological sex, whereas 'feminine' is used to describe those features which females are supposed to have (though, they do not necessarily do so) in a given culture. In this way gender – the social construction of the person – is separated from his/her biological sex; consequently a man may have what the cul-ture sees as 'feminine' qualities, and a woman may have mascu-line ones.

On the other hand, it has not been possible entirely to escape the biological imperatives of sex. The most fundamental differ-ence between men and women is that women bear children, and men do not. This 'natural', biological distinction between the sexes has been (and continues to be) the basis of many of the cultural constructions of 'woman', and turns the category of woman into a paradox. Whilst 'the biological facts ... have no determinate meanings in themselves [they] are invested with various symbolic meanings by different cultures' (Greene and Kahn 1985, 2). In Western societies, the symbolic significance of femininity

– the cultural meaning of female – is at least double. As the bearers, nurses, rearers of children, women are often inscribed as being closer to nature. The universal necessity for species to reproduce themselves – shared by all animals who organize their lives around the production and protection of their young – makes women appear to be closer to nature, more animalistic, less cultured than men. Yet, at the same time, women are also the nurturers of children; that is, another of women's roles is to turn the anarchic and animalistic baby into a civilized and ac-culturated human being, at least up to the point (in Western societies) where outside agencies take on the role of education.[8] So woman is at once a manifestation of nature and of culture. She lives inside the house which she tends; she teaches her young; and she provides a civilized refuge from the world outside the home where Man makes his living. But she also gives birth, aligning her with the irrational world of nature. She is simulta-neously bearer of nature and bearer of culture.

What has this got to do with Edie? The first thing that we are told in Edie's diaries is that her father has just given her 'such a splendid set of furs' (19). Edie claims that she has never seen anything so beautiful. The gift is peculiarly double-edged. The fur is expensive, and might therefore be seen as a gift which emphasizes Edie's value in her father's eyes: he has, one might assume, spent a large sum of money on her as a mark of his affection for her. The expense is certainly important to Edie, and seems to enhance the aesthetic (and perhaps also sensuous) pleasure which she takes in them. But as the story progresses, and negotiations are entered into for Edie's marriage, it becomes increasingly clear that Edie's father simply does not have the kind of disposable wealth to have bought the furs – it may be indeed, Edie speculates, that the Alderman's money bought the gift, perhaps as a bribe to her father. It also becomes clear that Edie's father does not value his daughter in affectionate terms, but sees her merely as a commercial proposition whose mar-riageability may get him out of financial difficulties. She becomes, therefore, as we have already noted, an agent of culture – an object of exchange like paper money, to be passed between men. And we see her resentment of this treatment: her suitors have not asked her first which she sees as an insult, and her father has merely said that she 'might have which [she] liked, it made no difference to him' (21). The choice is illusory, since in fact she wants neither of the men she is offered.

The furs represent Edie's exchange value; in normal circumstances, if the London climate were behaving as it usually does, fur would not be a necessity, but a luxury. And the woman who wears the fur as an adornment becomes in turn a luxurious adornment to the men who own, or who seek to own, her. Like Edie herself, in normal circumstances, the furs are useless – even she admits that they will be too warm for her purpose of wearing them to the theatre. They operate as a conventional sign of value between men: Edie is literally carrying the signs of patriarchal culture on her back.

Alongside the furs as signs of monetary value within culture, they are also to be read as evoking Edie's proximity to nature. The related facts that the furs originate from the skins of dead animals, and that they are seen as an appropriate gift for a woman, implies also that the woman is close to the animal nature which they signify. As the snow descends upon London, as nature attacks civilization, the furs come into their own as a 'useful' gift. Their original 'natural' function, of keeping an animal warm, which has been displaced by their symbolic function within patriarchal systems of signification, is reinvoked. When the Alderman is trapped in the snow, Edie is able to keep him company by the window because she has her fur jacket to wear: though even then, she sits shivering.

In this story, it is not that nature and culture operate as precise opposites. Edie lives in the midst of the culture which defines her. She is central to its perpetuation in her position as object of exchange. But even under 'normal' circumstances, that very centrality is also a form of marginality. Just as she is both subject and object – person and sign – within the games and the commercial transactions of the men, she is also a carrier of both culture and nature. Visually, the furs associate her with animal nature; symbolically they represent her acculturation into sign. The men who are attracted to her are therefore attracted along two distinct axes. Lord Bilberton sees her only as a symbol of culture. He is unable to see her as more than a sign, and is consequently unable to communicate with her except in empty conventional compliments which, if he were to win her, would be merely self-congratulatory, directed at his achievement rather than at her worth. On the other hand, the attraction between Edie and Phillip is an animal – a natural – attraction.

As a soldier, Phillip is a conspicuously manly man; he is masculine in terms of his ability to act, in contrast to the relatively feminized existences of a businessman (who acts only within the commercial sphere) and aristocrat (who clearly cannot act at all). When Edie thinks about Phillip, what she regrets is that her cultured father cannot understand her natural attraction to the 'penniless soldier': 'Why can't papa see how handsome Aurelles is?' (21) And she explicitly contrasts his physical attractions with the lack of them in the other two men: 'He is so tall and strong and noble-looking, such a contrast to wizened little Bilberton, and stout Alderman Thrigg' (20). She also describes him in animal terms: 'he is a kind of a Newfoundland dog of a man' (20). The Newfoundland dog is a very large breed, with a coarse coat; it is noted mostly for its intelligence and for its tenacity. It is a domesticated breed, but one primarily used for outdoor work whose presence inside the cultured space of the domestic sphere is the occasion of some risk. (It is Phillip who breaks up the furniture for fuel, wrecking the domestic aesthetic, but producing thereby the means of life.) In this sense, Phillip is cultured enough to be safe (he is not a wild animal), but natural enough to be both useful and exciting.

The animal imagery is reciprocated too – implying that the animal attraction works both ways. As the snow continues and Edie becomes increasingly lonely and bored, she muses about how pleasant it would be to have '*somebody* to chat with' ('somebody' being a euphemism for Phillip).

> I wonder if I had *somebody* here every evening I should get tired of him! I can just fancy him curled up on this rug at my feet (he raves about my little feet and little paws and littleness altogether, and wicked black eyes and and – but no matter). He would be on that rug like a great dog, and make love to me *so nicely*, I do believe, *forever*. (21–2)

It is precisely Phillip's marginal acculturation – the fact that, like Edie, he does not quite belong to the cultured world of the other men – that makes him so attractive. He at least is capable of genuine, disinterested affection, and of a dog-like faithfulness to the ideal, at least in this version of him. Edie and Phillip recognize the natural in each other: he raves over her 'little paws'. But Edie is a much more domesticated animal than Phillip is. Indeed as the situation worsens, her littleness and timidity turn her into a dormouse (28), an animal (and therefore natural) which is helpless in the face of a natural disaster. This is at once the attraction of opposites (her littleness in contrast to his largeness), and an attraction based on their joint recognition that they each occupy undervalued positions on the continuum which leads from nature to culture. This is signalled by the fact that both of them are marginalized by the dominant modes of masculine culture. Phillip is a 'penniless soldier', and as such, cannot participate in the masculine culture of the exchange of monetary signs (Mr Thrigg) or signs of inherited status (Lord Bilberton's coronet). On the other hand, when things get really desperate, the men band together and eat Edie's Persian cat, which like her, is a useless luxury (rats infest the house, but the cat is only mentioned when she becomes a meal). Sometimes, it is implied, the bond between men is stronger than the animal bond between the young lovers. Edie must be careful that male predation – whether in capitalist enterprizes or in foraging for desperately needed food – is not turned on her, another domestic animal in a pretty fur coat.

Edie, we might say, occupies a position which is *between* culture and nature, and is thereby able partially to break down the hierarchy implied by such a binary opposition, in what might be described as a deconstructive move which subverts the nature/culture binary without replacing it at the end of the story. Edie's story permits the reader to analyse her situation as an object, whilst at the same time, the voice in which the story is told is a confident assertion of her subjectivity. Nature, we are told, is simultaneously despised and dangerous: the snow has reduced masculinity to a shadow of its former self – even Phillip is 'fearfully thin and gaunt':

> What has become or will become of the poor people no one can tell. And all through a little snow – the despised snow – so fine and impalpable, yet strong enough to completely conquer our civilization. No trains can run. No ships can come up the river. No food, no light, no help. All through the weak, feeble despised flakes of snow! (27)

Like the snow, though on a far smaller scale, Edie is a force of nature. And, like the snow, she is, even at the outset, no real respecter of the functions of civilization and culture. Her rejection of the role of mere sign in an exchange between men and her dismissal of the cultured values of money or social status, alongside her assertion in the diary of her self, all drive a wedge into the culture which seeks to keep her in what it sees is her rightful place. Her very existence calls into question the paradigm of the gendered hierarchy of inequality inscribed by binary thought. In this story, nature, the feminine side of the equation, cannot be ignored, and cannot be read as merely passive and impotent. Whilst the narrative seeks to close up the fissures which Edie's story implies exist in patriarchal culture, with life returning to 'normal', and the story reduced to a fictional speculation about the workings of the modern city, what her story has done is to expose the vulnerability of culture or civilization to outside, unpredictable, disordered, natural – feminine(?!) – forces.

BECOMING A WOMAN

A final word on Edie's marginal position. We have discussed the ways in which Edie's language appears to be feminine in its resistances to the logic and order which is usually described as masculine. And we have also considered her place in society as being both central (when she is a sign) and marginal (when she is a person). A final question might be: in what sense is Edie a woman at all?

She tells us that she is nineteen years old. She laments the fact that being a woman has serious disadvantages: 'I never get any fun now I'm a woman' (21). But throughout the text, she also insistently describes herself as a girl or a child: 'a poor little girl like me has so much to think of' (20); 'A poor girl is just like a shuttlecock' (20); 'We girls never care about such nonsense' (21); 'a mere slip of a child like me' (26); 'I mean to settle down and be a good girl, and make Phil a first rate wife' (29).[9] Jill Barker, in the previous chapter, described Edie as a child–woman; Edie is, I think, on the cusp – occupying another kind of border space, this time between infancy and adulthood, between girlishness and womanhood. She is in the process of becoming a woman. Her acculturation – her agreement to act as sign rather than as subject – is not yet complete. It may be indeed that the snow acts as a terrible warning to her that she must finally grow up and accept the male-dominated world. The anarchy caused by the natural phenomenon of the snow on civilized society – the lawlessness of the streets full of roughs, Edie's fears for poor women and children in these circumstances – show her the dangers inherent in refusing the restraints of patriarchal culture. If civilization is so fragile that it can be easily destroyed, and if the destruction of it is dangerous not only to the men of her acquaintance, but also to Edie herself, she may have little choice but to become a sign, the price culture exacts from its ladies – those females who become women in the dominant class. If this is the case, then this is indeed a conservative story.

If, on the other hand, what we take away is the memory of the fissures in the text, the exposure of society's vulnerability and its reliance on the compliance of its womenfolk, then Edie's story is at least potentially subversive of the conservative *status quo*. Her contempt for the status of signs – she will marry neither the greengrocer ('very low') nor Lord Bilberton's title – and her partial victory in the matter of her choice of marriage partner, her ability to manipulate the men by rationing her attentions to them, are all strategies by which apparent weaknesses can be manifested as strengths. She may very well resolve to make Phil a 'first rate wife', but we do not see the completed product. Edie hangs forever now *between* girl and woman. She is suspended at the moment when her commodity value is at its highest, and when her estimation of her own value in personal terms has not been repressed through commodification. She is not quite then 'writing as a woman', and whilst her voice is only temporary, it is also subversive.

NOTES

1. There are many collections of essays and anthologies of feminist texts available. For an introduction to the basic elements of feminist theory, see Toril Moi, *Sexual/Textual Politics: Feminist Literary Theory* (1985); for an introduction which covers literary theory in the context of other theoretical models, such as anthropology and sociology, see Gayle Greene and Coppélia Kahn (eds), *Making a Difference: Feminist Literary Criticism* (1985). The best introduction to the complexities of French feminist theory is Elaine Marks and Isabelle Courtivron (eds), *New French Feminisms: an Anthology* (1980). A more detailed introduction to Julia Kristeva is *The Kristeva Reader*, edited and translated by Toril Moi (1986). There

are many good anthologies of feminist theory, including those edited by Mary Eagleton, and a more general (not literature-specific) anthology called *Feminisms: a Reader* edited by Maggie Humm (1992). Full bibliographical details of these and other works in the bibliography at the end of the book.

2. I have placed 'Richard Jefferies' in quotation marks because I wanted to signal that in this context, Jefferies is as much a character in his own text as Edie is: the views that we might ascribe to the 'author' – in particular, the closing remarks of the short story, signed by 'Jefferies' do not necessarily have any more authority than Edie's. On the signature effect, and its fictions, see Julian Wolfreys' chapter below.

3. Both Julian Cowley's and Jill Barker's essays also focus on the status of the game in this story. The structuralist approach concentrates on the idea of the rules by which games are played and by which language is understood. No point is made beyond the noting of the existence of such parallel sets of rules. The psychoanalytic framework concentrates rather on the psychic situation implied by the metaphor. In this case, the feminist approach is nearer to the psychoanalytic approach, and feminist literary theory has indeed been greatly influenced by psychoanalysis. See for example *The Kristeva Reader*, edited by Toril Moi (1986); and Juliet Mitchell, *Psychoanalysis and Feminism* (1981) which provides an invaluable introduction to the connections between these two discourses.

4. In the historical context in which Jefferies is writing Edie's story – in 1876 – her remarks about herself as a commercial proposition would almost certainly call to mind a subject of fierce debate from the 1850s onwards: the position of prostitutes in urban England. The eminent Victorian doctor, William Action, had very clear views on the subject. Nice Victorian women 'know little or nothing of sexual indulgences. Love of home, children and domestic duties, are the only passions they feel', he wrote in 1862 (Heath 1982, 17). Prostitutes, however, he castigated because they 'give for money what they should only give for love'. It is clear that what he objected to was the overt commercialization of the sexual relationship, a commercialization which Edie half-recognizes as being the basis even of respectable marriage.

5. Again, see Julian Cowley's essay, with his description of the functions of the characters in a fairy-story derived from Vladimir Propp's 'Morphology of the Folktale'.

6. See Julian Wolfreys' chapter below.

7. This point is also related to Structuralist analysis. If, as Cowley argues, Saussure's insights lead to the rejection of 'common-sense

notions that the structure of language imitates the structure of things in the world', by extension the critic may well also choose to reject the common-sense world apparently evoked by language. Structuralism has been practised ahistorically and apolitically; but one can equally choose to take a politically committed form of structuralism as one's theoretical basis.

8. As Jill Barker's essay shows, this process can also be described in psychoanalytic terms.

9. Again, see Jill Barker's essay on how psychoanalytic theory would 'read' Edie's problems of sexuality and maturation.

PART 2   POLITICAL AND IDEOLOGICAL ACCOUNTS

5

Agriculture and Anarchy: A Marxist Reading of 'Snowed Up'

JESSICA MAYNARD

MOVEMENT, TRANSITION AND CONNECTION

Any introduction to the thought of Karl Marx should, perhaps, begin with the concept of the 'dialectic'. Dialectic was the term used by Marx and Engels to describe their theory of social change, which occurred, according to Marxist theory, as a result of class struggle. This conflict itself was a result of the social formations which emerged out of the forms of economic production prevalent in any given society. Society was envisaged as passing through several phases, designated by Marx, the 'antique', 'feudal' and 'bourgeois'. In the bourgeois phase – the nineteenth century about which Marx and Engels were writing – it was the capitalist mode of production which prevailed. According to this system, the means of production (the factories, the land, the machines and so on) were owned and controlled by one class (the bourgeoisie), although that class depended on the labour of another class (the proletariat) to maintain production. However, the proletariat received very little of the profits of their labour, these instead being appropriated by the owners and ploughed back into the capitalist machine. Marx referred to this as 'alienation', since the workers were alienated from the end result of the production process – and not simply in terms of profit, but also in

terms of working conditions. Where the artisan or peasant of
the feudal era had enjoyed access to the *whole* production process – he had had his own strip of land to cultivate for instance, or as, say, a weaver he had overseen the production of
cloth from start to finish – now, under the increasingly mecha-
nized practices of capitalist production, he was denied access to
the whole process. On the contrary, the worker became simply
a cog in a huge machine, a factory 'hand', restricted in his activity to the unending repetition of one particular component of
the process, and receiving wages for his particular contribution.
His hands were no longer his tools; it was he who became the
tool, operating other tools (machines), subservient to a vast
impersonal system. Hence, according to this account, industrial
civilization was based on a form of contradiction. It differentiated tasks, splitting up the constituents of the labour process
(the factory production line is emblematic of this), making every-
one contribute a separate task in order to produce the finished
item. But, in doing so, it also presupposed a system, a scheme
that unified all these fragments. It presupposed co-operation, but
it did so at the price of dehumanization. This is an important
contradiction of the capitalist process: that in order to function,
it fragments society, it fragments people. At the same time as
being a rationalization of working methods, always aiming for
the most efficient exploitation of time and space, it could be
suggested that capitalism is also profoundly *irrational*. Capitalism is the economic system that brings people to work side by
side in factories, to live back to back in cities, and then divides
them against one another. Perhaps the crowd is the highest expression of this process: physical density combined with psychic
isolation. A new social imperative – that of self-preservation,
that of maintaining one's privacy – develops. And while capitalism produces disproportionate financial rewards for the minor-
ity, it produces poverty for the majority. The circumstances under
which a capitalist economy functions – breeding competition,
competition in turn lowering profit margins, decreased profit
margins breeding wage cuts, and so on – brings about a divided
society, riven by problems of unemployment, housing, starvation. Capitalist accumulation, in Marxist terms, is ultimately seen
as inimical to human interests and human life.

However, all this is not to assume a straightforward causal
relation between the material means of production, and the so-

ciety that is elaborated around it. It is slightly more complex than that. While the Marxist position is undoubtedly a *materialist* one – it sees 'the material conditions of human life' as determining social process (Coward and Ellis 1977, 62–3) – it need not necessarily be a rigidly deterministic one. It is true that Marx argues that the economic base gives rise to a certain 'superstructure', certain legal, parliamentary, educational and cultural institutions, all of which contribute to the maintenance of certain social beliefs and attitudes, but this superstructure can also, in turn, influence and change the economic base.[1] For example, the conditions of class struggle between bourgeoisie and proletariat will, for Marx, lead eventually to revolution. A purely deterministic model might suggest the prospect of unending oppression, a passive and defeated proletariat unable to challenge the prevailing system; Marx's dialectical model, on the other hand, proposes that the system will eventually produce the revolutionary 'subject' who will intervene in order to try and change the social system. As David Forgacs points out, this has long been a disputed area for Marxist theorists. The traditionalists have followed a 'reflective' model of Marxism ('vulgar' Marxism), interpreting social phenomenona unproblematically as a product of economic forces; others 'have placed more emphasis on the way changes in the superstructure (for instance political organization and party action) can influence and accelerate changes in the base' (Jefferson and Robey 1982, 137).

This second approach, which does not see the interaction between base and superstructure as consistently one-way, but also subject to anomalies, to uneven development and to the contradictory nature of capitalism (expansion and deterioration), is explained by Engels in *Socialism: Utopian and Scientific*. Engels, who believes nature is more truly to be conceived in terms of 'movements, transitions, connections' (Marx and Engels 1980, 405) than in 'the things that move, combine and are connected', finds it inappropriate to distinguish between cause and effect, between the privileged term and the secondary term. For him, it is not the separate categories themselves that are of paramount importance, but the continual movement between them, and he uses nature to demonstrate his point:

> [E]very organic being is every moment the same and not the same; every moment it assimilates matter supplied from without,

and gets rid of other matter; every moment some cells of its body die and others build themselves anew; in a longer or shorter time the matter of its body is completely renewed, and is replaced by other molecules of matter, so that every organic being is always itself, and yet something other than itself. (Marx and Engels 1980, 407)

This is an important point. According to Engels, who is obviously writing in the context of advances in biological theory, 'organic being', human or otherwise, is always somehow 'in between', always in a state of transition, and is therefore simultaneously itself and not itself. He goes on to suggest that cause and effect, by the same principle, cannot be detached from one another but are 'imbricated' [literally, plaited together]:

Further, we find upon closer investigation that the two poles of an antithesis, positive and negative, e.g., are as inseparable as they are opposed, and that despite all their opposition, they mutually interpenetrate. And we find, in like manner that cause and effect are conceptions which only hold good in their application to individual cases; but as soon as we consider the individual cases in their general connection with the universe as a whole, they run into each other, and they become confounded when we contemplate that universal action and reaction in which causes and effects are eternally changing places, so that what is effect here and now will be cause there and then, and *vice versa.* (Marx and Engels 1980, 407)

For Engels, a proper understanding of revolution was founded on an understanding of 'movements, transition, connection'. Revolution was *part* of evolution.

This is how natural and social change worked for Engels, and also, it seems, for Jefferies, who compared 'the invisible and subterranean stirrings of nature to the mood of public opinion, which is subtly but strongly moving towards Republicanism' ('The Man of the Future', quoted in Matthews and Treitel 1994, 43). The various mutations of capitalist organization in the end would bring about its downfall, while mutations in natural populations would in turn contribute to adaptation and the improvement of the species. But here we encounter a problem. Marx, and Jefferies, as we shall see later on, characterize life in urban concentrations as an ugly and dehumanizing affair. They appear to link capitalism, with its emphasis on competition, on the survival of the fittest, with Darwinian ideas. How, then, is it possible for

Engels to compare the inevitability of revolution with the inevitability of evolution, when at the same time it seems to be a society based on evolutionary principles that he wishes to see destroyed? The only way to avoid this problem is to accept it in all its contradictoriness. When Engels uses nature to demonstrate how revolution will occur, he is also saying that capitalism contains within it the principle of its own degeneration.

The evolutionary model is co-opted by both Marxist and capitalist. In terms of liberal democracy, which Marx designates as capitalism's mode of government, Darwinian competition at an economic level is regarded as beneficial for society as a whole. Free-market speculation, the values of *laissez-faire* individualism, also work for the general good. The robust individual, in pursuing his own gain, also sustains and strengthens the economy, just as for Darwin, natural selection, by which the healthiest examples of the species were reproduced, was for the good of what he called the 'aggregate'. Yet for Engels, evolution was used to demonstrate the inevitable obsolescence of capitalism, and here perhaps Engels raises another facet of evolutionary theory, but one that is always implicit: that, once the progressivist principles of Darwin have been accepted, then it is also maybe logical to accept the possibility of regression too. What Marxist theory does, in a way, is to envisage future catastrophe which will inaugurate a new reign of social justice.

Does this then suggest that progress, for the Marxist, can only occur through regression? This is an important question to consider. Both Marx and Jefferies take up anti-industrial positions, and they might be said to share in a romantic condemnation of contemporary civilization. Both are critics of modernity, both in different ways lament the loss of spiritual values that nineteenth-century progress entails. It might be argued that, to a certain extent, their visions of social change *do* depend on social decay, on the crumbling of the existing status quo. But where one takes the form of a democratic socialist utopianism, the other takes that of a conservative escapist one, based on a mythical appreciation of the land and a distrust of democratic movements. Jefferies was not always so sympathetic as he seemed to be later in his career to the inequalities suffered by the labouring classes. His journalistic reputation, it should be recalled, was founded on a series of letters written to the *Times* in November 1872, critical of agricultural workers who had organized themselves, under the leadership of Joseph Arch, into the National Agricultural Labourers' Union. The most striking feature of the letters is their traditionally paternalist stance. Jefferies finds the protesting labourers 'ungrateful', reserving his praise instead for the Duke of Marlborough's policy of 'only letting cottages to men who work on the farms where they are situated' (Thomas 1978, 74). Here, Jefferies champions the virtues of locality, of close links between work and land. 'Cotton, coal and iron cannot be eaten', he declares, 'but the land gives us corn and beef; therefore the land stands first and foremost . . .' (Thomas 1978, 77).

JOURNALS AND JOURNALISM

4th December 1881	Ragwort; bit still in flower. Weeping willows in leaf still. Just seen 400 peewits in large field.
8th December	1000 peewits – same field
29th December	Several jays in copse – seen from window
31st December	2000 peewits in same field
	(Jefferies 1947, 272)

In writing about the effects on the city of London of a freak snowfall in 'Snowed Up: A Mistletoe Story', Jefferies looks at cultivation under threat; he examines the nature of contingency, how one phenomenon may be dependent on the previous one, how one circumstance engenders the next.[2] The premise is a very simple one: that, in the event of the failure of the communications network which services the city (and communications includes telegraph, railway and road systems, and food provisioning), the great civilization of London would soon revert to Darwinian ecosystem, where, in most cases, the healthy prevailed and the weak perished. Jefferies exercises his faculties of long-range prediction, which is particularly appropriate to a story which is organized around the vagaries of the weather.[3] It is no mere coincidence that this survivalist fiction should be written at roughly the same time as innovations in meteorological mapping appear in the press. On 1 April 1875, *The Times* became the first newspaper to print a 'Daily Weather Chart', and other newspapers, including the *Daily News* and the *Pall Mall Gazette*, soon followed suit. That this is more than a piece of historical trivia may become clearer if we consider the following further details. Amongst the findings of the Report of the Meteorological Committee of the Royal Society for the year ending 31 December 1874 was the promotion of what were described as 'synchronous observations', whereby meteorological stations all over the world were linked into one global network. Hence the United Kingdom could receive daily information on the weather from colonies and possessions as far apart as Gibraltar, Bermuda, Natal and Colombo. Such synchronous observations were made possible by the spirit of international co-operation of which the Vienna Congress of 1873 was an example: 'It was stated in the last Report that the Office had entered cordially into the proposal made at the Vienna Congress in 1873, by Brigadier-General Myer, in a system of really synchronous observations at 0h. 43m. pm Greenwich meantime' (1875 Reports, Commissioners [13], XXVII, 23). This kind of accord brought hitherto geographically diverse and separate spaces into imperial alignment, and to some extent, by constructing a kind of imaginary community united by information and technology, it closed off the distance (the physical space that had to be traversed and the travelling time required for such a passage) between London and its imperial outposts. Furthermore, this initiative was founded on the assumption that meteorological monitoring was in the universal interest: there was a particular 'necessity for such simultaneous observations at times of atmospheric disturbance'. Here again, the improving and rationalizing tendencies of civilization seem to emerge from an anticipation of trouble, of 'atmospheric disturbance'. These measures are precautionary, and for that reason, beneficial. But precaution is also about added control, and here the heightening of imperial control is achieved through advances in the measurement, tracking and relay of information to the capital.

There is one other feature of note here, and that is the presence of Francis Galton on the Meteorological Committee. A few years later, in 1883, Galton was to coin the principle of 'eugenics', according to which biological vigour was held to be the key to a nation's social and economic vigour. The inherited physical and mental characteristics of the population were crucial to the national welfare, and ultimately could determine the fitness of that nation to maintain and administer an extensive empire. Such ideas, significantly, became current at a time when Britain was becoming all too well aware of other rival powers on the international stage, most notably Germany and the United States. As Britain faced a diminution in economic and diplomatic prestige, so the attention devoted to a perceived 'degenerative' tendency in the urban poor increased in its imaginative appeal to social and political commentators. It is important to identify, if only briefly, a continuity in Galton's scientific activities, the connection between his work on eugenics and his work on the weather. Arguably, both procedures hypothesize some future state of emergency, and they both, in different ways, endeavour to insure against such an emergency. On the one hand, eugenics attempts to iron out the regressive elements implicit in evolutionary theory, those social elements which threaten to taint and detract from civilization: on the other hand, meteorological monitoring hopes to guard against 'atmospheric disturbances' – which are occasionally catastrophic – by the acquisition of as much prior knowledge, as much data as possible. On the one hand, it is atmospheric chaos that is envisaged; on the other, social chaos.

All these issues are evident, in one form or another, in 'Snowed Up'. Formally, we are presented with a journal, a record, which, like the newspapers, presents a daily (or almost) report of the weather. By presenting a city in crisis, Jefferies makes the centrality of statistics and information services to the maintenance of urban/national administration stand out in artificially bold relief. A 'worst case scenario' adds illustrative value. Perhaps most immediately obvious to the reader is that this story is written in journal form. Perhaps not so immediately obvious, and something which it will be a theoretical task to explain, is the relation of Edie's journal to the burgeoning world of nineteenth-century journalism. Jefferies himself is part of this world, earning his living as a newspaper correspondent; both he and Edie are journalists. Jefferies generally follows nature; Edie follows the unfolding of urban catastrophe. Being a journalist here means constructing a narrative, reporting the development of a story over a period of time. It means charting the impact of the great snow on the city of London. In the absence of those tracking and communicative devices that are generally the bonding agents of civilization – the newpapers, the postal service, the telegraph – it becomes all the more important to replicate emergency structures in their place. 'Papa is fidgety and cross', says Edie, 'for he could not get his *Morning Post* this morning, and no letters came' (22).

Instead, Edie institutes her own journalism; she dutifully provides us with weather reports: 'Thrigg has kept a memorandum of the depth of the snow. The day before yesterday it was 21 inches deep in Cornhill'; 'It was 33 inches deep yesterday in Faringdon St., and Thrigg is quite sure that no trains will be able to get in tomorrow: because of the deep drifts – though thousands of men are at work digging. But as fast as they clear it away it fills up again' (22). Notice how rapidly she has learnt the value of comparison and the importance of forward and backward referencing. Like Jefferies the naturalist observer, she assesses the situation on the strength of the available data and postulates a future outcome.

This freak of nature is an educative experience for Edie. It should be noted that she acquires and hones her journalistic skills while she is 'snowed up'. As she announces to the imagined reader of her journal, she begins from a position of inexperience and ineptitude. She is, she tells us, no historian: 'I shall never be a good diarist, my last entry was a month ago. Oh dear whenever shall I reduce this giddy head of mine to something like order' (19–20). Edie's frivolity and femininity, signalled at the outset by her gushing admiration for the 'splendid set of furs' Papa has just given her, is also denoted in her inability to order experience accurately and rationally in a diary form. In explaining her shortcomings to us, she also obligingly displays her faulty memory and her lack of precision: 'It was old Mr., I mean the very reverend, at least I'm not sure about his title . . . who persuaded me to begin keeping a diary – he said it would help me to classify my ideas, and bring my mind into shape' (20).

Edie's initial inability to write historically is also seen as a function of gender and in setting out to 'classify ideas' she moves into a masculinist order of experience, where rationality prevails over flighty subjectivity. Where she has failed in the past to provide an account evenly distributed through time, an evolutionary narrative, she now attempts a more comprehensive approach which eliminates the gaps. Long intervals between events make the elaboration of a story more difficult, they produce an abrupt and fragmentary list which excludes the possibility of interpretation and meaning. This happened, and then a month later, something else, which may or may not be connected, no opinion being offered. So at first, it seems that the story is situating itself against that kind of disconnectedness and is promising that Edie will be properly socialized: she will be instructed in how to write a narrative *that makes sense.*

Jefferies' privileging of the land and his paternalistic views on rural communities might not seem consistent with the rational, historical perspective which Edie seems to adopt at the beginning of the story. The narrative – at least when it comes to Edie's journal – seems very much aligned with the progressive objectivism of nineteenth-century historiography. Newspaper reporting, as has already been established, is just one of the communication structures which supports and furthers the enterprise of civilization. Isn't this story all about what happens when such structures collapse? And wouldn't it be tempting to read it as a reinforcement of how important and how beneficial those structures are? That would be a reading which limits itself to what the text quite openly declares as its meaning, and which assumes that, once the critic has stated what this meaning is, there is nothing more to be said on the matter. This declaration – 'the story by Richard Jefferies means X' – can leave us a little dissatisfied, suspicious even: does it *really* mean that, was it always so simple? The moment a text is reduced to a bald formula, that formula seems inadequate, and somehow distorting, the 'work may seem rather threadbare' (Macherey 1978, 76). This, Macherey tells us, was a point raised by Plato in *The Republic,* and he quotes the following passage:

> For if we strip the works of the poets of the colours of poetry and recite them thus diminished to themselves, you know, I think, what they will look like.... They can be compared to those faces which, having no other beauty than their freshness cease to attract the eye when the flower of youth has withered. (Plato, 601b, quoted in Macherey 1978)

In *A Theory of Literary Production* Macherey argues that what the text leaves unsaid is also what it says: '... we must go beyond the work and explain it, must say what it does not and could not say' (Macherey 1978, 77). In the case of Richard Jefferies, this kind of reading will require that his story is not viewed in isolation, as an autonomous work of art offering itself for interpretation, but as something socially *produced* which the critic will *explain.* Macherey – and here he has something in common with Roland Barthes's position in 'The Death of the Author' – believes that the author is not a creator, but a producer, working with a certain range of 'determinate conditions'. This does not, however, mean that the work will be a straightforward reflection of historical conditions; rather, it will be endlessly diverse. This means that the work need not be consistent, it need not present some kind of ideological united front. On the contrary, it may well be rife with contradiction. This kind of reading will not be concerned with extracting a single, stable meaning or identifying a coherent scheme behind or within the work. There will be no anticipation of profundity or transcendence – the idea that the literary work contains some form of higher truth, a more perfect or total human experience than is available in everyday life, a glimpse of eternal value amidst the transience of worldly concerns. Instead, the *materiality* of the work will be examined: what is it made up of? What processes went into its production? This approach will be concerned to show how the work may at times undermine itself, how a writer, in setting out to say one thing, may also, unwittingly, say something else.

The surface ideology of Jefferies' text would appear to announce the frailty of nineteenth-century civilization, and to deliver a warning against complacency. This might be the humanist reading, which unearths what Macherey calls the 'ore' of meaning from the depths of the text, which distils the essence of the work. On the other hand, the proposition here will be that there is no particular essence, but instead a number of irreconcilable contradictions. Perhaps the main contradiction will be that, although Jefferies writes a cautionary tale about what happens when society is deprived of technological support, there also appears to be an unarticulated desire for such a catastrophe to occur, a desire for devastation and for reversion. The text contains liberal anxiety, admittedly, but also, as a conspicuous absence, a reactionary 'back to nature' impulse. In other words, the text is illogical and inconsistent. In exposing how reliant humanity has become on the technological extensions of civilization, Jefferies at the same time writes a critique of technology and, implicitly, speaks of his desire for a termination of modernity.

The 'illogicality' of Jefferies' ideology is made manifest in 'Nature and Books' in his distaste for 'the ponderous volumes of modern history, which are nothing but words' (1947, 238). Although himself a journalist and naturalist – a producer of causal and interpretive narratives – his preference is for 'the incomplete and shattered chronicles themselves, where the swords shine and the armour rings, and all is life though but a broken frieze' (Jefferies 1947, 238). Chronicle is the medieval precursor to modern history which, since it never properly concludes, instead breaking off abruptly, cannot be said to offer a full interpretation of the events it records (White 1987, 5). Capitalist culture, on the other hand, with its totalizing and centralizing effects, provides a favourable climate for a history of cause, effect and conclusion, a history that gathers, weighs and interprets facts. Narrative with a moral is dependent on social system governed by law, where actions can be registered as conformist or nonconformist, positive or negative, creative or destructive, right or wrong. Such assessment needs a 'social centre' against which to measure events. The less developed the institutions of central authority, the less feasible the kind of narrative which arrives at ethical or moral conclusions (White 1987, 10). It is this kind of decentred, feudal culture that is the absence of Jefferies' text, and it is this kind of culture that he promotes when he talks about the sovereignty of the land, the importance of locality, and the duties of the nobility and agriculturalist alike. This is why Edie's narration hovers uncertainly between chronicle and modern historical discourse. She may attempt to learn the techniques of reportage, but her disordered past, as an eminently *bad* diarist, is always there, always making sure her narrative is not quite the finished product it should be. Edie's delivery still retains some of the abruptness of pre-modern narrative, its lack of élan, its failure to sum up. Is it significant that, in the manner of a chronicle, her account simply breaks off with the words 'The Diary ends here' (29)?

TERMINAL CITY

I have no more faith than a grain of mustard seed in the future history of 'civilisation', which I *know* now is doomed to destruction. probably before very long: what joy it is to think of! and how often it consoles me to think of barbarism once more flooding the world, and real feelings and passions, however rudimentary, taking the place of our wretched hypocrisies. (William Morris 1885, letter to Mrs Burne-Jones)

For many a decade past the history of industry and commerce is but the history of the revolt of modern productive forces against modern conditions of production, against the property relations that are the conditions for the existence of the bourgeoisie and of its rule. . . . In these crises there breaks out an epidemic that, in all earlier epochs, would have seemed an absurdity – the epidemic of overproduction. Society suddenly finds itself put back into a state of momentary barbarism; it appears as a famine, a universal war of devastation had cut off the supply of every means of subsistence; industry and commerce seem to be destroyed; and why? Because there is too much civilisation, too much means of subsistence, too much industry, too much commerce. (Marx and Engels 1980, 40)

It was 'incomplete and shattered chronicles' that Jefferies praised in 'Nature and Books' – a kind of narrative rubble and ruination – and similarly in 'Snowed Up' he turns his attention to the shattered visage of civilization. He gives us a projection of social rupture, a society which 'finds itself put back into a state of momentary barbarism'. Here, he says, are the weaknesses that threaten the whole edifice of modernity, rather as Marx and Engels say that industrial capitalism – the ultimate 'modern Prometheus' aspiring for complete mastery of nature – will, in the end, consume itself: 'What the bourgeoisie . . . produces, above all, is its own grave-diggers. Its fall and the victory of the proletariat are equally inevitable' (Marx and Engels 1968, 46). The resulting fiction is a simulation, an experiment conducted to see how a given ecological community would react and adapt to a meteorological trauma.

This is how Jefferies charts the descent of the city into chaos. He incorporates it into a courtship narrative – which of the three suitors will Edie choose? – of the type which Darwin might have sketched in the *Descent of Man*. Here, according to Darwin, it was female choice that coincided with the best interests of the species. The female chose the strongest, healthiest, most handsomely plumed, most vigorous mate. Similarly, Edie, exercising her female prerogative – one which is consistently upheld in nineteenth-century narrative generally (Yeazell 1989, 33–53) – and at the same time guaranteeing the perpetuation of the species, will select Aurelles, the dashing military man, as her future husband. It is, of course, Aurelles, the penniless soldier who would at other, less critical moments and in other stories, be cast as the charismatic but unsuitable ne'er-do-well. But in these 'extraordinary' (in its fullest, emergency sense) circumstances, it is Aurelles who comes into his own, and wins the laurels. Jefferies prefers the military option for the continuation of the species, and this is significant. Aurelles defeats two rivals: Lord Bilberton, whose 'ancient, shivering body' can be considered landed aristocracy under threat; and Alderman Thrigg, emblematic of new entrepreneurial metropolitan capital, the power group in the ascendant, aligned with the doctrines of free trade, self-help and industry, but also liberal reform and civic responsibility (hence the 'Alderman', the signification of his involvement in municipal government and all the progressivist initiatives that implies). This tripartite structure is important. It enables Edie/Jefferies to reject the worn-out and no longer viable Lord Bilberton, and also the rather *parvenu* Thrigg, who has been in the habit, Edie tells us, of 'lending paper money' (20). Edie's choice of army over the options of nobility and trade is utterly in line with Jefferies' form of radical conservatism which despises modernity, and yet would also retain an evolutionary dimension to social transformation. The army offers both vitality/virility and destructiveness, both of which can be seen as part of the totalitarian dynamic of change. It can establish a new order, and wipe out the old, through sheer physical superiority. Together with the mob, the military provides the prototype of the totalitarian state, 'in which the police make common cause with the looters' (Benjamin 1992, 131). The army upholds the ideas of change and motion, by rooting out what resists the unalterable principle of change (the weak, the deviant, the insurgent), and it will, in the form of the totalitarian state, achieve this through violence. This kind of state might be viewed as ruled by a kind of organized mob, always changeable, often capricious, continually mobile in the Latin sense of mutable, volatile.

So it makes sense that Aurelles is the only effective protection against the looters of this story. This is because, as the closest there is in this story to martial law (always an integral part of totalitarianism), he is the counterweight to the mobs who terrorize the West End; as a soldier, he is the legitimate face of terror. If this seems an exaggeration, consider the bullying tactics Phillip uses to eliminate his opponents:

> ... to every demand of Phillip's that he would cease to ask my hand he [the Alderman] replied he would die first. So Phillip pushed him down again and I grew terribly frightened. I threatened

to call the police if Phillip did not help him out but he only laughed and said there were none within miles and miles. (25)

There are no police because Phillip is both self-appointed guardian and aggressor. In these conditions, the bodily vigour of the individual becomes an index of state health and efficiency: 'He is so tall and strong and noble-looking, such a contrast to wizened little Bilberton, and stout Alderman Thrigg' (20). This should be read especially in the context of an 1870s Britain glancing towards Bismarck's Prussia, where state-directed initiatives are taking the economy from strength to strength. French humiliation in the Franco-Prussian War of 1870–71, and the scenes of popular revolt in the Paris Commune of 1871, are very recent recollections. The end of protected markets with the repeal of the Corn Laws in 1846 opens Britain up to the import of foreign goods, and in these conditions it is all the more vital that the nation be able to hold her own in world markets. Disraeli's purchase of shares in the Suez Canal in 1875 (thus conferring the controlling interest on Britain) guarantees a trade route through to India, previously served by the Cape of Good Hope route, and inspires Queen Victoria to describe it as a 'blow at Bismarck' and his 'insolent declarations that England had ceased to be a political power' (Shannon 1974, 117).

With such a contention in mind, it becomes easy to see how the absent presence (as Macherey would have it) of such national anxieties makes itself felt in the narrative. The extremity of the scenario, however, elides economic survival of the species, with the most immediate concerns of life. London, temporarily immobilized by snow, allows Jefferies to indulge a fantasy which has much in common with William Morris's vision of 'barbarism once more flooding the world'.[4] This is the curative power of natural disaster, the purgative power of fire and water. Railways, telegraph and gaslight must go. Technology must go, so must the railways and the telegraph. If Jefferies does not, in his heart of hearts, like what he sees around him in the marketplace of the nineteenth century, he hankers after an end to all of it.

COMMODITIES, SPECTACLE, AND THE
COLLAPSE OF CULTURE

Edie begins by admiring her furs, and she looks forward to showing them off at the theatre. Here is a perfect summation of the capitalist society of spectacle, where woman is commodity, whether wife or prostitute. 'I suppose I am to be a commodity bought and sold like the Alderman's onions', notes Edie (29), and, in being spared marriage to stout Alderman Thrigg, she will eventually bypass the commodities market. But at the beginning, she is still on display, part of capitalism's theatre of production and consumption. The world of competition – in manufacture as well as marriage – necessitates that the product show itself off to best effect, demonstrate its superiority over its competitor. Hence capitalism has an *aestheticizing* effect, it endows an aesthetic value on the product in order that it may be sold, that what are essentially the same, may be differentiated from each other. It is the same, initially, for Edie, who, in her enthusiasm for her furs, identifies herself as object for visual consumption:

> I shall wear the jacket to the theatre tonight, Lord Bilberton escorts me, perhaps its not *de règle*, but I *must* wear it, it is so pretty and so warm, and new, and I can take it off. How *can* people keep their new things a month before they try them on? (20)

This fur, absorbed into the superficial world of commodity exchange where value no longer has anything to do with utility, will later revert to its use-value when used functionally, and not aesthetically: 'So I put on my fur jacket and wrapped myself up well, and sat at that window in the cold room shivering, till it became dark' (25). The snowfall has a de-aestheticizing effect,[5] and it suggestively restores furs to their stone-age serviceability.

The first casualty of the snow is Bilberton, the weakest contender for Edie's hand in marriage. His vulnerability is also that of the city, and his physical decrepitude is spatialized. So frail is he that he has to be carried to the house, while we hear that 'Piccadilly is quite impassable with the snow, and Curzon St blocked up' (22). The biological dead-end of Bilberton's 'poor shivering ancient body' has its geographical counterpart in the clogging of two of London's most prestigious arteries, Piccadilly and Curzon Street. It is the fashionable quarter that is the first to become congested. The financial district is the next to be affected. 'The day before yesterday it was 21 inches deep in Cornhill (some stupid place in the East I think)' (22). Edie's feminine ignorance of the commercial quarter is already vindicated: Cornhill *is*, through the effects of the snow, well on the way to losing all significance. Edie is inadvertently right. Later still, culture and constitution are both submerged, the National Gallery and the Houses of Parliament. The courtship narrative is the model for all these changes to the social map of London. Ownership – whether traditionally located in the land, as with the aristocrat Lord Bilberton, or in mercantile activity, with the bourgeois Thrigg – has been utterly superseded as a concept, rendered null and void. 'Ownership' loses all meaning, and all influence, in this extreme situation, is revealed in all its artificiality and impotence. Since the concept, and all the social relations that go with it, are the products of ideology, they only have a limited life in this evolving community.

Communications follow: 'The Scotch express never reached town at all, and there's no news of them, for it seems a rough wind has blown down the telegraph poles and snapped the wires' (22). Then, Faringdon Street, as the map of capital is gradually erased, gradually rendered irrelevant and redundant. 'Papa in his nasty way says it serves us right for attempting to reach the North Pole – it's a judgement', says Edie (23), and it might be suspected that Papa's views echo those of Richard Jefferies.[6] Civilization, as Marx and Engels said, digs its own grave. Macherey, writing about Jules Verne, makes a similar observation: that the voyage to the Pole is the final venture, the attempt to penetrate Nature at her most resistant; it is the 'most pointed representation of totality' and therefore the explorer's highest aim. Once conquered, it confers full mastery of the globe.

Take technology away, and the city is no longer viable. Thrigg tells Edie 'all the provisions people eat in London are brought in daily – the meat and everything else, his darling cabbages and onions included. . . . If the railway service be blocked for one week like this, all the stores will be exhausted' (23). This modern catastrophe is not provided for, unlike Joseph's Egypt (23), an earlier civilization to be besieged by nature, in the form of seven years of famine. The scriptural analogy recurs once more later on, when Edie records the sighting of a hansom cab and compares it to 'the olive branches brought into the Ark showing that the dry land had reappeared' (29). She reminds us of the *penal* quality of the catastrophe, sent down by God or gods to rectify mankind, and she sounds suitably rectified by the end: 'Certainly *I* shan't forget it. It has sobered me. I mean to settle down and be a good girl, and make Phil a first rate wife.' But Jefferies declines the opportunity to reinforce the message with scriptural sonority, and the codicil he provides seems curiously ill-adapted to the devastation that has preceded it. By attempting to reintegrate itself into the register of common sense, the narrative, which secretly would court the irrational, would lay waste to London, concludes with limp banality. It fails to convince:

> It's quite possible that a lady's fright may have exaggerated matters: but it is also pretty certain that if a fall of snow four feet deep occurred in London and remained on the ground – being supplied by fresh falls – for only one week, the great city of London depending as it does on stores brought in by rail day after day, would find itself in a very awkward position. (29)

Is that really all there is? Or is there much more that is never said, at least not directly? Jefferies, ever the naturalist, believes the city to be subject to its own principle of destruction, just like the overreaching capitalist machine. But this can be taken one step further. The city does not even have to *descend to barbarism*; it is barbaric here and now.

NATURALIZED CITY

> And still they crowd by one another as though they had nothing in common, nothing to do with one another, and their only agreement is a tacit one, that each keep to his own side of the pavement, so as not to delay the opposing streams of the crowd, while it occurs to no man to honour another with so much as a glance. The brutal indifference, the unfeeling isolation of each in his private interest becomes the more repellent and offensive, the more these individuals are crowded together, within a limited space. And, however much one may be aware that this isolation of the individual, this narrow self-seeking is the fundamental principle of our society everywhere, it is is nowhere so shamelessly barefaced, so self-conscious as just here in the crowding of the great city. (Engels 1973, 69)

Jefferies is by no means the first Victorian writer to envisage a barbarian London, a city given over to the pursuit of the basest needs, the unending fight for the most fundamental requirements of survival – food, shelter, warmth, or simply space. Engels before him, for example, had quoted an East End clergyman on the squalid living conditions of Bethnal Green, whose inhabitants may as well have been South-Sea islanders, for all that the rest of the population knew of their plight.[7] The East End of London would often, especially later in the 1880s, be conceived by journalists and urban explorers as the dark side of industrial capitalist culture, as analogous, in its distance from civilized values, to a wilderness inhabited by savages. They would comment, with mingled fascination and horror, on the proximity of such abominable living conditions to the financial, political and cultural institutions of the British Empire. London seemed to contain within it the extremes of both progress and decline, truly a society split into two nations.

For Engels, the ravages of capitalism seemed to produce their own brutality, their own particular kind of savagery: the 'unfeeling' selfishness of the individual, a 'brutal indifference' to his or her fellow human being. It was the fragmenting culture of capitalism that destroyed the values of community, which divided labour on every front: in the workplace, on the crowded street and in row after row of slum housing. Individualism, the ideology of the liberal bourgeoisie which promoted the virtues of private enterprise, hard work and non-state-interventionism, concealed beneath the trappings of civilization a crude barbarism. When Engels talks of the 'streams of the crowd', he equates the crowd with a state of nature, and he superimposes the template of nature over the map of the city. London is already an ecological battleground, and Jefferies' snowfall only makes that point a little more pronounced.

In Jefferies' story the snow comes from the east. It is therefore typical of the zoning of the city which echoes the geography of the civilized world itself: west as developed and enlightened; east as underdeveloped and benighted; west as open, visible and rational, east as closed, invisible, and irrational. The east is the source of mystery, danger and suspense, and it is these properties that Jefferies enlists when he has a bitter wind bring snow from the east into the sheltered precincts of the West End in order that they may be obliterated. The snow in this story is all that is savage and 'uncivilized', and it graphically conveys the sense of social atomization that Engels and other social explorers found so repellent. If the masses are so many atoms, then the snow might be seen as another 'mass' phenomenon, a powerful and anarchic accumulation of indistinguishable units. It belongs, in this story, alongside the rats that overrun the city – 'We could hear them all over the house – they came up the sewer no doubt, and were made bold by starvation and cold' (26); alongside the looters – 'After a while the roughs began to plunder the houses . . . and there were some fearful scenes in the city' (26); alongside the demon of alcohol – 'The beer barrels were out – the servants having nothing to do had emptied them' (24). Rats, roughs, east wind and alcohol: all are significantly juxtaposed; they work together to unseat civilization, and this because they *are* the savagery of civilization, they are 'the people':

> The bitter east wind drives the hard frozen snow along so swiftly that it cuts the face – it struck [Phillip] like the pellets from a shotgun. The draught through the narrow portals of Temple Bar kept them clear of drift but so savagely and fiercely did the frozen grains of snow drive in his face there that he could not get by. The people are mad – at least those left are. They could not light bonfires in the huts for the wind, so they set houses on fire, and stood near to warm themselves. Some prophesied about the end of the world – but I can't write these horrid things. The bonded warehouses and spirit stores are full of drunken men who have broken in. (27–8)

The text is secretly affiliated with this reversion, even though Edie says she 'can't write these horrid things' (27). The anxiety it expresses regarding the ferocity of the east and its destructive elements cannot really be resolved through the customary liberal expedients of reform, which represent merely another stage in modernization and guarantee the maintenance of industrial culture. Rather, the story sees catastrophe as the more extreme but also the more effective solution, the east at once as civilization's punishment and salvation. 'The people are mad – at least those left are' (27), goes the diary. Those last few words, apparently an afterthought, might perhaps go unnoticed – and this is precisely why they should be questioned: because they seem so casual. 'At least those left' points to an extermination that, for the most part, goes unrecorded and is only ever touched on briefly, as a solicitous thought – 'What has become or what will become of the poor people no one can tell' (27). Edie persistently evades answering that question fully. Is it because the 'horrid' but none the less expedient truth is that the majority of the poor will die? When Edie says she 'cannot write these horrid things', she gives us a clue to a more general textual unwillingness to say the unsayable: to say what Jefferies could articulate with impunity in an *agricultural* context: 'We should like to see them torn up . . . thoroughly cleansed, the rubbish burnt – for nothing else but fire will destroy such stuff as this' (Jefferies 1948, 174).

Edward Said sees a similar connection between ruin and reconstruction in Romantic notions about the regeneration of Europe by Asia: '[Schlegel and Novalis] . . . said it was Indian culture and religion that could defeat the materialism and mechanism (and republicanism) of Occidental culture. And from this defeat would arise a new, revitalized Europe: the Biblical imagery of death, rebirth, and redemption is evident in this prescription' (Said 1991, 115). Jefferies, while he pays lip service to the necessity for modernization, has much more in common with these Romantic 'revisionists' than with liberal champions of improvement. For him, the city is most acceptable, not as the highest form of human culture and as site of democratic freedom, but as a natural wilderness. His fear of the 'rank mass' is worked out, perversely, by invoking degeneration; only then will the conditions be right for renewal.

In Jefferies' writing the city is essentially a phenomenon of nature. It is immense and infinite; it is savage; it engulfs the individual. 'How very little value has the individual, his life and aims!' notes Jefferies. Public transport is often a graphic illustration of this point: 'What a sermon on this is to be found in the carriages of the Metropolitan and District Railway which run deep under houses. At the stations people are shot about – and quick in the current – are lost. They rush on – with no attention.' Unlike those commentators who would object to this depersonalization on liberal grounds – the mass swamps the individual, and so on – Jefferies does not necessarily catalogue these city sights in order to rail against them. There is much more of an ambivalence in this writing. Admittedly, there is criticism of the 'mechanical' mode of living that goes with urban agglomeration (note the 'lack of attention' of the tube travellers to each other, and the way they are absorbed into the machinery, 'shot about'). But at the same time, these processes seem almost to be considered as if they are a prelude to a transformation of the city, as if, taken to extremes, they will be their own undoing.

Again and again, we hear him apply his naturalist's techniques and terminology to the swarming crowds of the city, the great hive that is London. It is suburbia that is anathema to Jefferies, since it represents a hinterland, neither one thing nor the other. He has a word for this, 'villadom': everything hypocritical, mediocre, and insipid. Whether such views are held because or in spite of his residence in latter years in Surbiton and Sydenham, is a matter for speculation. The main objection presumably was to the conformity of suburbia, to its obedience to convention. In the city, on the other hand, it was possible for the solitary explorer to lose himself, just as it was it was possible for the human observer to be dwarfed by the grandeur of nature. Jefferies invokes an *urban* sublime, where loss of self takes place, not in the forest or in a rugged mountain landscape or under the stars, but in the crowded street. He returns continually to this idea of city-as-nature, city-as-savage: in 'Snowed Up', in the image of an iceberg aground in the river Thames; in a similarly atavistic moment, in 'The Great Snow' (unpublished, probably written about 1875, Jefferies 1980b, 243–8), Jefferies compares the dome of St Paul's, the only part of the cathedral to remain visible, to an 'Esquimoux hut'. There is concealed delight here, a near-pagan appreciation of this image of regress: 'The great gilt cross on the top had been torn off by the violence of the wind' (1980b, 244).

If we turn to Jefferies' other occasional writings about the city, we see him quite consciously elide natural with urban landscape. 'In London I can always find the way,' he says. 'With me it is largely instinctive. I have the instinct of direction alike through courts and alleys and in country lanes and fields' (1980b, 244). Navigating the city calls for the same suspension of conscious effort that rural orientation called for. Noticeably, neither require rational thought. Even in the minor observations, this tendency to perceive the city as more of a natural outcrop than as evidence of cultural development, is evident. Jefferies describes how, in an urban context, 'a living hop rose up, twining round the wire stay of a telegraph post, just as the hops twine up the poles in Kent or the wild plant rises up the growing poles in copses' (1980b). Even the telegraph post, then, under Jefferies' gaze, is reoccupied by nature. These are not innocent observations, but ideologically loaded.

Social atomization – the London of impersonal tube travel, of fighting to secure a place on the omnibus, of 'Human beings reduced to mere hurrying machines ... to the condition of the wooden cabs ... pulled along by the irresistible horse Circumstance' ('A Wet Night in London', 1908, 234) – is the condition required for a reinstatement of natural hierarchies. If the mechanization of the human body in factories was, in Marxist theory, the precipitant of revolution, then these same phenomena, for Jefferies, foreshadow the next, higher stage – higher because all that was learned has been unlearned. The working man, transformed as he is into an automaton, presages this future state of natural (because non-rational) wisdom:

> A man works at night and sleeps by day: he lies yonder as calmly as if in a quiet country cottage. ... The man who lies sleeping so calmly seems to me to indicate the immensity of the life around more than all the rest. He is oblivious of it all; it does not make him nervous or wakeful; he is so used to it, and bred to it, that it seems to him nothing. When he is awake he does not see it; now he sleeps he does not hear it. It is only in the great woods that you cannot see the trees. He is like a leaf in the forest – he is not conscious of it. (Jefferies 1948, 234)

Here again, urban scene is converted into rural: the worker's house becomes 'a quiet country cottage', the worker himself, 'a leaf in the forest'. Far from attacking this loss of identity, Jefferies seems to suggest that this quality brings the worker closer to a state of natural grace. In the end, the effect of this naturalizing discourse is to lift the city beyond the realm of social and economic effects, to remove it altogether from political debate. 'The Red Roofs of London' closes with a meditation on our universal yearning for romance, and it moves from one forest of labour to another: that of the ships' masts that cluster by the dockside: 'they stand in groups as trees often grow, a thicket here and a thicket yonder' (Jefferies 1948, 235). Jefferies does make clear that they also testify to a network of productive relations – 'Labour to obtain the material, labour to bring it hither, labour to force it into shape – work without end' – but his impulse is to move away from this, to lay emphasis on the romantic content of this view.

Jefferies may recoil from the effects of urban accumulation, but he recoils back into a fantasy of wilderness, of adventure, of a soul overwhelmed by the magnitude and unreason of nature.

His projections of an urban future are permeated by a desire for restoration, for a situation in which feelings may once more be 'real', life once more 'lived'. 'Snowed Up' is only half the story of Jefferies' aspirations, it is only half-way towards the total ruination of *After London*. It masquerades as a cautionary tale, when it is really wish-fulfilment. 'Masts are always dreamy to look at', says Jefferies, because they are an intimation of infinity:

> ... they speak a romance of the sea; of unknown lands; of distant forests aglow with tropical colours and abounding with strange forms of life. In the hearts of most of us there is always a desire for something beyond experience. Hardly any of us but have thought, Some day I will go on a long voyage; but the years go by, and still we have not sailed. (Jefferies 1948, 235)

Are these perhaps the regrets, the unfulfilled ambitions of a reluctant suburbanite speaking here? The Jefferies who looked for recognition as a novelist, but earned it as a newpaper man? The passage seems to betray the weariness of one who has, at least latterly, eked out his days in a state of dreary 'villadom'. This takes us back to an earlier contradiction: that Jefferies as an agricultural journalist was a part of those forces of modernization, of mass circulation and capital accumulation which he destroyed in his stories. Jefferies was the naturalist who painstakingly recorded the seasonal mutations of the landscape, who reported the ecological effects of weather, who made predictions and issued recommendations. In all this, he seems the model of progressive scientific thought. But, if we seek to *explain* this story, if we look at it against the body of Jefferies' work as a whole, against his notebooks and his newpaper articles, we see something other than a simple fantasy, a piece of throwaway prophecy. Sheltering beneath the paraphernalia of civilization, we see a kind of nineteenth-century vandal, one who would sack London and watch the vines twist round the telegraph posts, one who would see history replaced with shattered chronicles.

This is why the appeal to nature is so strong in Jefferies' work, because it speaks of harmony, wholeness, eternity, and not the linear imperative of mechanical civilization, always improving, always replacing. Jefferies reminds his reader that there is 'but a thin, transparent sheet of brittle glass' between human civilization, with its luxuries 'brought from the utmost ends of the earth, with the telegraph, the printing press, the railway at immediate command', and the wilderness outside ('Nature and Eternity', Jefferies 1980b, 304). If, as Macherey recommends, we should make the silences of the text speak, then it is not the lame conclusion of 'Snowed Up' we should attend to, but those almost gloating words: 'And all through a little snow – the despised snow – so fine and impalpable, yet strong enough to completely conquer our civilization. No trains can run. No ships can come up the river. No food, no light, no help. All through the weak, feeble despised flakes of snow!' (27) The silence here speaks far more eloquently than the words: it says that there is no escaping nature, and it looks forward to a new idyll.

NOTES

1. It is out of the discourses and activities of and between the various institutions of the superstructure that ideologies emerge, and, most importantly, the dominant ideology of a given culture. Ideology can be defined as the cluster of value and belief systems that support and perpetuate society. Ideology need not be formulated as a set of overtly stated principles; it is not necessarily as clear-cut as that. It can be interpreted more subtly to mean the range of standards applied in all areas of everyday life, from significant to apparently insignificant, from law court to family home, from work to play, and so on. For example, it is by ideology that, in Marxist terms, a worker is persuaded of his/her freedom (he has his labouring power to sell), when in practice this 'freedom' amounts to exploitation (the worker is forced to sell his labour, since he is deprived of the means of production). This could be termed a 'representation' of freedom, since it is 'the product of ideological practice' (Coward and Ellis 1977, 65). The ideological productions that concern us here are those of nature and the city. What 'representation' of the city does Jefferies give us, and how does it relate to nature? To say something is 'natural' is immediately ideological; it takes for granted that nature is accepted as the primary term of value, the standard against which everything else is measured. But the objection to this might be that nature does not exist, out there somewhere, as a given, but is culturally constructed as an idea which only *seems* to need no explanation; nature is *ideological*, in other words.

2. Jefferies' concern with the examination of cultivation under threat is taken up at some length in one of his agricultural commentaries entitled 'Weeds and Waste' which is worth commenting on (Jefferies 1947). While Jefferies appears to be writing about the city In 'Snowed Up', he may also, implicitly, be writing about the countryside and

its crucial relation to the city. There is a certain economic and social relation between country and city in 1870s Britain, and in a Marxist reading, this historical context should be included in any consideration of the text.

As with 'Snowed Up', Jefferies, in 'Weeds and Waste' is dealing with a potentially decadent community, but in this case a natural one. In 'Snowed Up', Jefferies imagines the fate of an overextended urban civilization: it will be overrun by its own impure offspring, its *human* waste. In 'Weeds and Waste', we also see hints of this avenging host, this mass which will sweep through the city, but in an agricultural context:

> The rain . . . has so stimulated the growth of weeds that in many places the fields seem quite choked with them. Operations for their removal before the crops get too high were checked and even altogether prevented by the downpour just before the summer opened. They therefore got a firm hold, and the consequence may now be seen, and will be felt for some time afterwards. . . . If the reaping machine or the sickle and the scythe could go to work without constant interruption from storms, the greater part of the weeds would be cut off before they could ripen their seeds, but as this has not yet been possible, *a future source of trouble is being prepared.* (Jefferies 1948, 172 [emphasis mine])

Here, we are given the causes and the consequences of the problem, and a prediction based on that data. Jefferies' reforming zeal, in this case applied to the problems of land management, arises from a forecasting of future decline. In urging the farmer to move forward with the times, to be competitive, Jefferies is also issuing a warning. He envisages a loss of balance, the reversion of the land to a state of nature untamed by human cultivation, where '[t]he wild convulvulus and bindweed cling to the wheat'. Is there anything more we need to know about this? Arguably, there is. There is a historical context for Jefferies' concern, and there are specific social and economic factors which we may wish to consider. In what ways is this piece of journalism an ideological production?

It might first be pointed out that at this time, in the late 1870s, agricultural production in England is undergoing a depression, which is symptomatic of the general trend in the national economy towards an income based on manufacturing industry, and away from a land-based income. This contraction of the rural sector is reflected in the decrease in population, as agricultural workers migrated to towns and cities. In 1851, the rural population still accounted for 49.8 per cent of the population, while in 1871 this was reduced to 38.2 per cent, and in 1881 to 32.1 per cent (Read 1979, 15). The fall in prices is more pronounced in grain than in dairy or meat products – reflecting the growing importance of urban markets – and while the amount of land under arable cultivation decreases, the amount allocated to pasture tends to increase (Keuchtwanger 1985, 116). Similarly, sanitary legislation during the 1860s begins the move of slaughterhouses and meat markets out of the city, though this does not happen immediately. The city is increasingly reliant on provisions transported in by rail. Jefferies himself comments on how milking times, once fairly uniform throughout the country, have been gradually adapted to fit in with train timetables, and he points to a growing mechanization and rationalization of farming generally (Waller 1983, 52). Urban developments – fear of disease, fear of revolt, new sanitary measures – have a material impact on rural practices, on the shape of agriculture itself. The influence of the city spreads far beyond its boundaries. This is one way to read Jefferies' journalistic interventions, as a straightforward response to economic conditions. Jefferies identifies a need for adaptations in agricultural practice to accommodate such changes, adaptations that are necessary for survival. But if we choose to consider 'Snowed Up', which quite explicitly deals with all these same issues – the provisioning of the city, the reliance on foodstuffs transported in by rail, the industrialization of agriculture (Thrigg with his potatoes and onions) – alongside 'Weeds and Waste', then a slightly different ideological position begins to emerge.

'Weeds and Waste' is a discussion of the deterioration of the stock which finds that only the most radical action will halt the tendency towards decline; weeds must be 'torn up ... thoroughly cleansed, the rubbish burnt'. Only such catastrophic solutions are capable of wiping out what Jefferies suggestively calls 'a rank mass of vegetation creeping out from the hedge' and, even more biblical in its moral *gravitas*, 'every kind of abomination'. Traditionally, cities of vice and depravity have plagues, blights and tempests visited upon them, and that sense of retributive justice seems to have its echo, however faintly, in Jefferies' agricultural writing. Purification of corrupt communities, whether vegetable or human, is achieved through destruction; the conditions for renewal and rehabilitation are founded on extermination. This is why it is worthwhile to pay attention to that apparently innocent 'rank mass of vegetation creeping out from the hedge'. It may recur elsewhere. Jefferies would like to see this 'rank mass' rooted out, the land thoroughly cleansed of such an abomination. It is possible that his fiction shares this nervousness regarding mass phenomena, but fails to articulate it thoroughly.

3. This interest in long-range prediction is particularly evident in *After London*, which gives a detailed picture of the ecological adaptations.

4. See also Morris's utopian narrative, *News from Nowhere*.

5. Ruth Robbins makes a similar point in her chapter, above, when she points out that Aurelles, in breaking up the furniture for firewood, also breaks up the domestic aesthetic.

6. There was a real Arctic expedition in 1875.

7. Engels quotes Mr G. Alston, preacher of St Philip's, Bethnal Green: '"I believe that before the Bishop of London called attention to this most poverty-stricken parish, people of the West End knew as little of it as of the savages of Australia or the South Sea Isles. . . . [A] nation like ours must blush that these things can be possible"' (Engels 1973, 69).

6

Power and its Representations: A New Historicist Reading of Richard Jefferies' 'Snowed Up'

JOHN BRANNIGAN

The 'populace', poor souls, having been goaded all the summer for not making any demonstration in favour of Reform, wished to hold a big meeting in Hyde Park to-day to express such an opinion. In a most un-English fashion the meeting was forbidden, the gates of the park shut at 5, and all the police had to come out to guard them. There was not the smallest pretext for believing there would have been any riot; but naturally this tyranny produced one among the roughs, who *uprooted the rails* (probably they were pushed down, being rotten), and remained masters of the field. The Life Guards were called out, which was not done in '48, and which was truly absurd as they did nothing whatever; and the people dispersed in time after some knocks had been exchanged. We might as well be French authorities, screwing down the safety-valve! and very nice and high-minded it will read on the continent.

Lady Frederick Cavendish, London, 23 July 1866
(1927, 14–15)

One of the preferred methods of beginning a New Historicist reading is the depiction of a scene or piece of writing which yields a microcosmic image of what the critic seeks to elaborate in relation to the main text of discussion. So Stephen Greenblatt begins 'Invisible Bullets', his acclaimed article named after the false understandings that American Indians had of the ways in which Europeans were destroying them (believing that the smallpox which was obliterating them was in fact the invisible bullets of the Europeans), with a story of how red spots on the face of the dying mathematician, Thomas Harriot, were falsely believed to be proof of revenge from God for Harriot's alleged atheism. Whether Harriot was an atheist or not we have no way of knowing, for, as Greenblatt reminds us, '[t]he historical evidence, of course, is unreliable' (Greenblatt, in Wilson and Dutton 1992, 84).[1] In its first published form the article also began with the story of an Italian miller tried of heresy by the Inquisition who, having finally renounced his atheist views, was allowed to return to life in his village, albeit branded as heretic, but on returning to his atheist views was then burned at the stake. The point of this story is to allow Greenblatt to introduce ideas of subversion and punishment, or containment: 'My interest in what follows is in a prior form of restraint – in the process whereby subversive insights are generated in the midst of apparently orthodox texts and simultaneously contained by those texts, contained so effectively that the society's licensing and policing apparatus is not directly engaged' (Greenblatt 1981, 41). This manner of opening the discussion is not just an anecdotal breaking of the ice; it is also a neat way of pointing out the fact that history, what we know of one text or event, is dependent upon a number of texts. History is only that which is written, and it is the manner in which it is recorded, whether this is by means of a Shakespearean drama or a merchant's diary, that interests New Historicists. The Elizabethan age, and particularly Renaissance drama, has been the focus of New Historicist attention, and this attention has been characterized by the reading of Shakespeare's plays, for example, as 'embedded in other *written texts*, such as penal, medical and colonial documents' (Wilson and Dutton 1992, 8). Read in relation to such texts Shakespeare's plays began to acquire new aspects, of being sites of power-struggles, of being the sites of emerging classes and ruling orders, of being the sites of national, political and cultural demarcation.

If these aspects seem to be familiar as concerns of a Marxist reading, it is largely because New Historicism is heavily influenced by Marxist analyses. What distinguishes it from Marxism is that is also heavily influenced by the work of Michel Foucault. Foucault's notions of 'power' and 'discourse' were particularly formative of New Historicist thinking. 'Power', in Foucault's work, is the fundamental force which drives all human experience, the desire to dominate and control. Derived from Nietzsche's 'will to power', Foucault's conception of the basic truth of human existence explains the interest with social hierarchies and colonialism that we subsequently find in New Historicist work. To gain control over others, one must be able to legitimate one's own claim to power. In the absolutist state, power was legitimate if it was believed to be divinely appointed. This concept of 'power', and the corresponding legitimation of that power, is to New Historicists what the idea of class-struggle is to Marxists. The concept of 'discourse' is closely related to 'power', in the sense that 'discourse' refers to a form of language that is socially controlled, and that is used to legitimate the claims to power of certain customs or institutions. 'Discourse' is a kind of official language, signifying some kind of privileged access to truth or power, and consisting of regulated forms of speech and writing. Different discourses indicate privileged strands of official language; hence, we accept the importance accorded 'science' over the humanities. Science makes a claim to knowing and controlling the world in a certain way, and to be accepted as a scientist one must speak, write and act in a 'scientific' manner, that is, within the discourse of science. Science is valorized over the humanities as a study because it is supposed to be an objective discourse, reliant not on aesthetic evaluation but on the discernment of the truth. Language and representations are crucial, as a consequence of Foucault's conception of 'discourse', to New Historicist analyses of power struggles. This emphasis on power relations as they are inscribed in language and representations shifts the focus of attention from the Marxist privileging of political contest to the New Historicist privileging of ideological contest.

The opening extract from the diaries of Lady Frederick Cavendish describes an event which highlights contest between the authorities and the 'populace', the occasion of a riot resulting from the prohibition of a public meeting. The diary records Lady Cavendish's thoughts and anxieties about the event, beginning with her appearing to take the side of the '"populace", poor souls'. The important point to note here is how she responds to a public disturbance, the violence of which is threatening to the social order, and to the corresponding reaction of the authorities. Clearly she disapproves of the strong-arm response of the authorities, who prevent the assembly with police and cavalry. The grounds on which she disapproves of this response is that it is 'un-English' and that there is no 'pretext' for regarding the event as threatening. The repressive apparatus of the State should not be used at times when no threat is visible. Lady Cavendish is not then objecting on the grounds of the inherent tyranny of using armed forces to prevent public disturbance, but of the inappropriateness of such a move in this case. Moreover she contests the *signs* of rioting, reading what she has italicized, *'uprooted the rails'*, not as proof of disorder, but of an accident owing to the rails being rotten. This re-reading gives the appearance of siding with the populace against the authority of the State, but a New Historicist reading would direct us to observing how possible and actual subversion is being contained within writing. Lady Cavendish's diary, in reporting the event, is the site of the contest between the authorities and the people, but it is serving the interests of the authorities in, firstly, dismissing the threat of subversion, and secondly, masking the repressive act of prohibition and mobilization of troops as a mistake. In this way a riot, direct contest over the authority of the State, is read as an accident and the possibility of real subversion is glossed over and concealed. Cavendish reinscribes herself as an agent of authority in writing: 'We might as well be French authorities' (my italics). Her concern is not then with highlighting injustice to the 'populace', as at first perceived, but with how the English authorities *appear*, how 'it will read on the continent'. The diary entry, then, is a record of anxieties about the image that is produced by the State, but more than being the expression of anxieties it also reinscribes the legitimacy of state authorities. The diary expresses state power, and only records the threat of subversion in order to contain and dismiss that threat. Lady Cavendish is free to record these threats because they are already undermined, and her reading is, then, a further undermining of the *signs* of subversion, a further effacement of the threat in order to strengthen the authority of the State. Her diary exhibits the power of the State, just as surely as the Life Guards display power to the 'populace'.

The diary entries in Richard Jefferies' 'Snowed Up: A Mistletoe Story' record the threat to state power as the threat unfolds rather than after it has happened, but this makes the contest between power and subversion even more important and dramatic. Lady Frederick Cavendish's diary reveals a similar event in the threat of public disturbance being heightened by the effects of heavy snowfall:

> Holker, *January 22nd*, 1867 – Bitter grey cold: snow again tonight. A poor postman near Compton Place was found frozen to death in his cart holding the reins, when the horse stopped at the post-office. And there have been several other deaths from the same cause. . . .

> Holker, *January 27th*, 1867 – . . . There is terrible distress in London. . . . There have been actually bread riots in the E.; baker's and butcher's shops rifled: the Poor Law as usual at a dead-lock. (Cavendish 1927, 23–4)[2]

Richard Jefferies' story utilizes this idea of the snow or inclement weather as a force of social disruption as a means of suggesting the ice-thin nature of the grounds on which the social structure is founded (a point made by other essays in this volume). The story is explicitly concerned with the possibility of society being threatened, moving as it does from a record of a present of furs to an expression of anxieties and fears of starvation and mob rule, and Jefferies could be said to have stated his intention for the story at the end in portraying how 'the great city of London' might 'find itself in a very awkward position' (29). 'Snowed Up' is a record of social crisis, and the social, and therefore political, conflicts that are brought to the fore by this crisis.

New Historicist critics would be concerned to examine the relationship between writing and society in this text, or, as Richard Wilson calls it, 'the textuality of history'. Although there are notable studies of nineteenth-century textuality from a New Historicist perspective, such as those by D. A. Miller, Catharine Gallagher, and Hillary Schor (all from the United States), it is relatively rare for a New Historicist analysis to be used as a basis for interpreting a Victorian text, especially in British literary studies. New Historicist critics are more frequently Renaissance specialists, focusing particularly on Shakespearean drama. A number of reasons have been suggested for this. At least two critics have suggested that the historicist E. M. W. Tillyard's book, *The Elizabethan World Picture* was influential on New Historicists in that it set a precedent for viewing Renaissance literature from the perspective of its wider cultural context.[3] It is also likely that Michel Foucault had something to do with this focus on Renaissance times, in that this period for Foucault marked some definitive transitions of the social structure towards modern capitalism and modern political hegemonies.[4] It is the transitionary and conflictual nature of Elizabethan society that has fascinated the New Historicists, in particular the evolution of the modern State, initially foregrounded as the establishment of the legitimacy of monarchic rule, but also as the evolution of the modern idea of the individual as a complete knowing subject. The modern idea of the individual as autonomous, free and self-representing was contentious and new in Renaissance times, and therefore the emergence of this idea produces ideological conflict in Renaissance literature. This provides, then, very important and useful material for the New Historicists who wish to analyse how writing, and representation in general, is shaped by social structures and ideological discourses.

The Victorian society which New Historicists would say is in the foreground rather than the background of Richard Jefferies' 'Snowed Up' may be less contentious in terms of the modern state of society, but certainly provides equally significant trends regarding the evolution of the State and the idea of the individual. Since the early 1800s trade and commerce were becoming more important as sources of wealth and privilege than the traditional ownership of land, and hence the middle class was developing in strength, and a bourgeois hegemony was emerging. This new social class was at first the target of upper-class snobbery, but gradually came to be taken more seriously as the political power of the bourgeoisie grew with its economic power. The Victorian era then becomes a period of contest and conflict between the older, landed upper class, and the developing, commercial bourgeoisie. Alfred Tennyson characterized the main thrust of nineteenth-century Britain in his poem 'On the Jubilee of Queen Victoria' (1887):

> Fifty years of ever-broadening Commerce!
> Fifty years of ever-brightening Science!
> Fifty years of ever-widening Empire!
> (52–4)

Tennyson's view of the Victorian era is one of immense social and political change in which the State is continuing to expand and evolve. The diarist of Jefferies' short story quite clearly draws attention to her position within this changing social structure: 'Papa has just given me such a splendid set of furs' (19), and relates the social status of each of the names mentioned in the story: 'Lord Bilberton has immense influence with the Ministry, and papa wants to be an Ambassador, and Alderman Thrigg has mountains of gold which he made by selling green peas in the city somewhere, and papa's estate is encumbered' (20). Only one of the three individuals described above has derived his wealth from trade, the others are either titled or landed. The diary serves the function of locating each of these individuals in terms of their position in the social structure, the story then serving as the site of interaction between these social positions. Thrigg signifies the emerging bourgeoisie and, as such, has been accepted by the upper class in terms of his being titled 'Alderman' and in being accepted into the company of Lord Bilberton and 'Papa', but is also the object of ridicule in the story, the diarist mocking his trade and referring to him as 'bigger than Falstaff', '[s]uch a spectacle' (22). Unlike Phillip Aurelles, Thrigg has acquired the wealth and status which should enable his incorporation within upper-class culture, but the upper-class ideology of inheritance and rank prevent Thrigg being completely accepted. Thrigg's bid for acceptance can be seen in his proposing himself as 'suitor' to the diarist, and his lavish attempt to buy himself into her favour is the utilization of his commercial wealth to gain admission into upper-class culture and status. But his wealth is not in itself the key to acceptance, as it is the source of this wealth which is derided in the upper-class discourse: '[Alderman Thrigg] is a kind of gigantic greengrocer, I think – very low' (23). Alderman Thrigg, however, is not the only suitor, and the diarist seems to be the centre of the social structure as constructed in the story. This is not in the egotistical sense of being central, but instead her role is that of classifying and defining the role of those around her:

> A poor girl is just like a shuttlecock or a tennis ball with all these gentlemen tossing her from one to the other. It *is* laughable when I think of it to see fat Mr Thrigg jump up and open the door for me, and Lord Bilberton screwing his face into a

smile of approval (though he hates the Alderman) and Lieut. Aurelles scowling at them both, and trying oh, so hard to play chess – which he does not understand – with papa and all just because. Well, I suppose I *am* pretty. (20)

As the scene of social inscription, the story constructs contest between competing ideologies, and their competition can be read in the above passage. Thrigg as the enthusiastic newcomer to wealth and privilege, struggling to gain entry to upper-class discourse, must 'jump up and open doors'. Bilberton is in the more comfortable, established position of only having to smile approval. His is not an ascending aspiration but a condescending, subliminally spiteful, complacency. Aurelles is the lowest of all of the group, the guardsman with no fortune, who, struggling with difficulty in even trying to be the equal of papa, therefore has the most to prove and consequently is the most aggressive, 'scowling at them both' (20). It is at the end of this passage and in the line following it that we see the roles of both the diarist and papa: 'Well, I suppose I *am* pretty. I think papa wants to play chess with me as the queen' (20). The diarist is the point of attraction for other elements of the social structure, and is therefore secure as the anchor of power in the sense that the others are taking her to be the object of their desire. As papa's 'queen' she is the servant of his power as 'householder', and, as the house is the society of the story, papa is then the power of the ruling class. The diarist, serving in the interests of papa's power, is powerful herself in being the agent of change, alliance and downfall. It is she who will facilitate the one who is to be incorporated into upper-class power. As the object of the three men's desires, she is the status symbol of the upper class, complete with furs. Possessing her signifies acceptance within the ruling ideology. But as the agent of 'papa's power' she is also the guardian of the stability and dominance of power. The crisis of disruption which threatens the social structure in the story serves only to provoke the three suitors into action which will be the basis for judgement by the ruling ideology. Papa sets the scene of the real crisis, of which the snow is only a mask:

> Papa said in his nasty cynical way that I might have which liked, it made no difference to him. Cool! As if it made no difference to me. He said the ancient name of Audeley was in danger of disgrace – bankruptcy, or something, and either he must get a

good appointment under Government, or his mortgages must be paid off. His dear Edie – me of course – would not let our house tumble down, that's not how he put it but I can't remember the fine words. (21)

With the ever more apparent threat of the bourgeoisie gaining dominance, the house of the upper class is in danger of disgrace, sinking in fortune behind those with commercial ties. Papa sees the future of this house as dependent upon two eventualities: the strengthening of his power by moving to a more central position (government), thereby reinforcing the political power of the upper class, and simultaneously the consolidation of power through the marriage of his daughter to one who will bring fresh power. The latter is the underlying story of Edie's search for a suitor. The choice for Papa is either the incorporation of the emerging trade wealth of the bourgeoisie in the figure of Alderman Thrigg, or of the aristocratic base of government power in the figure of Lord Bilberton. Excluded at this stage, of course, is Phillip Aurelles who is but 'a penniless soldier'.

There are three different kinds of subversion which appear in the story which threaten the social order of the house. Firstly, there is Edie's rejection of her father's choice of partners, and her desire instead for the forbidden Aurelles. That she desires Aurelles threatens subversion in the sense that Aurelles is not an acceptable member of the dominant class or power. Secondly there is the threat to the dominant male order in that it is *she*, the passive, submissive female, who desires Aurelles. It is she therefore who begins in her diary to control the future of their relationship, who expresses her own desires and wills. This is contrary, of course, to the ideology of the male order in the sense that woman is not supposed to express desire but instead is to accept and submit to male desire. Thirdly, then, there is the threat of the masses, the roving mobs, who threaten to raid the house and to overturn ruling-class stability. It is important to recognize that for New Historicists the snow is not the main source of crisis in the story. The real fear expressed in the diary is of poverty and vulnerability to mob rule. But these are anxieties already in place with papa's fear of financial ruin due to his estate being encumbered. The real crisis of this diary is the approaching economic ruin of the traditional ruling power, and the snow is literally a masking or clouding of this crisis. The snow, far from being the crisis, actually provokes the solution to the problems of the ruling power. In this way Edie's diary serves the same role as Greenblatt's view of Prince Hal in *Henry IV*, as the *agent provocateur* in society. The diary invents the notion that a natural disaster threatens the social order, whereas in fact it is the internal crisis of the dominant order that threatens to leave this order vulnerable. This is a central feature of New Historicist readings, that power incites its own subversion in order to contain subversion and to preserve its authority.

Lieutenant Aurelles, 'the penniless soldier', proves of course to be the solution to the problem. The threat of mob rule is contained by his display of power:

> ... three or four of the roughs found us out ... Phillip had a revolver fortunately (how nice it is to have a soldier by one's side!) and he fired till they went away. But this morning about three o'clock the rats came up and ran over our beds, we all rushed about in *deshabille* [in nightclothes] and I thought we should have been gnawed to pieces, but thoughtful Phil had foreseen this attack for sometime, and opened a great tin of pepper which he flung over them. This held them at bay, but we can hear them all over the place ... (28)

In New Historicist thought, the 'individual' is not inherently unique or complete, but is produced as an effect of the social order. Therefore heroism exists not as the sign of inherent individual courage but as an effect which is produced by the action of social forces around the individual. The 'hero' is then invented by the ruling order to promote an ideal image or stereotype, and this image or stereotype is constructed entirely along the lines of what the dominant order requires for its own perpetuation at this time. In this case the 'heroism' of Phillip Aurelles is that he represents the incorporation of raw, repressive power with the ailing upper class in order to stabilize and maintain that class and its dominant social order. In denying 'the roughs' their attempt to gain access to the house, he is also reasserting the elitism and power of the ruling class. The crisis which the diary produces, of snow, of social disruption, has precipitated the end of the real crisis of the upper class and its threatened loss of power in finding an ally of strength and power, Aurelles, who in defending the house is also defending the values and order of the house.

Subversion has been contained therefore. The diary which provokes subversion – the desire for Aurelles, the idea of female desire, the threat of the masses – is also the diary which contains subversion. The threat of the masses results in Aurelles's defence of the social order and his incorporation within the upper class. This in turn means that Aurelles is no longer a threat. The upper class have maintained their power but have changed the basis of their power from that of property to that of political and repressive power. Aurelles, who was just a penniless soldier to the upper class prior to crisis, is now 'better than gold' (28, 29). He has saved their order and therefore Edie's desire for him can now be accepted. As for the fact that Edie desires at all, the diary quickly recovers the norms of the male order and female desire has given way to Edie's 'not objecting' to Aurelles's desire: 'I may as well agree. . . . I mean to settle down and be a good girl, and make Phil a first rate wife !' (29). Her desires are then glossed over and she is no longer the key player in the drama of their relationship.

This is an important ideological function of the end of the story: to gloss over any appearance of the dominant culture's efforts to renew and maintain its power: 'Papa says people will think this storm most extraordinary, but its nothing at all to the convulsions of nature which the geologists have shown to have once taken place' (28). Power needs to conceal how it *operates*, but simultaneously needs at certain times to make its *presence* visible. Greenblatt says in 'Invisible Bullets': 'Elizabethan power . . . depends upon its privileged visibility. As in a theatre, the audience must be powerfully engaged by this visible presence while at the same time held at a respectful distance from it. "We princes", Elizabeth told a deputation of Lords and Common in 1586, "are set on stages in the sight and view of all the world"' (Greenblatt, in Wilson and Dutton 1992, 108). The Victorian context of Jefferies' story differs only in that crisis needs now to be as visible as power. The crisis which haunts Jefferies' 'Snowed Up' is of the imminent danger of society collapsing back into barbarism, and as such it shares its anxieties with other texts of the late Victorian era, most notably H. G. Wells's *The Time Machine*, and Jefferies' own *After London*. But making visible the imminent danger of 'reverting' to barbarism is a device through which power validates the value of 'civilization'. Following Foucault's ideas on how the self is constructed by defining it against what is alien or 'other', sanity determined by institutionalizing and defining insanity, freedom established by imprisonment, the New Historicists posit that power secures the value of its order by sanctioning glimpses of disorder. Kelvin Everest thinks that the New Historicist insight into how the dominant order uses binary oppositions is one of its most fundamental contributions to critical and literary theory:

> This tendency to take on the guise of the enemy is exactly the danger about which the new historicism has succeeded in making us so vigilant, with respect to our general encounter with the texts of Romanticism. Romantic texts seeks to constrain us to read as Romantics. Frequently their internal structures mirror the external relations between text and reader: Caleb and Falkland in Godwin's *Caleb Williams*, or Frankenstein and his monster in Mary Shelley's novel, provide archetypal instances of such structures, in their modelling of an antithetical relation whose ostensibly opposed terms mirror and feed upon each other. (Everest 1991, 5)

Within Jefferies' story itself a series of oppositions are set up precisely for the purpose of reinforcing the dominant ideology. The individual hero opposes the anarchy of the masses. Jefferies' narration at the end of the story sets up his own male objectivity in relation to the exaggeration of a lady, his own male rationality in relation to her fright. The order represented by furs and the welcome sign of the hansom cab is opposed to the disorder of blockage and looting. The values and order of the dominant culture are made visible and dominant precisely through the textual presentation of the 'other', the dialectically opposed margins. The dominant and the margins, of course, are the same oppositions which are set up in the discourse of colonialism. One of the most eminent of Foucauldian critics, Edward Said, could be said to be New Historicist in his analysis of how the text is the site of the dialectic opposites of European and Oriental. Said's most celebrated work, *Orientalism*, claims that colonization operated through such mediums as academic disciplines and literature in using the idea of 'the Orient', or 'darkest Africa', as sites of negative characteristics and identities in order to reinforce the positive and desirable in the idea of 'Europe' (Said 1978). Within this construction of dialectically opposed cultures, 'Europe' is always found to be rational, enlightened, liberal and dutiful, and this is in direct opposition, and is defined in opposition to, 'the Orient' which is irrational, incompetent, savage and untrust-worthy. 'The Orient' in European literature was the imagined 'other' which helped to reinforce the power of the dominant ideology and culture in Europe as well as in those parts of the world that Europe was colonizing. Louis Montrose deals with similar issues when he writes of how sixteenth-century travel writings recreated stories of an Amazonian culture dominated by women, where the women were 'norished and trayned' in armies, and where the daughters inherited the political and military power, led by a witch-queen who 'feeds on the flesh of young boys':

> This cultural fantasy assimilates Amazonian myth, witchcraft, and cannibalism into an anti-culture that precisely inverts European norms of political authority, sexual license, marriage practices, and inheritance. The attitude toward the Amazons expressed in such Renaissance texts is a mixture of fascination and horror. Amazonian mythology seems symbolically to embody and to control a collective anxiety about the power of the female not only to dominate or reject the male, but to create and destroy him. It is an ironic acknowledgement by an androcentric culture of the degree to which men are in fact dependent upon women: upon mothers and nurses, for their birth and nurture; upon mistresses and wives, for the validation of their manhood. (Montrose, in Wilson and Dutton 1992, 115–16)

Montrose's essay focuses on how Elizabethan culture involves bringing oppositions and otherness into visibility so as to re-inforce the norms of the dominant, of Elizabethan power. The important dimension that he adds to the essay is to say that this dialectic structure does not just appear complete within one text, but is dispersed across a whole range of texts, dialectically related to each other. Montrose is describing the depressing absence of grounds for breaking away from or radically subverting the dominant culture when he says that a text 'creates the culture by which it is created, shapes the fantasies by which it is shaped, begets that by which it is begotten' (Montrose, in Wilson and Dutton, 1992, 130). Since texts operate in the mode of rep-resentation, and representations are determined in social con-sciousness by texts, a vicious circularity of formation and confirmation maintains the stability and power of the dominant culture. For the New Historicist, in other words, the text is the depository of the fantasies and fears of the ruling power of a society. This does not just mean the upper class as it is constructed in and by Jefferies' story, for, as Foucault maintained, power is everywhere. This is the crucial difference between Marxist literary analysis and New Historicism, in that Marxism – or a certain version within literary criticism – views class relations as the focus of political contest, and the economic base of society as more important than ideological factors,[5] whereas in New Historicism it is ideology, among other non-concrete figures and tropes, which is more important. Classes can transform, as in Jefferies' story, incorporating other elements. For Marx the future of proletarian revolution lay in the upper class's accumulation of excessive wealth and property, economic greed which would reveal their dominance as intolerable. The proletariat would then unite and collectively assert their will to power. New Historicism belongs much more evidently to the media-driven world of 1980s America in asserting that political power will remain in the hands of those who control representation. No revolution is possible where power can manufacture crises, wars and revolution towards its own ends. The *representation* of Saddam Hussein or Colonel Gaddafi as threatening and dangerous is much more important for New Historicists than any *actual* historical threat which they might present, and it is the representation of this threat which serves to validate American cultural and political power. Similarly the factual existence of riots or the collapse of the social infrastructure in Victorian Britain is of less importance to the dominant power than the textual representation of such events or possibilities. Jefferies' 'Snowed Up', like Lady Frederick Cavendish's diary entries, is the site of the struggle for power and to reinforce ideological constructions of 'normality'. We have, then, only the textuality of history, history as a series of narratives. Reality, or fact, does not exist outside of the text, outside of constructions which are always, either implicitly or explicitly, textual.

By the late 1980s it was clear from the kinds of articles and books appearing on Renaissance drama that the critical practice known as New Historicism had become prevalent, but it was unclear whether this constituted a movement or even whether there was such a thing as an agreed New Historicist critical practice. Calls began to appear for the 'New Historicists' to articulate and defend their own practices and positions. Carolyn Porter, in an article entitled 'Are We Being Historical Yet?', writes: 'All of us who are concerned with fostering a more fully historicized view of literature . . . deserve a more serious discussion from those in the forefront of new historicism of the critical methods, theoretical assumptions, and political implications of their work' (Porter 1988, 751). Porter then went on to question whether the kind of critical practice evident in Greenblatt's 'Invisible Bullets', and demonstrated above, was really the work of a 'New Historicism' or whether it was the work of a 'cultural poetics', the phrase Greenblatt uses in his book *Renaissance Self-fashioning* to denote criticism which recognizes that culture is a self-fashioning system of signs (Greenblatt 1980). Her point here is that the analysis performed by New Historicist critics such as Greenblatt, Montrose and Goldberg fails to link instances of power containing subversion in texts to anything specifically historical at all. In 'Invisible Bullets', a colonial encounter with Algonkian culture, a tale of an Italian heretic, and the political dynamics of Shakespeare's *Henry IV*, all supposedly confirm the model of containment that Greenblatt says is, on the one hand, 'a primary expression of Renaissance power', but which, on the other hand, is 'the very condition of power' (Greenblatt 1981, 57). Porter proves that the lack of historical specificity, and the analogous way in which one text is found to 'confirm' the dynamics of another, renders any claim to 'historicism' a little weak, and that instead Greenblatt is performing a poetics of cultural power. History, that is to say the historicity of texts or phenomena, is precisely what is being evaded. Whereas the old historicism viewed history as a series of periods which unfolded the great march of progress and evolution, the 'New Historicism', Porter says, 'projects a vision of history as an endless skein of cloth smocked in a complex overall pattern by the needle and thread of Power. You need only pull the thread at one place to find it connected to another' (Porter 1988, 765).

Whether influenced by Porter's article or not, New Historicists at this time began to articulate their positions and to identify themselves as practising 'cultural poetics' rather than 'New Historicism':

> Stephen Greenblatt, who is most closely identified with the label 'New Historicism' in Renaissance literary studies, has himself now abandoned it in favor of 'Cultural Poetics'. . . . In effect this project reorients the axis of inter-textuality, substituting for the diachronic text of an autonomous literary history the synchronic text of a cultural system. (Montrose, in Veeser 1989, 17)

Both New Historicism and cultural poetics are opposed to analyses which read terms like 'text' and 'context', 'literature' and 'history', as distinctive and diametrically opposite (the kind of binary oppositions already mentioned in many of the essays in this collection), and both are opposed to 'histories that have been abstracted from their social matrices' (Montrose 1989, 17). The difference, what little there is, between the practice of New Historicism and the practice of cultural poetics, is that cultural poetics is more adamant that culture is a hermetic system of signs, complete in itself, and that any notion of reality or history was an effect of this sign system and entirely determined by representations. Greenblatt takes as paradigmatic of his argument Caliban's retort to Prospero:

> You taught me language; and my profit on't
> Is, I know how to curse. The red plague rid you
> For learning me your language! (I. ii. 363–5)

It is language that defines Caliban as 'deformed, lecherous, evil-smelling, idle, treacherous, naive, drunken, rebellious, violent and devil-worshipping' (Greenblatt 1990, 25–6), language which colonizes him and subjects him to Prospero's rule, and not the material or historical act of colonization. Representations (whether called literary, cultural or textual) are the agencies of power, and are, therefore, used to produce subversion only in order to contain that subversion.

Often mistakenly identified as the British derivative of New Historicism, cultural materialism takes up the study of how dominance and dissidence are constructed both materially and culturally. Deriving from the work of critics such as Raymond Williams, Richard Hoggart and E. P. Thompson, as well as Foucault and Louis Althusser, a cultural materialist reading focuses on how the text is the site of struggles which do not necessarily end up with the incorporation of the subversive within the dominant ideology. A cultural materialist reading of Jefferies' 'Snowed Up' would focus not just on how the text was producing crisis so as to invoke order, but also how the text itself was being constructed within the material forces around its production at the time of writing, and its production in the present time of the critic and reader. Central to this latter part of its interest is, then, the idea of literature and canonical literature that is prevalent at any one time. Shakespeare has been of enormous interest to critics such as Alan Sinfield, Jonathan Dollimore and Catherine Belsey not so much because of the interest of the Elizabethan era but because of the traditional canonical status of Shakespeare in ideas of English literature and culture. Sinfield, for example, begins his formidable study, *Faultlines*, by saying that his aim is 'to check the tendency of *Julius Caesar* to add Shakesperean authority to reactionary discourses' (Sinfield 1992, 21). The reason for this is that cultural materialists believe that 'power' operates as much through material institutions like schools, theatres and universities as through 'texts', and it is how these texts are negotiated and communicated through these kinds of institution that are important, at least as much as what these texts can be made to mean interpretatively. Jefferies' story, as a relatively unknown text, would be of little interest to cultural materialism as the story has not been assigned any special ideological or cultural function within the social structure, unlike Shakespeare or Wordsworth or Tennyson. Where a writer or a text has been made to support the interests of the dominant culture either by its institutionalization or by the production of dominant readings (e.g. Shakespeare's plays read as insights into the universal characteristics of human nature), Sinfield proposes that it is the job of dissident critics to challenge this incorporation of literature within the dominant ideology and suggests a number of strategies that the dissident critic might adopt for this purpose:

1. Rejection
Simple rejection of a respected text for its reactionary implications can be stimulating, it can shake normally unquestioned assumptions. . . .

2. Interpretation
Interpretation has been the dominant means by which criticism in general handles awkward texts: they are 'analysed' so as to yield acceptable meanings. . . . Such slanted reading is, of course, available to the socialist critic. . . .

3. Deflect into Form(alism)
One may sidestep altogether the issue of the version of human relations propounded by the text by shifting attention from its supposed truth to the mechanism of its construction. . . .

4. Deflect into History

History affords a better route away from the embarrassment of the text . . . [T]he literary text may be understood not as a privileged mode of insight, nor as a privileged formal construction. Initially, it is a project devised within a certain set of practices (the institutions and forms of writing as currently operative), and producing a version of reality which is promulgated as meaningful and persuasive at a certain historical conjuncture. And then, subsequently, it is re-used – reproduced – in terms of other practices and other historical conditions. (Sinfield 1983, 48)

The last method is a preferred method of Sinfield's, and of cultural materialists in general, of putting the text in its contexts, whether the contexts of production or the contexts of reception, so as to expose the process by which it has been rendered in support of the dominant culture. Once this process has been exposed then the text can be interpreted by dissident critics 'against the grain' of the dominant reading.

Sinfield and Dollimore in particular have worked on a number of ways in which dissidence and subversion can be read in a text. Sinfield's *Faultlines* claims that 'the social order *cannot but produce* faultlines through which its own criteria of plausibility fall into contest and disarray' (Sinfield 1992, 45). In contrast to the New Historicist reading above, which was based on the idea that power produced the crisis recorded in the diary in order to sustain itself, a cultural materialist reading might focus on how the dissident perspective of Aurelles, and of Edie's desire for him, is enabled by the widening crack in the dominant ideology, a crack or faultline which is exposed, even if momentarily, while the dominant works to maintain its power. The basis for this reading, or alternatively perhaps of a reading focusing on the subversive threat of Thrigg's wealth overcoming the traditional power of the upper class, is Sinfield's belief that 'even a text that aspires to contain a subordinate perspective must first bring it into visibility; even to misrepresent one must present' (Sinfield 1992, 48). This is the crucial difference between cultural materialism and New Historicism on the issue of subversion, that the latter believes that subversion is always produced to be contained within the text, whereas cultural materialists work from the more positive belief that even where subversion is contained, traces of it remain which enable the dissident critic to articulate this subversion and thereby contest the meaning attributed to it by the dominant culture.

A New Historicist reading of Richard Jefferies' 'Snowed Up' provides a useful insight into the story's relationship to the discourse of power. We gain a sense of how the text operates in relationships with the other texts of this period towards producing subversion and subsequently containing it, reinscribing and sustaining the social order in which it is fully implicated. Borrowing from the work of Foucault, Catherine Belsey suggests the following questions should be included in any new Historicist analysis of texts:

> What are the modes and conditions of these texts?
> Where do they come from; who controls them; on behalf of whom?
> What possible subject positions are inscribed in them?
> What meanings and what contests for meaning do they display?
> (Belsey, in Wilson and Dutton 1992, 39)

To find the answers to these questions, Belsey writes, 'is to relativize the present, to locate the present in history and in process' (in Wilson and Dutton 1992, 40), the effect of which is radically to alter the way in which we think about the relationship between and the nature of literature, history and politics.

NOTES

1. Wilson and Dutton's collection of essays is very useful, and each of the essays are separately introduced. Another useful New Historicist collection is edited by H. Aram Veeser, entitled *The New Historicism Reader* (1994), not to be confused with a collection of more critical and self-conscious essays which Veeser has edited entitled *The New Historicism* (see Bibliography).

2. Another snowfall, similar in effect to that of Jefferies' story, is related in the Lady Cavendish's diary on 17 January 1881 (277).

3. Raman Selden in his *Practising Theory and Reading Literature: An Introduction* (1989, 94), and Catherine Belsey in 'Literature, History, Politics', *Literature and History*, 9 (1983), 17. The full title of Tillyard's book is *The Elizabethan World Picture: A Study of the Idea of Order in the Age of Shakespeare, Donne and Milton* (1943). Tillyard's historicism is of the nineteenth-century variety of regarding history as a series of general overarching cultural and political movements, as opposed to empiricist history which regarded history as a series of isolated and isolatable events.

4. See Foucault's *Madness and Civilization: A History of Insanity in*

the Age of Reason (1971), where he says of madness: 'When man deploys the arbitrary nature of his madness, he confronts the dark necessity of the world; the animal that haunts his nightmares and his privation is his own nature, which will lay bare hell's pitiless truth. . . . In such images . . . the Renaissance has expressed what it apprehended of the threats and secrets of the world' (23–4).

5. See also Jessica Maynard's Marxist reading of 'Snowed Up' in this volume, above.

Encore

7

An 'Economics' of Snow and the Blank Page, or, 'Writing' at the 'Margins': 'Deconstructing' 'Richard Jefferies'?[1]

JULIAN WOLFREYS

STRATEGIC JUSTIFICATIONS: WHY THIS IS NOT A DECONSTRUCTION OF 'SNOWED UP'[2]

We must begin somewhere, but there is no absolutely justified beginning (GR, 162; M, 6–7). One cannot, for essential reasons that we shall have to explain, return to a point of departure from which all the rest could be constructed following an order of reasons (POS, 4) nor following an individual or historical evolution (POS, 48–9). At most one can give a *strategic* justification for the procedure. (Db, 15)[3]

Geoffrey Bennington

. . . there is no separate 'Derrida' in the form of theory who might *then* be applied to something else. Insofar as 'Deconstruction' tends to become a method or a school, we might say that it has forgotten this, and has begun at least to make Derrida into a theory which it wants to put into practice.

Geoffrey Bennington, 'X'

> So, on the one hand, there is no 'applied deconstruction'. But on
> the other hand there is nothing else, since deconstruction doesn't
> consist in a set of theorems, axioms, tools, rules, techniques,
> methods. . . . There is no deconstruction, deconstruction has no
> specific object. . . . Now 'Derrida applied'. That is something
> else. . . .
>
> Jacques Derrida

> 'deconstruction' is a notoriously difficult subject to introduce.
>
> anon.

You might think people would have listened by now. But they
just don't seem to be able to do so. So, in this essay, after
Jacques Derrida, I am going to argue that there is no programme
to 'deconstruction' which I can demonstrate to you. There is no
programme, model or code which I could define which would
provide you with the tools for 'deconstruction' as a theory to
be applied to literature; or to 'deconstructive criticism', a phrase
which can be read as saying 'forget the theory, let's just get on
with the criticism, let's just talk about texts'. The 'deconstructive'
is that which escapes the programme (as I hope you will see,
this essay is itself internally 'deconstructive' inasmuch as it constantly overflows the limits of the conventions of an introductory, expository essay). At the same time, I am going to attempt
to introduce you to a very small amount of the thought and
work of Jacques Derrida, whose name is mistakenly recognized
as being sometimes synonymous with what is understood in some
quarters as 'deconstructive criticism'. The mistake is in the idea
that what Derrida does, the ways in which he reads and interprets, is theoretical and not already involved in active interpretation; this mistaken reading of Derrida suggests that Derrida
can somehow be 'boiled down' to a theory, a collection of axioms,
which, once rendered, can then be applied.

   This 'introduction' is, therefore, designed to contest any simple
notion of 'deconstruction'. In the process of attempting this
introduction, I shall offer a partial reading of Richard Jefferies'
short story 'Snowed Up', as that story becomes illuminated by,
or as it in turn helps to illuminate, certain features of the work
of Jacques Derrida. Because of such an approach this reading
will be necessarily fragmentary, for the reason that I am not
seeking to suggest to you that there is some neat, seamless dove-
tailing going on between 'the text of Jacques Derrida' and 'the

text of Richard Jefferies'. The other reason for the fragmentation that you will find here is because while by rough analogy one can explain a particular moment in Derrida's thinking (as I do below with the concept of the gift), one cannot raise this to the level of a general principle. However, even the announcement of a fragmentary reading cannot, of course, be laid out in advance, for the reasons Derrida and Geoffrey Bennington suggest in the epigraphs of this essay, and in many other places.

As we move through the fragments of readings which this essay contains, you'll notice that I return to various terms, themes and ideas, folding them back into the text, and changing your perceptions as you proceed. In pursuing these tasks or trajectories, I shall argue that 'Snowed Up' cannot be understood through any single theory or theoretical approach to what we call literature. In fact, it calls the category of literature into question. One of the reasons for this is that 'Snowed Up' is made up of undecidable elements, unpredictable, anomalous figures and structures, ambiguous and equivocal tropes, images, voices; all of which make this narrative fascinating, and all of which make this text singular, irreducible to any conventional definitions of what literature is, and at the same time, typical of all literature in its irreducibility; what I have just said about 'Snowed Up' can be said about any work of literature; the singularity of literature, its irreducibility to a definable form known as 'Literature' in effect renders the distinction 'Literature' problematic at the very least. My purpose in proposing such an argument for you as readers interested in literature, literary studies, and literary theory – or literary *theories* – is that I want you to comprehend how each text requires that we give our attention to *its* own functions, paying attention to those functions, structures, features, even in their moments of paradox, contradiction, *aporia*, without seeking to make those functions conform to a particular model of what literature is, or to make the text understandable only according to a thematically organized programme of a particular theory.

If this sounds off-putting, rather than intriguing, or if you want to be able to approach this essay with more confidence, it might be advisable, before you read any further, to read note 5. You might then wish to read the previous note, to which note 5 refers; I would suggest, however, that you come back to here and continue, reading note 4 when you come to it, and then re-reading note 5.

●

For those readers not familiar with a certain rhetoric the title may seem rather obscure and confusing. How, for example, can there be an economics of snow? What is writing at the margins? Why 'margins' at all, and in what sense? Why are the terms in the title and subtitle marked off by inverted commas? The 'rhetoric' of the title, that is to say its 'style' and the concerns it articulates in the manner in which it does, might be taken at first glance to indicate what is sometimes referred to by literary critics as 'deconstruction'. Deconstruction, as a form of literary criticism, taken initially from the writing and thought of philosopher Jacques Derrida (Derrida has said that, while he does teach philosophy, he is not happy with being called a philosopher, as a term or definition for the ways in which he interprets texts [Derrida 1984, 107–26]), is concerned with exposing the structures of thought and the ways in which those structures come to be manifested in, for instance, literary texts. Furthermore, what is termed 'deconstruction' (again I am marking this off with quotation marks for a specific reason which I shall explain further on), through various strategies involving close reading, explores and exposes the ways in which structures of thought, which can be described at least momentarily as discourses or, again, philosophical ideas or concepts, become hidden through rhetorical devices and other techniques of expression and inscription, so that readers fail to see the structures and assume ideas, thoughts, beliefs and values to be natural, normal, just there and not necessarily open to questioning. The thoughts are embedded in such a fashion in our language that we do not even notice that they themselves have structures, are articulated by other thoughts and concepts (which in turn are constructed, and not ever simply points of origin, from which other ideas seem 'naturally' to spring).

But let me start again (like Edie, I appear to have a giddy head). All that I have already said implies that there is a body of knowledge or a theory called 'deconstruction', to which we can apply for a series of rules and regulations; and which, once we have learned these devices, we can use as tools on a literary text (or any other form of text). Were this so, matters would be relatively simple, even if some of the ideas were, initially, difficult, because all that would be required would be an eventual mastery of a method or technique; of something, in short, called 'deconstruction'. Like Edie's old Mr Whatsisname in the diary entry of 2 January, there are those who will insist that we can 'clarify' our ideas and bring our minds into shape, concerning the subject of deconstruction. Such thinking is inimical to the way I am proceeding here and is based on certain misconceptions however, and, like Edie, we may not really want to pay too much attention to such voices of authority.

What Jacques Derrida has to say about 'deconstruction' and the dream of a methodology is sometimes overlooked. But, as Derrida has insisted, what has been called 'deconstruction' is 'neither an *analysis* nor a *critique*'.

> It is not an analysis in particular because the dismantling of a structure is not a regression toward a *simple element*, toward an *indissoluble origin*. These values, like that of analysis, are themselves philosophemes subject to deconstruction. No more is it a critique, in a general sense. . . . I would say the same about *method*, Deconstruction is not a method and cannot be transformed into one . . . it is true that in certain circles (university or cultural, especially in the United States) the technical and methodological 'metaphor' that seems necessarily attached to the very word 'deconstruction' has been able to seduce or lead astray. (Derrida 1991, [270–6], 273)

Although this passage is taken from a very short piece, a letter on the subject of translation (what might be called one of several key topics in Derrida's writing) in general and the translation of the term 'deconstruction' in particular, it is, none the less, perhaps one of Derrida's most important statements on what deconstruction is or is not. This statement is important because, directly or indirectly, it forms a critique of and challenge to what passes as 'deconstruction' or deconstructive criticism (or the even cruder terms, 'deconstructionism' and 'deconstructivism'). It even challenges those who would teach 'deconstruction' as a method or theory of criticism.

Now, you'll notice that as I move on in the effort to define what 'deconstruction' is not, my use of conditional, hesitational clauses, parenthetical commentary, and, of course, quotation marks has become more pronounced. This is not merely a pastiche of Derrida's 'style' (if there is such a thing) as some old Mr, I forget his name, might suggest, but an attempt, in the spirit of Derrida, to try an incorporate all along the way, all of the problematic issues which should be announced at least, if not discussed fully. The hesitations, the clauses, and, most immediately, the quotation marks, mark those places where our acts of reading should be most vigilant, on guard against the kinds of seduction of which Derrida writes above. For example, consider the seductive or tempting qualities of a particular metaphor, which is seductive because it allows one to give up thinking and come to rest on a certain term as a tool and shorthand for a form of interpretation. The hesitant markers proliferate as a strategy of this writing in order to announce concepts, ideas and so on, for which we should maintain a distrust, of which we should ask questions, and concerning which we should consider carefully and perhaps maintain a distance, in order to see how they operate within the structure of thought. But if this is seen as an attempt to maintain a certain distance, then it is also, equally, an effort to create a degree of proximity to ideas with which we are involved. Taking nothing for granted, we have to place ourselves, in our reading, as close as possible to, or within, the structure of the discourse; we have to fold ourselves into the movements of thought and writing. In this way, not only am I talking about a certain subject, but also involving my discourse in it, recognizing the performative element in my own thought, an element which articulates the thought as it speaks of it.

For instance, these very remarks (and the ideas which make them possible) in which you find yourselves immersed are undergoing a process of articulation, iteration, even as I write 'of' those self-same ideas. This is very similar to the manner in which Edie constantly writes of herself as being involved in a narrative of events. Recognition of this double practice is crucial to understanding the nature of diary-writing in general, where one is both author and character, one who is produced by one's own narrations but who also serves the narration directly (more on this below in the section concerned with the title). Edie's writing throughout the diaries plays between her positions of actor in and analyst of cultural ritual (Derrida 1995, 3). This is most immediately apparent throughout the diaries when Edie offers often ironic commentary on the economic game of marriage in which she is being played like a chess piece, and in which she herself performs. Similarly, Edie is an analyst of the effects of the snow on culture and civilization, whilst also being the narrator of the story, to the generation of which the snow is incidental *and* being an actor in the same melodrama. However, these positions are never clear-cut, never wholly separable; Edie has both distance *and* proximity. As Derrida suggests, the boundary between being actor and analyst 'appears uncertain. Always permeable' (Derrida 1995, 3).

As Edie interprets, analyses, translates, she crosses the boundary between positions in order to narrate her role *in* the narrative. She participates in the rituals she analyses. Edie's positions are multiple. In such positions one writes oneself as someone other than the self which writes; one thinks of oneself as another person, divided from one's writing self, the activities of whom one is recalling in the act of writing a diary entry. Edie's always being doubled in this way, and being more than doubled, always being other than herself, is seen in the following remark:

> His dear Edie – me of course – (21)

Edie reiterates her father's remark and interjects with her own commentary, as if we should forget that 'his dear Edie' is 'our Edie', the one whose diary addresses us even while it is being used to address herself. Furthermore, if you return to the story, you will notice that Edie's positions are not simply delineated. Her reference to herself as having to be like another Edie, a heroine from 200 years ago (21) involves and implicates Edie in role-playing and narrative structures. At the same time, this gesture demonstrates the overflow of 'narrative' and 'fictive constructs' on to what we call 'real life'. The figures of the fold, of the weave, and of *the place between* – between 'fiction' and 'reality', between actor and analyst, between distance and proximity – between supposedly identifiable positions are implicated in the figure of Edie. Edie's narrative functions are constantly folded onto one another, they are of great importance and should be born in mind throughout.

Edie's positions are, as others in this volume have already observed, marked by a degree of self-reflexivity about the act of writing, especially in relation to what is called literature (see particularly Mark Currie's essay, above). Consider the following remarks of Edie's:

> I shall never be a good diarist. (19)

> There – I shall be a poetess some day. (20)

> I must be a heroine like Edith my namesake two hundred years ago. (20)

> I've got a fire in my bedroom tonight, and am writing cosily before I retire as the books say. (21)

> he is bigger than Falstaff was. (22)

> ... he broke down fairly for want of poetical language and left his absurd similes unfinished. (22)

These are merely a few of Edie's literary references, comments which others might call *metafictional* or *intertextual*. Edie's supposedly private diary is already 'contaminated', to use a Derridean word, by the traces of the literary, in what are clearly arch-reflexive gestures on her part. Nor are the references all of a piece, Edie's comments pertaining to aspects of poetics, direct and indirect textual allusion, general literary practice and language – notice her knowing reflexiveness in relation to her use of the word 'retire' – and literary criticism. And more than this, what is also, always, traced by the mark of 'literature' is not just the diary, but also Edie's identity. We cannot assume, paraphrasing Julian Cowley on Roland Barthes above, that 'Edie' is a signifier within the text for some extra-textual 'real person'. Edie's self-referentiality, her nods in the direction of what constitute the literary, do not allow us that luxury. The (self-) revelation of Edie's identity through her acts of inscription is always textual, always involved in the production of the text and the construction of identity as being written. What Edie makes us aware of, through the act of 'writing the self', is the inscription of being and its necessary relationship to the subject's identity. This clearly observable intrusion, of the gestures and traces of writing, is part of an attempt to make the reader aware of the 'writtenness' of both text and subject, a point acknowledged by Mark Currie, above (in an essay which might be described as a 'deconstruction' of Edie's story). Edie's acts of inscription show how texts are not merely transparent media through which the reader has direct access to either the voice or the presence of the 'author'. Once again, this kind of recognition of involvement is important in Derrida's writing (as will be shown at the end of this reading of 'Snowed Up; A Mistletoe Story'). And where this is going to lead us is from 'literature' to 'writing', from a restricted economy to a general economy, an economy without reserve.

But let's return to that long quotation of Derrida's on deconstruction and what it is not (this giddy head of mine!); it's worth reflecting further on what he says concerning 'deconstruction'. It is to be stressed that Derrida insists one cannot reduce the term 'deconstruction' to being just one more metaphor, a substitute or supplement, for analysis or critique. Like Edie, like Edie's writing – like Edie's *being written* – deconstruction does not have a stable, single identity. The construction of Edie is dependent on the discursive contexts which change with every diary entry; this change is not equivalent to a progression to maturity, as Mark Currie argues in his chapter. We construct Edie as we read, although the ways in which we structure her identity are not always in our control. Our reading may be influenced by other factors of which we are not aware. Similarly 'deconstruction' is a term the appearances of which are not governable, predictable, hence Derrida's insistence that the word is not merely some substitutable technological metaphor. And the reason Derrida gives for this is equally straightforward: the terms 'analysis' and 'critique' imply processes of interpretation whereby, through techniques of reading, one arrives at the supposed essence, the truth, or meaning of a text.

In the broader picture of Derrida's writing, this is a point on which he has always insisted. Through close reading of what are conventionally defined as 'philosophical' and 'literary' texts (that is to say, belonging to particular traditions, disciplines, fields or genres, the parameters of which we often accept as given), Derrida has shown how we rely on unquestioned assumptions, values or truths; what he calls in the passage above *philosophemes*. By this, Derrida means the particular philosophical units which make up, construct or structure our ways of comprehending ourselves, our identity, our world; those ideas, for instance, which inform the *ways* in which a narrative is structured 'conceptually' or 'philosophically'. And, Derrida elsewhere argues, philosophical figures, language, *philosophemes*, are always present, even in literature:

> in literature . . . philosophical language is still present in some
> sense; but it produces and presents itself as alienated from itself,
> at a remove, at a distance. This distance provides the necessary

> free space from which to interrogate philosophy anew; and it
> was my preoccupation with literary texts which enabled me to
> discern the problematic of *writing* as one of the key factors in
> the deconstruction of metaphysics. (Derrida 1984, 109)[4/5]

One of Derrida's points here, as above – a point he has always
argued for – is that there is no thought, idea, concept which is
not constructed out of, or contaminated by, groups of other
thoughts, ideas, concepts.[6] 'Literature' permits access to the
workings of 'philosophical' language because the philosophical
language is not hidden away within its own discourse or discipline,
pretending to some truth value or seemingly 'natural' logical
progression. Similarly, what we call literary is open to questioning
from non-literary vantage points, even while the 'literary' may
contaminate 'non-literary language' (as though there were
something so pure). The perception on the part of the reader of
what Derrida calls philosophical language in literature is a perception of the structuration of thought. It is in this recognition
or perception that one can recognize those moments which are
paradoxical or contradictory, where aporia open up in the
structure, and which upset the logic or quasi-organic quality of
the text. Thus, in looking for the *philosopheme*, one witnesses
the operation of what Derrida had momentarily called 'deconstruction'. Therefore deconstruction is not a way of reading which
we can control or master in order to get at the truth.

This is not to say that there are no truths, but to put it in a
somewhat convoluted manner, the truth of Truth is that there is
no truth; this is Truth's truth. Truths are to be understood as
moments in a structure of thought, or philosophy, where the
process of articulation, or questioning, critique, or analysis, comes
to rest. And it is a mark of our cultural and 'historical' (a term
of which Derrida has always been wary because of the metaphysical baggage it carries) positioning that we assume a concept or value to be an absolute, uncontestable or natural value.
A truth of 'Snowed Up' is that, if all means of transport into
London failed, and all commercial distribution of food 'dried
up', civilization would quickly collapse and anarchy would emerge;
no one, from Richard Jefferies to Edie, to Alderman Thrigg and
Lord Bilberton, questions the sequence of events as anything
other than the 'truth' of the situation (see Jessica Maynard on
this hypothetical scenario, above).

But to return, yet again, to the passage above. If 'deconstruction' is neither analysis nor critique, it is certainly not a method, states Derrida; as already mentioned, one cannot learn a set of techniques which are equivalent to 'deconstruction'; one cannot 'deconstruct'. In this short letter and elsewhere, in essays, books and interviews, Derrida has always insisted on the fact that the term 'deconstruction' was only ever chosen by him in passing, as it were, being an old French word which was a suitable translation at the time for the term *Destruktion* found in the text of German philosopher Martin Heidegger. Derrida has never privileged the term as a metaphor, nor has he ever reduced it to a metaphor for reading in a certain fashion. In addition, Derrida has insisted that deconstruction is merely one term amongst many which he has used as a name for an event, a movement, a moment of non-logical problematization, whereby a text reveals its own textuality; that is to say, the structure is revealed through an internal paradox or contradiction which dispels the illusion of truth, origin or absolute value.

But how might we demonstrate this, and particularly in relation to 'Snowed Up'?

EDIE AND THE GIFT

Let's take a relatively recent text by Derrida, which will have a certain, strategic, though limited, relevance and resonance in relation to 'Snowed Up', particularly the 'gift' of a fur coat for Edie: *Given Time: I. Counterfeit Money* (1992b). In this, Derrida takes a long, close look at the concept of the gift, of what it means to give gifts, and what is involved conceptually, 'theoretically', 'philosophically', in the process of giving gifts. Derrida points out that no gift-giving is ever simply that, it is never just a giving. For Derrida, implied in the act of giving a gift, implied even in the concept and logic of gift-giving is a moment of deconstruction; which is that the concept is always – always already[7] – problematized by another type of logic which has nothing to do with gifts, gift giving or 'giftness'. And this 'logic' is the logic of economy, of economics. For, argues Derrida, in the act of gift giving and in its attendant concepts, in the philosophy of the gift, there is suggested and already in place, the possibility, the implication of a necessary return and of indebtedness. If I give you a gift, you feel obliged, you *are* obliged (at least in Western culture) to acknowledge that gift, to give something back to me, whether that something is another gift, or merely thanks. This obligation, says Derrida is economic in its condition, it has a structure similar to other economic forms of exchange. And so 'the gift' is deconstructed by an inherent troubling of its own premises, by that other logic which 'contaminates' the logic of gift-giving.

In Edie's case the gift of the furs which is announced in the very first diary entry is clearly overdetermined by an economic network involving free trade, the Government, and a potentially arranged marriage, property. This network also involves house and home, for let us not forget the etymological root of economy and its related terms: οἰκο–s + νέμειν, 'oiko(s)' meaning house or household, and 'nemein' meaning to manage or control. We may be tempted to ascribe the entire unfolding and re-marking of the text to these two ancient Greek words and their subsequent translation into Latin and English. One of the things forgotten in the translation, certainly the *English* translation, is the domestic scene inscribed in 'economy, of which the Greek reminds us. And 'Snowed Up' serves to bring back to us this very scene. For all of the 'action' of this story takes place in the house, in Edie's father's house; and all the action takes place, including the act of 'gift-giving', around the economic issue of Edie, whose house she is to be installed in, whose domestic economy of which she is to be the manager. The narrative is economic through and through, the gift of furs being merely a sign of this economics written otherwise.

We can see this throughout 'Snowed Up'. Despite the rhetoric of gift-giving by which Edie receives the furs, her writing reveals – 'deconstructs' (?) – such rhetoric by unveiling the various local economic mechanisms, direct and oblique, involved in the event of the 'impure' gift. We can follow this trace in order to see how the thread traces the story from its very beginning to its abrupt end:

> *January 2nd.* Papa has just given me such a splendid set of furs. I never saw anything so beautiful. I do believe they must have cost three hundred pounds. (19)

> ... Why are guardsmen always so nice and why have they never got ten thousand a year like Mr Alderman Thrigg, who I believe

has been lending paper money, and now I think of it I shouldn't wonder if these furs were bought with some of it. (20)

I wish papa would let us go to Nice as we used to. (20)

If guardsmen would only manage to be rich; but I'm not going to be sold exactly. (20)

Jan 3rd. . . . They have both done it. I hate them both, ugly, old – . . . . Why didn't they ask *me* first, I call it an insult. I shan't marry either of them. . . . Papa said . . . that I might have which I liked. . . . He said the ancient name of Audeley was in danger of disgrace – bankruptcy or something, and either he must get a good appointment under Government, or his mortgages must be paid off. (21)

These extended references of the first two days' diary-keeping are amongst the more obvious allusions to economic matters and Edie's position in the network of concerns. All of the characters are introduced, the reason for the gift of the furs revealed, and the entire marriage subplot laid bare in its relation to economics, power, and the question, the secret of the household. From 4 January the snow makes it impossible for Edie to leave the house, somewhat ironically perhaps. At the same time as the snow begins to accumulate, the financial references decrease, although they are still present.

Jan 6th. Alderman Thrigg is in despair – he declares he shall be ruined . . . he might have made his fortune . . . at such a crisis if he could only have got his onions and potatoes in. (23)

The reference is now to Thrigg's financial matters rather than having anything to do with Edie's marriage. The next time this is mentioned is in the face of Thrigg's having become stuck in the snow, at which Edie writes, '[i]t served him right for daring to ask papa to marry me;

but I couldn't see him left like that. So I put on my fur jacket and wrapped myself up well, and sat at that window . . . (25)

The fur jacket is again mentioned in relation to marriage, although this time with an ironic twist. Finally the references only coalesce once again in the last of the diary entries:

Mr Thrigg is closeted with papa, what for I can't imagine.

Well I'm sure, I am to be a commodity bought and sold like the Alderman's onions. He has bought me – for Phil. He has just handed me over to Phil as he would a basket of vegetables! 'Better than gold' he repeated again. 'Better than gold Mr Audeley: this is the man for your daughter Sir.' They never stopped to ask me first and even Phillip seems to take it as a matter of course that I shan't object. On the whole as a means of escaping Lord Bilberton perhaps I may as well agree. So the snow was not such a bad thing for – for Phillip. The Alderman showers his gold on Phil and me, and we are to be married in May – if ever May comes any more. (29)

As Thrigg had had dealings with Mr Audeley at the beginning of the story, resulting in the purchase of the furs, so Edie is now subject to a similar deal between the same two men, she now being the 'commodity', the 'household goods', which has supplemented the furs as that which connects marriage and economics through a gift: Edie is a gift for Phillip. But all this can only occur once the snow has gone, for the snow had stopped all commerce, all normal routes of exchange. In fact the snow had made it possible for Edie to write, while the return to economic activity puts an end to Edie's writing.

However, it is not that there has ever been in the story a concept of the gift detached from economic dealing. The gift, whether the furs or Edie, are always already implicated in the economic circuits, as I have just shown. Snow disrupts those circuits and introduces into the text an *aneconomic*[8] figure of excess, non-exchange, supplement; it provides the opportunity for the suspension of trading and for Edie to open her diary at a blank page and begin writing in her own terms. The snow is pure gift to Edie; it is the blank page which effaces the operation, albeit temporarily, of all those textual traces which traditionally figure so prominently as the dominant structural features of the English realist narrative tradition, and which can be economically signalled under the terms 'Money' and 'Marriage', for which the gift has conventionally been a ruse. The snow disrupts not merely the local discourses of the story 'Snowed Up'; it also effectively snows up, partially erases, the dominant tradition of English narrative fiction (of which more at the end of the chapter). The snow is thus a gift without reserve, without return, turning the blank page, making possible writing *against* literature. The snow thus shows us through its intervention the aporia in the logic of gift-giving.

What we can therefore see is that the idea of the impure gift is structured in particular ways by other discourses which determine gift-giving. Edie has always already entered into such economic discourses, and acknowledges her indebtedness, albeit obliquely. She is part of the annulment of the 'giftness'; for, as Derrida puts it, '[f]or there to be a gift, *it is necessary* [*il faut*] that the donee not give back, amortize, reimburse, acquit himself, enter into a contract, and that he never have contracted a debt' (1992b, 13), and Edie has already contracted the debt. Furthermore, as soon as Edie keeps the gift as gift, then, as Derrida says, there is no more *gift* (1992b, 15). Edie has thus entered into the 'circle of debt, of exchange, or of symbolic equilibrium' (Derrida 1992b, 16). On the other hand, Edie owes nothing to the snow; she owes it only to herself to write, this being the gift of snow, which is to say the gift of the blank page which has erased the history of literary authority. And the snow maintains its purity as gift because its giftness is hidden from Edie, as its secret. Others in this collection of essays have noted that Edie's expression becomes more mature, less banal, less clichéd, the more she has to write from necessity, rather than out of mere social convention; indeed, she comments at one point (15 January) that she must write out of a sense of urgent necessity, *in spite of being snowed up* (26–7). It is the secret gift of being snowed up that brings Edie's being into writing. 'Snowed Up' therefore gives us to understand that there is no true 'gift' value, there is no truth to the gift within the conventional narrative. Even here, using the metaphor of 'value', I am admitting to a certain 'economic' structure by which we understand concepts and truths. My writing is 'contaminated' by a metaphoricity announcing the philosophical structuration of the (concept of) the economic.

STRATEGIC JUSTIFICATIONS (CONTINUED): TO SPEAK OF DECONSTRUCTION, AND TO LEAD ELSEWHERE

What deconstruction is not? everything of course!
What is deconstruction? nothing of course!

Jacques Derrida

It should start to become clear now why the term 'deconstruction' is placed in quotation marks in the title above and elsewhere, if only in order to resist such misleading metaphorization and to mark my resistance to making the term a metaphor with certain functions. I am not pretending that this essay is a deconstruction of Richard Jefferies' story; nor will I pretend to be offering you either a deconstructive reading or a lesson in deconstructive thinking. The brief analysis of economics, the gift, and snow just followed are not abstractable into a method of interpretation. The analysis relies for its cogency and authority on a certain analysis of Derrida's, and it works by taking the logic of gift-giving as described by Derrida and looking at gift-functions in the text of 'Snowed Up'. But this is clearly not a methodology which one can apply to all works of literature equally. If I am to be faithful to Derrida's statement above – and to other similar statements made by him elsewhere – then neither can I, as I have already insisted, use Derrida's reading of 'giftness' as a general principle of analysis; and nor can I call it a deconstruction, turning the term deconstruction into a metaphor or simile for analysis, critique or method. If I have recourse to any particular term or phrase, that may well be the phrase 'Derridean', as in the sense of 'Derridean thinking' or 'Derridean interpretation'. But this still suggests a particular strategy, technique or protocol for reading, for interpretation or translation as a 'theological' process in search of an origin.[9]

Also this is merely to use a particular proper name as you would use an author's name such as 'Richard Jefferies' as a meta-phoric or metonymic figure in phrases such as 'Jefferies says that . . .' or 'Derrida suggests . . .'; when, in fact, you mean that you have read and interpreted the following in a text which has been attributed to the person bearing that name.[10] Furthermore, such phrases are not strictly accurate, inasmuch as, instead of readings where the meaning or origin was a particular truth or value (such as Reason, Logic, God), the meaning or origin has now become the person named 'Jacques Derrida' or 'Richard Jefferies'. Proper names, standing in for the absent author, announcing that absence and yet appearing to guarantee a yet-to-come, always deferred, presence, serve as origins or unifying signs, economical means by which various ideas, discourses, phil-osophies, ideologies which come to figure in any given text are gathered together, as though the name guaranteed the meaning or truth or definable source (again, you'll notice, I hope, that I have had recourse to terms such as 'economical' and 'guaranteed', terms which suggest an economic logic; like Edie we are always caught up in that which we attempt to analyse and criticize). They suggest, in the words of Geoffrey Bennington, 'a certain passage between language and world . . . indicat[ing] a concrete individual, without ambiguity, without having to pass through the circuits of meaning (Db 104).[11] It is precisely such a function of the proper name which Edie's diary complicates. The diary of 'Snowed Up' always positions Edie ironically with regard to the other characters, informing us that there is no passage between word and world which is not ambiguous, and nor is there a neat separable distinction between the two. Nowhere is this more clearly announced than in Jefferies' cautionary caveat, his attempted closure, which seeks to define Edie. There is a problematized question of origins in Jefferies' addendum.

So, to talk of either Jefferies or Derrida as the origin of a text or thought misleads. To take the example of Derrida, this thought, this writing and text, which we are calling 'his', itself has a history, several histories, from Derrida's own history, his education, to the intellectual history and tradition out of which 'Derrida's' work comes, such as the other philosophers and philosophical discourses to which Derrida has applied. Were we to suggest as shorthand the proper names or signatures Kant, Hegel, Socrates, Plato, Saussure, Structuralism, Freud, Psychoanalysis, Heidegger, Merleau-Ponty, Husserl, we would no doubt acknowledge certain textual traces 'in Derrida', so to speak (Bennington Db 4). We could do the same with 'Snowed Up', seeking out the source of literary references, the origins of the 'style', and so place the text either in Jefferies' own *oeuvre* or within the wider field of literature itself. But still this would not be to exhaust all the traces – in either Derrida or Jefferies – even were we to study the texts being signified here. Take an example from 'Derrida's sources': 'Freud' is neither an origin nor an end in himself; the 'Freudian' text is not a point either of genesis or destination, being informed as it is by both other intellectual and cultural philosophemes from its past, the 'present' moment of its production in the late nineteenth century, and the 'future' moments of translation, in, say, Derrida's or our readings of Freud.

And, to go further, using the proper name in a phrase such as

'Derridean thinking' implies discernible strategies, techniques, devices for interpretation across a range of texts which are predominant in the texts signed by the name 'Jacques Derrida'. It is perhaps true that we could, reading the writings of 'Jacques Derrida', see certain features in common, but what of the features that are different? What of a feature which might appear in a single text, but in no other? Would we merely write such a feature off as 'marginal', not a 'dominant' theme? And, as Derrida himself has recently suggested, there may always be that which escapes us in our reading, in our translation or interpretation of his work, that for which we simply cannot account in any account of what we call 'his' work.[12] If we think of Edie for a moment, her forgetfulness concerning Old Mr – offers us a brief though valuable lesson in avoiding the source head on. She concentrates on his discourse and not on his personality.

This all seems to delay further the moment of interpretation once more, and you may well wonder why I am not getting on with interpreting 'Jefferies' story (by the way, you should now begin to understand why the name 'Richard Jefferies' is also in quotation marks in the title of this chapter [and subsequently]). You'll have noticed that I have made numerous references, some passing some more sustained, to 'Snowed Up', but do these constitute a reading in the manner of Derrida, are they an *application* of Derrida's thought? Is such a thing possible?

Before we 'return' to the short story,[13] I should acknowledge that seemingly most of what I have told you so far is what you should not do, or be wary of doing, even as I have avoided the pretence of (the) beginning (of) a reading, of, for example, 'Jacques Derrida' or 'Richard Jefferies' in these strategic justifications; at which point, it might be worthwhile re-reading the first of Geoffrey Bennington's two comments, cited as epigraphs to this essay. Were you to push me as to what 'kind of a reading' this will have been, if it is not a deconstruction, I might be tempted to say that, following the programme and title of one of Derrida's texts, this aspires in a very limited fashion to being a 'grammatological' reading, inasmuch as my attention is directed towards writing, text, traces, the formation of these forms and structures, and (a few of) the philosophical concepts which articulate those forms and structures, which help weave the fabric, the text-ile. But I'm still not happy with defining this 'reading' in this manner, because that would still be seeking to be 'true' to Derrida, and thus fall short of truth. It would still imply the possibility of imposing a programme of reading on 'Snowed Up' ahead of the text.

Another possible, provisional, definition of this reading, a definition which marks its singularity, and yet which also acknowledges the debt to Derrida's writings, is to describe it as a 'hymenography' (Derrida 1981a, 213), a term which is also appropriate as a description, if not an explanation, of the structures of 'Snowed Up'. The meaning of the term 'hymenography' will become clear, in the section given that name. Yet we still must keep in mind that, as Geoffrey Bennington has announced, the only way of respecting 'Derrida's' thought is to betray it (Db 316).

Much of my introductory justification so far, then, has seemingly been involved in negating, denying, deferring, avoiding. Why?

Some may say that this is 'typical of deconstruction' (just another way of pinning something down, of presuming to identify a resemblance, and, thus, a *telos or logos*), 'the kind of thing Derrida does' or 'typical of imitators of the Derridean text'. There may be a little truth to this, in that, as Derrida is scrupulous and rigorous in trying to announce all the possibilities of a textual instance, as well as announcing some of the possible contexts within which he is writing or presenting his ideas, in order to show the structures within which thought and writing are produced, so I may be seen as also having tried to be both scrupulous and rigorous. Except that this introduction does not begin to measure up to the rigour of a Derridean reading. Nor does it pretend to; nor could such a reading be feasible in the space here. Furthermore, if I have not set out a programme of reading, if Derrida does not set out a programme of reading, how can it then be claimed that this is typical of something or someone, something called deconstruction, someone called Derrida? You might just as well say that it is typical of someone called Richard Jefferies that he doesn't tell you the end of the story at the beginning. Granted, this is what is called criticism, and Jefferies writes what we call literature, but the act of criticism is essentially an act of reading, and every time something different is read, is not the only responsible act of criticism one which writes according to what has been read, responding to the call or demand made by this text which is other? Or are we only interested in mastery, in control, in making things safe and comprehensible?

Again, it is true that I will have tried, am trying, to expose

some of the contexts and concepts involved in 'Snowed Up' as
well as those within which this chapter is written, within which
I think. Such an approach I believe I may have learned in part
from what we call the texts of Jacques Derrida, but this is not
to say that this is a 'deconstructive' text. Nor is this to announce a 'kind of practice', in Derrida's words (Derrida, in Brunette
and Wills 1994, 9–33). As Derrida points out, if his work and
thought have been ossified into a kind of practice that is immediately recognisable, then they are already dead, of no use. The
chance of 'deconstruction', of a 'deconstructive mode', of 'that
kind of practice' is in transformation, translation from 'the same
thing each time'; Derrida argues that one should be able to recognize the process without recognizing it, by which I take it
that he means that there should be certain similarities which are
recognisable inasmuch as the process involves the development
of a kind of on-going internal critique; yet the transformation
should involve something not recognisable as 'deconstruction'
or 'Derridean thought', which 'needs to be transformed, to move
elsewhere' (Brunette and Wills 1994, 28–9).

So, hopefully, there will have been that, in both the introduction and interpretation (of 'Jacques Derrida', of 'Richard
Jefferies'[14]) which betrays Derrida and which is recognizably
Derridean, which transforms 'deconstruction', directing it elsewhere. In the title and introduction, in the citations and the
marginalia of footnotes I have, either directly or obliquely, announced certain themes which find themselves occurring in
Derrida's texts: themes such as economic structures, writing, signatures, proper names, margins and the concept of marginality,
limits, boundaries, borders and frames; what constitutes such
figures, how we define, say, a margin as opposed to a centre.
For instance, how are we to comprehend that short paragraph
at the end of the story by Richard Jefferies which appears to be
a commentary on both Edie's diary and her personality? Is this
an external margin or an internal parenthesis? What status do
we accord it? Is it crucial or marginal in our reading? What, in
short, is its authority, and what authority, as readers, do we
grant to this signature, 'Richard Jefferies'? Think about your
reaction when you first read the story and got to this point.
How is such a last-minute incursion meant to be taken? As I
have stated, these themes find themselves announced, in different contexts and with different emphases, throughout what might

be conventionally termed Derrida's *oeuvre*. Interestingly enough these are also themes of importance in Richard Jefferies' short story.[15] I would suggest that such themes are amongst those to which we should turn our attention, which we should trace in the text of 'Snowed Up'.

SNOWED UP

> Among so many other things, Jacques Derrida has taught us to look at titles and to consider their frequently strange topology. This attention is particularly rewarded when the title in question entitles a work of fiction. . . .
>
> Peggy Kamuf

You should notice that I have used one of the possible titles of the story as the title of this section of the chapter. You might wonder why. In this section I want to discuss the function of titles and their relation to what we call literature and the literary. The title marks a certain frame, boundary or limit (this is true as a general principle of all titles), and we should perhaps begin there, titles being, after all, a conventional starting-point. To repeat, I have chosen the title of the story as the title for this section. This gesture calls into question the place and function of titles, even beyond the question of frames. Titles exist as borders between the supposed 'outside' and the 'inside' of the text, borders to which we are called but which we may never actually pass, in some senses. This is so because, throughout our reading of a text, we always have the title – which had served as an entrance point, an official recognition of the 'beginning' of a particular text as opposed to 'textuality' in general – as the horizon, the *telos* or meaning (one of several, including the author's proper name, already discussed) of the text. Thus while we keep the title of any work in mind, our reading habitually ignores the title, the title's function. All the while we are subject to the law of the title, the law which dictates the ways in which a title will work, to which law we submit ourselves unquestioningly.[16] Yet as Derrida says, a 'title occasionally resonates like the citation of another title. But as soon as it names something else, it no longer simply cites . . .' (1992a, 183).

The question of the title, then, is a double question concerning both function and placing, function being a result of placing, and placing, in turn, being an indicator of a possible function or several functions. The very possibility of discerning the 'outside' and 'inside' of the text has been (and will continue to be further on in this chapter), even at the self-same moment that the title is put in place, suspended in its 'proper place' at the head of the text.[17] But function has already been problematized through this essay's reduplication of the title of the short story as one of its (the essay's) titles. I haven't placed the title in quotation marks, as convention of titular notation of short stories in literary-critical essays demands (I am disobeying the law), so the question has to be asked, following Derrida's remark cited immediately above, am I in fact referring to the story? In naming something else – this section of the essay – I am no longer simply citing the short story. This all raises other questions, bringing into focus a degree of undecidability which it is important to acknowledge operates throughout 'Snowed Up'. The questions being raised include the following: am I referring to the story as a whole? am I referring to the title merely or the contents as supposedly distinct parts of the text? Does my illicit reference – a skewed citation – refer to or announce in some oblique fashion what is to follow in this essay? and in what fashion, what manner? What had been previously the sign of a certain knowable referent, the title, has become, through the simple act of reiteration, unstable; its context shifted, its meaning is affected. All of which begins to demonstrate through disproof what Derrida calls a few axioms or presuppositions concerning what we think we know of literature and its laws (Derrida 1992a, 184).

These axioms or suppositions are:

(1) That a text has a unity or singular identity which we consider, *a priori*, before the event of reading, in Derrida's words, 'inviolable' (1992a, 184). The accepted, conventional function of the title, its supposedly immovable place at the border of the text is supposed to prove the text's unity, to assure us of the uniqueness of the text being named. (2) The text is supposed to have an author, another so-called guarantee of unity and singularity. This author is understood not as a fiction, or a character of fiction, but as 'real'. Indeed, the manuscript is signed 'Richard Jefferies, author of "A Midnight Skate"' (29). Jefferies, in a private moment of composition, asserts his right to be recognized as a literary persona, which is doubly asserted through the act

of naming another text composed by him. The title of an absent fiction supposedly asserts and guarantees the author's property and authority. Richard Jefferies has what Derrida calls a '*presumed* reality', whereas Edie does not (except that the form of Edie's writing – a diary – complicates the possible interpretation, as I have already hinted and will discuss below [Derrida 1992a, 185]). As Derrida says, there is a cultural consensus as to the these 'qualities' of literature. (3) The third axiom of 'literature', writes Derrida, is that all the events within the text gathered together by the name 'Snowed Up' are related and that 'this relation belongs to what we call literature' (1992a, 186). Yet, once again, this consensual opinion is challenged by the fact that the text is partly represented as a diary, and diaries do not always belong to the category of literature; nor do all diary entries relate to one another, and certainly not in the same manner as events governed by narrative logic in literature are supposed to do. There is something in the diary as a form which exceeds both the generic distinctions and requirements – the laws – of 'literature'. As the snow has been shown above to overflow the limits of the economic logic behind the initial narrative structure, so the diary, as a supplemental structure – a structure always predicated on the potentially infinite supplement of yet one more day always arbitrarily following previous days without narrative economy – overflows literary form. Indeed, Jefferies anticipates the modernist nature of James Joyce's *A Portrait of the Artist as a Young Man* which relies on diary entries to mark the arbitrariness of formal closure.

Now Derrida points out what seems obvious but which seems to need pointing out none the less: that there are forms of narrative, fiction, history, parable and so on which we use all the time which cannot be defined as literature, according to conventional or institutional definitions of what literature is; these forms or types are not specifically literary. Yet you will notice in all the previous essays of this collection that, despite the fact that several allude to the diary form, to Edie's narration and so on, none of the essays ostensibly challenges the 'literariness' of the text; it is assumed implicitly to be 'literature' and all of the essays, despite their various, often diverse theoretical programmes, leave the status of the text unquestioned as such. All the essays obey the Law, which is most immediately questioned through our interrogation of the 'title'. This essay is not seeking to question the short story as 'literature', in the sense of 'good' or 'bad' literature, but to demonstrate, through a reading of the various levels of ambiguity and undecidability of the text, how what we take for granted as 'literature', what we assume unproblematically to have a unity, is always already problematized by its non-literary relations. Furthermore, what this essay proposes is reading which, through attention to moments of undecidability, refuses the desire for mastery, containment and authority, which titles try to install, and which is signalled by the last paragraph of the story. But for now we need to return to the title.

The title conventionally serves a purpose similar in its performance to the signature and the proper name (see Bennington Db 241ff). The title installed, a law is enforced. Let us see what Bennington, in interpreting Derrida, has to say:

> Whatever its grammatical form, the title of a text functions as its proper name. Inscribed on the outer edge of the limit or frame that circumscribes the text (and whose empirical figure is the cover) the title identifies the text, and, like any proper name, permits one to talk about it in its absence. Without a title, be it only a classification number in a library, or the recitation of the first words of a text with no title, or even the word 'untitled' – one would be unable to make external distinction between one text and another and all the disciplines of reading would collapse. The title, more still than the attribution to an author's proper name, is the very operator of textual normality and legality. (Db 241–2)

Fine; axiom No. 1, the title guarantees unity and singularity. Except that, as Bennington goes on to show, titles while acting in the name of the Law of language are, none the less, not as unequivocal as we would like to believe. Notice that, above, Bennington talks of library call numbers and the institution of the title 'untitled' both as manifestations of institutional normal-izations – laws – of the textual frame, that which marks off the 'inner' and 'outer' places of the text. There is in Bennington's discussion the acknowledgement of the text-become-public, the propriety of the text, the text as public property, and the text institutionalized *qua* singular, unified text, available for certain functions, types of performances; and all this through the title.

This raises another question however: what of the 'private' text, the text which is either not yet published, or is not necess-arily ever destined for publication, as in the examples, say, of a previously unpublished manuscript, intended perhaps for publication, but 'silenced' for a certain time (perhaps initially rejected by a publisher and subsequently forgotten)? Or what about diaries? We certainly make the assumption that 'Snowed Up' is a short story, a work of literature, because of certain marks which, through the already-in-place consensus about what constitutes literature, govern our interpretation of the text. In this particular case, there is the signature of 'Richard Jefferies', a name we have been taught to associate with literature, with the production of novels, novellas, essays and short stories, journalism concerned with agriculture, and other forms of 'documentary', 'imaginative' and 'journalistic' prose. We also understand 'Richard Jefferies' as the proper name assigned to a relatively minor figure in the literary canon. We therefore judge (notice the legal, juridical metaphor) the text as literature because of the signature rather than through a translation of any other 'internal' textual elements, and we assign that literature (and its author) to a certain position within the general economy of what we know as 'Literature'. These are not merely idle questions or overstatements of the facts, as Derrida has himself reminded us elsewhere, through his critique of Jacques Lacan's reading of Edgar Allan Poe's short story 'The Purloined Letter'.[18]

This particular text, which also talks at some length about the question of the title, takes the Lacanian reading to task for having overlooked the literary form of Poe's text, and having simply assumed 'The Purloined Letter' to be an example of writing in which the 'Truth' of psychoanalysis is found, supposedly. Without going into detail about Derrida's reading at this point, this particular essay serves as a highly important argument for always bearing in mind the formal conditions of the text;[19] how does it present itself, what are the recognizable markers of the genre to which it seemingly belongs, and, to go back to the question raised by the essay 'Before the Law', what is literature? Here we are with a previously unpublished text, now in print for the first time since it was written approximately one hundred years ago, and its form, as we receive it, is shaped as a fragment of a diary, with an unfinished last section, an apparent editorial comment, a choice of titles, and, equally apparently, missing pages; several 'days' are missing in fact: the diary-text begins on January 2nd and ends on January 25th, but the 7th, 8th, 9th, 11th, 12th, 13th, 16th, 20th, 21st and 23rd are not present; did Edie forget to make entries? Were these pages destroyed? Did Richard Jefferies deliberately leave out these days? (Derrida has given careful consideration to dates and we shall return to this subject after this section.)

As you can see, Richard Jefferies failed to decide on a title, and the editors of this volume have now reproduced the possible title permutations at the beginning of the story. These are:

Edie's Avalanche: Snowed Up

or

Snowed Up: A Mistletoe Story

We shall never know what the final title would have been, even though all of the essays in this collection (including this one) have settled on 'Snowed Up'. Notice in the citation above the play of terms between the two titles. Both obey certain conventions, both have title and subtitle, separated by the mute sign of the colon, a sign which, despite its being mute, still interprets the various terms of the title and their relationship to each other, providing hierarchical organization. Notice also how each title contains the words 'Snowed Up'.

However, the different placement – as subtitle and title, and the repetition – suggests different possible meanings or values. We have presuppositions which we share about titles and subtitles. Conventionally, a title is considered evocative, while a subtitle is more prosaic, descriptive. Yet here we have the same words, drifting like snow from title to title, making access to a single, unified meaning less likely; 'Snowed Up' is marked by equivocality. In fact, the ambiguity around the title suspends the title-function. To borrow a pun of Derrida's about titles, the story/diary is decapitated (1981a, 178),[20] its head already off before we have even begun to read. The title and the title-function are suspended *a priori*, before the reading has begun. And this suspension, this decapitation, is authorized, ironically enough, by the 'author' Richard Jefferies. Thus the text is readable as a network of interwoven traces without a heading. The very condition of the story – if it is a story, if it is literature and not merely a curiosity of a diary, as the 'editor' named Richard Jefferies would have us believe – even now, after publication, is one premised on the radical destabilization of the convention of the title, and this will be important as we read the text.

All of which is, still, to assume, quite unproblematically, a relationship between title, all possible titles, and the text, the 'inside' text. The majority of the text is supposedly a diary, as has already been stated (certainly, as Julian Cowley's chapter on structuralism observes above, the conventions of the diary are observed through the presence of consecutive dates, the references to the writing being a diary, the condition of private writing being announced, the self-reflection of the writer who appears to address herself, rather than any particular audience, and so on). But we need to ask, do we give diaries titles? The answer is, for those of is who keep diaries for private purposes or the registration of engagements, probably not. Diaries of this kind, which belong to one of those forms of narrative alluded to by Derrida in 'Before the Law' not commonly understood as 'literature', share a common, generic title: Diary, the very generic quality of which in its generalizing economy hides the singular, the unique, and all the possible intimacy contained therein. The Diary (of this kind) does not even require the presence of an author's signature, being the anonymous temporalization and spacing of the self-made-writing, writing-as-identity, identity as différance.[21] The title 'Diary' announces privacy and acts as a border patrol. If we read someone else's diary, in this case, Edie's, we are transgressing the laws of the diary. However, this provisional definition of the diary is not the only one, this is not the (only) truth of the diary. There are, of course, diaries which are published, often posthumously, such as those of writers ('professional' writers such as novelists, dramatists, poets, politicians, and officers of the armed forces, if they are sufficiently famous). Some even publish diaries – or selected highlights, at least – while they are alive.

But Edie Audeley, the diarist *in* 'Snowed Up' the short story, the diarist *of* the diary subsequently named 'Snowed Up', is not a public figure, far from it (even though her father wishes he were, and Edie associates with fairly public figures, an alderman, a dignitary in the church, a lord, and a lieutenant, all figures more likely than Edie to publish their diaries sooner or later). So, as far as we are to understand the conventions, someone such as Edie, a private diarist, would not normally, usually, give her diary, even a fragment such as we have, a title such as 'Snowed

Up'. There is, though, an apparent rationalization at work, if we move for a moment to the end of the text, where the diary runs out and someone imposes an apparently editorial presence, in the form of the final paragraph and a signature.

> The Diary ends here. It's quite possible that a lady's fright may have exaggerated matters; but it is also pretty certain that if a fall of snow four feet deep occurred in London and remained on the ground – being supplied by fresh falls – for only one week, the great city of London depending as it does upon stores brought in by rail day after day, would find itself in a very awkward position. *Richard Jefferies* ... (29)

This 'editorial commentary' is signed 'Richard Jefferies'. What are we to believe, then? That Richard Jefferies 'found' or was given the diary, missing or edited-out pages and all? Here we see the signature at work, guaranteeing us an ending, a *telos*, as well as a unity for the text; in short, assuring us of the literariness of the text. From a text without end, with possible arbitrary beginnings and endings which deny textual specificity or singularity (this being one possible definition of a diary), we have emerged into a signature apparently guaranteeing, or attempting to guarantee, us closure. There is also the suggestion that the hand which signed the signature also wrote the possible titles, that a unified frame has been constructed out of title and signature.

Even this suggestion is, however, a gesture which seeks after unity, seeking to provide a teleological structure which, properly speaking, the diary of the text, neither acknowledges nor obeys. It is the law of literature which we obey unquestioningly when we allow ourselves to make such assumptions. As we can see from the wobbling framing devices and the sudden imposition of the signature, this text bears within it the possibilities of reading a potentially dizzying instability and undecidability. This is attested to by the violence[22] of the final commentary, a violence reproduced by the institution of the signature, even though the application of the signature is meant to hide the violence in its implicit claims to being a legal marker of the propriety of the text. And paradoxically, perhaps even 'deconstructively', Richard Jefferies, in authorizing the diary as diary at the end of the text (even though he attempts to discount Edie's account as exaggerated through fright), is readable as authorizing us to ignore his authority by 'testifying' to the 'fact' that this *is* a diary. You'll notice that Jefferies can say nothing very certain, couching his comments in conditional phrases such as '[i]t's quite possible' and 'fright may have exaggerated . . .'. Jefferies only succeeds in making matters even more undecidable.

What then is at stake in such a text as a young girl's private diary, that it should be so clearly curtailed and enclosed?

The possible titles wobble, as I have said; they shake and, in so resonating, reveal to us the structures of literature as constructs and not natural laws, not fixed, immobile Truths. The structures we see are composed out of movable parts and Edie's writing acknowledges the precarious nature of the structure of literature. Her writing of the narrative of events over a number of days is a particularly bald exposure of literature's structural–narrative devices. Throughout there are 'literary allusions' (to which I'll return). Her diary entries show, through being internally framed by dates, the arbitrary arrangement of events which apparently are subject to a presumed reality beyond literary fictions; narrative ordering thus becomes subsumed by chance, thereby denying the author as origin or unifying presence. Edie is apparently subject to the movement of days, rather than controlling their narration.

Dates in diaries also act as titles. But in this case, these are titles which deny the specificity or uniqueness of the event and the 'literary' quality of titles; this being for the reason that dates are common to us all, and do not sign a particular text but the shared writing or signification of the real. Dates in diaries also serve to confuse by making narrative connections in a purely arbitrary manner, and thus destabilize even further the inside/outside structure which a title promises to uphold, by being both within and without simultaneously.

In the case of Edie's diary, the dates mark off subsections, they function as subtitles, much as 'Snowed Up' functions as a subtitle within this essay; except that, with dates once again, the subtitle is shown to have no have no particularly literary quality. And Edie, in her writing, talks of things, people, the city, being 'snowed up':

Jan. 5th. . . . It will be fun if we really do get *snowed up*. . . . (22)

Jan. 6th. Alderman Thrigg is in despair – he declares he shall be ruined. All his vegetables coming to London from fifty different places are *snowed up* on the way. (23) [my emphases]

Here we have what we have taken to be the title, repeated twice, on separate days, in separate diary entries, with different contexts, which substantially alter the possible meaning, whilst also overflowing the economy and limit of the title-function, while folding the title back into the text. The phrase drifts like snow, literally, across the story, across the diary and its narrative. You should not, however, mistake this as an act of mimesis, of writerly imitation of 'reality'. For what the drifting 'title' does is refer us back to textuality and writing. The first reference comes from a purely self-interested entry on Edie's part in the diary, which describes how the snow has made it impossible for Lord Bilberton to go home, and how it is equally impossible for Lieutenant Aurelles to ride by Edie's house. Edie's use of the phrase is generated by her own immediate affairs and relationships, and her sense of the possible loss or gain of pleasure. The second use of the phrase is in relation to economic matters, appropriately enough, specifically those of Alderman Thrigg, who will be ruined financially because the vegetables he sells are 'snowed up' and cannot be brought to London to be resold.

Through these entries we not only understand how unstable the phrase can be, but we also understand Edie's double role, which can be described as 'a narrating narrator and a narrated narrator', to borrow Derrida's phrase from a discussion of Edgar Allan Poe's 'The Purloined Letter' (Derrida 1987, 431). Edie narrates, she tells and writes the events, she is their 'author' and she also narrates herself inside the events, as one of the characters of her narration. Her status is different, however, from the other characters, Bilberton, Thrigg, Aurelles, her father. Edie has consciousness of herself. She writes of herself, and writes of her (in)ability to write, acknowledging the limits of her authorial powers, albeit in a seemingly coy manner. Importantly for us, though, we see that Edie remarks herself as always doubled, as both herself and as other than herself. Furthermore, with her reference to her keeping a diary, she also tells us that she is telling us the events. Although the circumstance of Edie's narrations are quite different from those of the narrator of Edgar Allan Poe's 'The Purloined Letter', there occurs through these various positions of Edie what Derrida calls, again in relation to the Poe text, 'a problem of framing, of bordering and delimitation, whose analysis must be very finely detailed if it wishes to ascertain the effects of fiction' (1987, 431). Edie's two comments above mark out the different kinds of commentary, which allow us to see the levels of narration, while complicating further the outside/inside boundaries of which I have already written, and which will again be taken up below, in relation to an exposition of Derrida's use of the figure of the hymen; and this is made no less problematic by Edie's use of the phrase 'snowed up', which we had previously assumed to have been a possible title, however unstable. Edie's narratorial oscillation echoes the oscillations and resonances of the titles, taken up by her use of the phrase. We see, as Derrida has suggested, that 'the same group of words would not have the value of the title were they to appear elsewhere, in places not prescribed by convention, for example in a different context or in a different place within the same context' (1992a, 189). If we are to accept for the moment the suggestion that this is a diary 'edited' by 'Richard Jefferies' (as I have already suggested this is implied by the form of the text, which is nothing less than the evidence before us), then we can imagine that Edie (having a 'presumed reality' and a status different from that of the other characters) used the term 'snowed up' prior to its use (by Jefferies?) as a possible title. Furthermore, she used it without understanding its potential status or implied power, that is to say, without according it any special value. This means that the title comes to the text, after its internal presence. The title, rather than being a point of origin, is merely a supplement to a text which plays with, and unsettles, the 'truth' of literature. Above I outlined three axioms or presuppositions put forward by Derrida in his essay 'Before the Law'. I omitted the fourth, even though I have talked about it more or less throughout this part of the text. Let's now, as we conclude this section, turn to Derrida, as a way of summarizing, and returning to the point of departure, as another strategic justification:

> We think we know what a title is, notably the title of a work. It is placed in a specific position, highly determined and regulated by conventional laws: at the beginning of and at a set distance above the body of a text, but in any case *before* it. The title is generally chosen by the author or by his or her editorial representatives whose property it is. The title names and guarantees the identity, the unity and boundaries of the original work which it entitles. (1992a, 188)

Edie's writing does not seem to acknowledge the guarantee.

SNOWED UP

> ... the excess of evidence demands the supplement of inquiry.
> Now we must come closer, reread, question.
> (Derrida 1987, 425)

I mentioned above that the phrase 'snowed up' is made equivo-cal by its reiteration in different contexts. The phrase is a homonym of the title; it sounds exactly the same when read out, yet cannot be taken as the same (by implication then the meaning of all language is unstable). It certainly does not serve the same function twice in any of its manifestations. If we argue that the context *is* the same – that the phrase 'snowed up' appears in the context of a diary – we must still acknowledge that its placing alters its sense, a sense even more altered precisely because the contexts are so different. Broadly speaking, we may determine the contexts of the uses of the phrase 'snowed up' as 'pleasure' and 'economics', two terms which could be construed as belonging to an oppositional pairing. In the overall context of the diary-text, we may say that these contexts are also discourses, traces or threads, in the writing which surface repeatedly, the value of the discourses altered each time they make an appearance, while yet causing an accretion throughout the text. The text threatens to become 'snowed up' with the traces of the discourses of pleasure and economics (even though the snow does supplement such a pairing). One of the many meeting-places of these discourses occurs early on:

> *January 2nd.* Papa has just given me such a splendid set of furs, I never saw anything so beautiful. I do believe they must have cost three hundred pounds. I must make a note of it, but I shall never be a good diarist, my last entry I see was a month ago. (19)

As you know, Edie receives pleasure from the furs, but is also mindful of their cost, perhaps thereby indicating that pleasure and economics are not necessarily binary opposites, as might be suggested, but inextricably linked, the one having its meaning determined by the other (we have to ask 'what joins the two'?). But the two discourses lead to another frame of reference, already briefly mentioned, the literary. This frame is decidedly troublesome, having been worrying at this essay throughout. In deciding to note the value of the furs – or does she mean the present, or both? Edie's 'it' is not clear; and notice that, in writing that she must note 'it', she already has noted it, in the act of noting that she must note it – Edie notes also, in a moment of self-reflection, that she will never make a good diarist. This of course leaves open what is meant exactly by the term 'good'. What value does Edie place on the term 'good' in this context? Does she refer to a diarist who is good because she makes consistently regular entries, or does she mean the 'writerly' or 'literary' quality of the entry? Perhaps, once more, she means both. It is, then, never possibly to decide on an unequivocal meaning. What we are witness to, and what our reading produces, or seems to produce, is the resistant nature of the text, its resistance to being controlled through the search for a single meaning. And we are therefore also witness to the text's affirmation of its textness, and of a certain otherness, through its resistance.

Yet this otherness, an otherness resistant to the naming of a particular identity, can be found in the very act of writing the diary itself. In the essay 'Force and Signification' Derrida suggests that such resistance, such otherness, is the very 'thing' in writing, or in any structure, whether biological, linguistic, or literary, which denies the effort of certain procedures or protocols of interpretation, as in a structuralist reading for example, to reach closure in the act of interpretation (Derrida 1978, 27–30). The structuralist reading aims to bring together all the elements of a text and account for them through demonstrating that the text has a structural unity; furthermore, such readings – and we can see the evidence of this with our own eyes in the essays contained in this collection – aim to replicate the text's movements, structures and trajectories as part of a homogeneous whole. Literary interpretation seeks to perform a teleological act of reading which produces wholeness and unity, closing up the text in the production of a single meaning, where all that is seen as significant in the story is said to aim at generating this single meaning. And this is effected by placing various elements of the text in particular places relative to other textual elements, while, at the same time, ignoring, overlooking, other textual elements and figures which cannot be interpreted along the lines proposed by the particular protocols of that type of interpretation.

However, as we see already from the reading of the 'title's' reduplication (and will continue to see), and also from the interweaving of certain disparate figures, tropes, ideas, concepts, and so on, in 'Snowed Up', the connections which are made do not provide a sense of unity. Rather, through their 'illogical' concatenation, these figures maintain a level of heterogeneity through the foregrounding of the chance randomness of structural relationships which cannot be made into a unified whole, whilst still being connected. We can even suggest that the snow becomes the figure *par excellence* for all such figures, its fall being random, unplanned, its effects achieved wholly by chance; yet it is also what connects in its ineluctable, aleatory fashion. Indeed, it is the very connectedness which tends to dissolve and dismiss easily identifiable 'positions', such as 'inside' and 'outside', 'author' and 'character', 'narrator' and 'narrated', 'economics' and 'pleasure', 'private' and 'public' writing, 'fiction' and 'documentary', 'fiction' and 'truth', 'narration' and 'performance'. Meanings slide and shake, drifting like the snow, and are unsettled from a secure location because they are not discretely located or stable. Nor, as I hope I am showing, can they be though of as such. Theirs are chance meetings, connected and yet arbitrarily divided.

DATING EDIE

The diary-text begins on January 2nd and ends on January 25th, but the 7th, 8th, 9th, 11th, 12th, 13th, 16th, 20th, 21st and 23rd are not present . . .

Julian Wolfreys

All of the absent dates are from the period of being 'snowed up'. Ten missing days. Edie seems to take a perverse delight in not keeping her diary at the moments of potentially greatest narrative excitement. But we shall never know. All we can say for sure is that Edie's diary habits are as unpredictable as the weather itself. In this brief section I want to look at the dates of the diary and their function as part of this reading, and in order to explore Derrida's writing further. The dates and their function are a feature largely passed over by most of the essays in this collection. However, the diary as the narrative form which we must read dictates that we must respond to the dates in our reading, and not merely look at the more obvious features of the narrative and its contents, features which, including a man – or, to be precise, two men – being in possession of a good fortune and being in want of a wife, might just as well be taken from Jane Austen's *Pride and Prejudice*. From examining the dates, and exploring the date-function, I will then turn, in the final sections of the chapter, to the figure of the hymen, to the diary as hymenography, and the figure of writing in the broad sense.

'[D]ating', says Derrida, 'is signing' (Derrida 1992b, 259). Yet what, we might ask, is being signed? Every date, like every signature, marks that which is dated or signed with an apparent uniqueness or singularity. Thus each day of Edie's diary is marked off from every other. Yet we can re-read the date, as we can the signature, and thus the date and the signature are paradoxically re-markable outside of the singular context of their initial inscription. Derek Attridge, editor of a collection of Derrida's essays, *Acts of Literature*, explains the paradoxical logic of dates further:

> ... all writing is a dating (as it is a signing) ... the date, like the signature, exhibits the counter-logic of iterability: serving to fix for the future a specific and unique time and place, it can do so only on the basis of its readability, which is to say that it has to remain open to repetition and reinscription; its repeatability is a condition of its singularity. (Derrida 1992b, 371)

Inscribed in the very singularity of the date is the possibility of its being reinscribed elsewhere. The condition of the date is, therefore, an enigmatic condition according to Derrida (Derrida 1992b, 378), precisely because it resists thematization and cannot be theorized due to the paradox or aporia in its logic. Yet the memory of the date is 'rooted in the singularity of the event' (Derrida 1992b, 381). Each day which Edie records is a singular event, each having its own date. For us to recognize the singularity of those events, such as the event of Edie being given furs or going to the theatre, or making a pudding with the Alderman, we have to be able to re-read them, to reiterate them outside of their singularity. We cannot therefore theorize how each day, each date, functions.

This is, you will no doubt say, true of any diary, any dating, so what makes Edie's diary special, unique? Nothing precisely, except that it bears the trace of Edie's identity as uniquely, irreducibly hers, whilst also demonstrating how that identity is in

fact several identities, each composed on different days. Paradoxically, Edie only becomes a singular character through our
act of re-reading, through our acts which make her other than
she is. Edie exists because she can be re-read, and because she
writes of herself. Edie's *Being* is therefore written. She is thus
like every character in literature and every piece of literature,
none of which can lay claim to singularity, uniqueness, unless
they are reiterated, re-read and rewritten. What this suggests is
that each work of 'literature' in its singularity is paradoxically
unique only inasmuch as it can be seen to belong to the general
category of 'literature'.

Yet Edie has always already acknowledged this in keeping her
diary, through references to the literary. In keeping her memory
of the specific date, and her relation to the specific date through
the inscription of memory (for each diary entry is not the event
itself but the memory of the event), Edie traces her Being, which
is other to and opposed to her mere animal existence. Each date
of each day in the diary confirms this inscription of Being. Edie
assigns her Being to particular dates, writing of herself as a
memory; she re-members herself, attempts to put her self together
through memory, writing, signing and dating. This re-membered,
re-marked inscription, available for reiteration, re-reading, shows
Edie inscribing herself, her Being, as other. The date of a particular diary entry is the co-signature of the other Edie. Edie's
Being is therefore signed, written, with each day; it is not homogeneous but marked through the inscription of dates by difference.

Each date, like Edie, already speaks of itself, to paraphrase
Derrida (Derrida 1992b, 382). Yet the date, in the act of 'preserving its memory . . . by the inscription of a sign as memorandum, will have broken the silence of pure singularity' (Derrida
1992b, 382). This is true of Edie, also. In the act of writing
down her memory, using her diary as a series of memoranda, a
collection of dated signs, about herself, Edie has located her
Being as other, her Being as not simply the subject of a 'given
year, month, day, or hour', but also as located at a 'given place'
(Derrida 1992b, 387). This otherness is not a simple opposition, part of a binarism, but dispersed among a series of arbitrary days and locations. Writing a diary entry, Edie confirms
the date's and her own iterability through the 're-marking of
place and time, at the point of the here and now' (Derrida 1992b,
391). At the same time, Edie's acts of inscription also reveal the

constructedness, the structuration, of all narrativity. Dating merely reveals to us the truth of narrative, or, to put it another way, narrative truth. Yet it is not only a narrative truth but also the truth of Being: which is that there is no original, no single Edie, no centre from which all is generated. Each diary entry performs the contingent strangeness of identity. Identity is never fixed, but written and rewritten – re-marked – by the discourses which trace it and which memory traces in turn. Each date of the diary thus signs an other Edie, other Edies, who are reiterated through our act of re-reading. This act is one which brings back Edie to us as other than she is. And we can connect Edie to the date so precisely, without theorizing either, yet still noting that both are subject to inscription, by acknowledging, along with Derrida, that the date is 'always bound up with some proper name' (Derrida 1992b, 390).

Each date of the diary, each date which has its hitherto blank page filled in – and don't forget that there are still ten missing days – acts as a form of key or cipher for memory. We are given access through dates to Edie's memory and to the memory of Edie's Being manifested as a written trace. And this access is to a series of discontinuous events, brought together by the hypothetical situation of the snowstorm. Edie's Being is left strategically incomplete, fragmentary, absolutely unknowable, and therefore strange, contingent, provisional, because of those ten blank pages which have never been filled in and remain, like the snow, outside of any economic determination. The absent dates are, as much as those which we have, part of 'Snowed Up'. Yet their pages are missing, absolutely other to the diary entries which remain to be read. These blank pages seem to suggest a wholly other Edie, unreadable, unknowable. They dispel any possibility of a full presence, haunting the fragments which we have.

In talking of Edie and the dates of the diary I seem to have shifted ground from talking about 'literature' to talking about what is ostensibly a far more 'philosophical' topic, 'Being'. This might in itself strike you as inappropriate to 'literature'. But this is exactly the kind of argument levelled at Derrida; for some literary critics he is too 'philosophical', while for philosophers he is not philosophical enough, bringing literature into his discussions. Yet what is going on here is a fundamental questioning of the ways in which we read and write, the ways in which we ask questions. Edie herself doesn't know the correct ways of writing about certain discourses and admits as much. This does not prevent her from continuing to do so, however. And if (you think) I have shifted the ground, without theorizing Derrida or, for that matter, theorizing Edie – not to mention Richard Jefferies – still, I have been making comments, assessments, arguments which, as I have admitted, are equally applicable to the specific topic of 'Snowed Up' and the general category of 'literature'. Often the most interesting way to discuss a topic is not to approach it head-on.

In discussing Edie's Being in relation to the diary entries as dates, I have pointed to the diary as being fragmented within itself because of its blank pages, The diary is, like Edie, a non-unified Being composed of a non-predictable series of signatures of Being and, specifically, *Being other*. The diary resists theorization as a complete entity, because of its aporia. So too does Edie. The diary is randomized through elision, omission, absence, unpredictable difference within itself, and we have no way of knowing how the diary has come to be constructed as it is. We cannot, therefore, define it unequivocally as *Diary* any more than we can say it is unquestionably 'literature'. Form and content are iterable yet not wholly definable. Indeed it is iterability which defers definition. In this they are connected to their narrator. And what else can be said to connect Edie and the diary? The snow (otherwise I wouldn't be pursuing Being here). The diary's fragmented narrative is concerned with the snowstorm, and it is the snow which allows Edie the possibility of re-marking herself. All three – the diary, Edie, the snow – are written in an aleatory fashion.

Immediately above I wrote of the contingent strangeness of Edie's Being, a condition, by the way, of all being (Edie's Being is, like a date, like a signature, both singular and iterable; the condition of Edie's Being is the condition of all Being). In doing so, I was aware of how Edie is at odds with the dominant economic discourses of the text, those discourses which seek to pin Edie down, fix her meaning through money and marriage. I want to conclude this section by tracing a few heterogeneous connections. Edie's being at odds with economics is re-figured, re-marked, in certain ways by the fragmentary construction of the diary, the supplementary excess of the snow, and in the aleatory configurations of Edie's Being and her supplementary otherness. Edie's otherness is not merely one half of a self/other binarism, and we should not make the mistake of thinking of it in this fashion. The reason for my describing Edie's otherness as supplementary is as follows: this supplementarity, the excess and overflow of Being, is traced not only by the unpredictable diary entries but also in the oscillation across the non-fixable positions between actor and analyst, and narrating narrator and narrated narrator. Furthermore, Edie's supplementary otherness, that which the economic discourse cannot allow, is given a figure of alterity *par excellence* in the aneconomic figure of the snow, a space which, like the blank pages of the diary, suggests a possible, unpredictable writing always in the future, always to come, and always on the way to Being. We can thus imagine the possibility of an other Edie always writing in the future, always inscribing the strangeness of Being *contra* economics. I can only suggest this hypothesis to you, however, by finding suggestions of it traced throughout the story. I have just commented on the connections between Edie, the diary and snow, but let's take this one stage further.

Edie's identity is marked, we know, by a strangeness. Always in her home, always writing her diary in her home, she is not *at* home. Her diary entries reveal much about the interweaving web of economics, even while she is interwoven with them. Yet in her proximity is a certain distance also, and it is this which allows us to read the possible strangenesses of the text. Like the snow, then, Edie does not belong completely to the economic configurations even though there are tangential connections. Like Edie, the snow is also strange, a stranger to economics; both have an improper relationship to the economic. Indeed, it is Edie's writing, Edie's diary, which makes possible the violent yoking of the two in the text.

What I am suggesting necessitates that we return to and remember the etymology of 'economic' once more noted above. We must re-mark the 'control of the household' which figures in the narrative economically, and in which Edie is so crucial a figure. The snow is outside the house (although Edie's writing does in a sense bring it in), while the discourse of the economic is what has been present inside, appropriately enough. Once the snow starts to shut things down neither market nor household economics function. The snow is not of the house, not of the economic figure, because it is, to borrow a Freudian term, *unheimlich*. The English translation for this term is usually 'uncanny', and, certainly enough, such a snowfall as the one imagined by Richard Jefferies is uncanny enough, if not in the supernatural or spectral sense, then at least in the less familiar sense of being unreliable, untrustworthy, unsafe, or of an unsettling intensity, as the *OED* puts it. However, if we go back to the German term used by Freud and translate it literally, we find – uncannily enough, if you bear in mind the sense of household in the Greek root of economy – that *unheimlich* translates as 'unhomely', not of the home. I would suggest that we read Edie as being *unheimlich* also, at least in part, for it is her memory and narrative in the form of the diary, which fold and unfold the various economic concatenations, snowing them up all the while. For is it not true to say that if the diary *is* 'Snowed Up', then Edie, Edie's Being, is also equally both 'Snowed Up' and snowed up. Edie's Being is her text, her writing – the unpredictable diary entries tracing her being in fragmentary and aleatory ways. And because of this, both the discourse and web of economic traces and, along with them, the conventional, clichéd figures of realist narrative, are equally snowed up, subject to the threefold supplementary otherness of writing, Being, and snow.

HYMENOGRAPHIES: WRITING EDIE

The hymen is thus a sort of *text*ile [emphasis added]
> Jacques Derrida

Edie's writing is what connects, making connections without homogenizing. It is the trace which makes connections between apparent opposites, seemingly discrete and disparate, self-contained positions. For instance, Edie connects snow and economics, outside and inside, word and world. We may suggest, then, that Edie's writing offers a series of connections which can be read as hymeneal (in the sense given the word by Derrida). In this final section, I am going to consider Derrida's use of the figure of hymen in relation to a few elements and motifs of 'Snowed Up'.

In the giddy course of this essay I have mentioned the words 'hymen', 'hymeneal' and 'hymenography', in the context of Derrida's thought, without explaining either my use or their function in Derrida's discourse. Derrida himself first discusses the figure of the hymen in the poetry and writing of Stéphane

Mallarmé in *Dissemination*. 'Hymenographies' and 'hymenologies' are described in this work by Derrida as writings, treatises, on membranes (1981a, 213). Despite my own use of the terms in question as provisional metaphors to describe particular qualities of Edie's writing and my borrowing from Derrida, I have avoided definition as part of the obliquely expressed responsibility I feel to being faithful to the spirit of Derrida's reading, writing, and thinking. This avoidance is, once more, one of those strategic tactics designed to necessitate the various detours, the folds, the unfoldings, the various crossings, counter-crossings and crossings-through of the many discursive traces you find weaved together here: those of this essay, those of 'Derridean' thought, those of 'Snowed Up', and those of the reading of 'Snowed Up', to name only the most obvious. (Although this 'reading' is fragmented and fragmentary and does not meet 'Snowed Up' head-on, it would not be difficult to show how this is a Derridean reading – and writing – of 'Snowed Up' through and through.)

Yet despite or, perhaps, because of the various detours and driftings – what, exactly, does a snowdrift *do*, what is its effect on Edie's writing? – the foldings and unfoldings of this writing, the hymen is an important figure for comprehending what is at stake in 'Snowed Up'. At the same time, though, I want to stress once more that you cannot abstract from its use here a general theory of the hymen as it pertains to literature. This particular connection, this textual and textile conjunction has come to me from the story, and what I am going to suggest and pursue throughout the rest of this chapter is that Edie's diary and Edie's act of writing the diary together constitute a hymenography, a writing on and at the margins, at the limits of various conventional scenes of writing, such as literature and diary-keeping, literature and *belles-lettres*. Edie's writing confuses definition, refuses theoretical assimilation by weaving together its disparate threads, by folding into one another apparently separate spheres of discourse. As I shall show, this is not merely a play on words or a somewhat violent appropriation of the term 'hymen', with its possible etymological echoes, as a suitable metaphor for my analysis. As we shall see, Edie's writing is intimately connected with the maintenance of her virginity and the preservation of her hymen; and her writing and its abrupt breaking by someone who comes to sign himself 'Richard Jefferies' is related to the foreseeable loss of the hymen, beyond the text, but already inscribed in writing, in the figure of writing, which Edie acknowledges from the outset in her remarks about diary-keeping and marriage.

Since 1968 at least the figure of the hymen has been appearing repeatedly in Derrida's writing, from the influential essay 'Différance' onwards. In this essay Derrida produces the figure of the hymen as one of what he calls the 'nonsynonymous substitutions' for the key term *différance* (Derrida 1991, 65).[23] In the 'Letter to a Japanese Friend' (that text which serves as my strategic starting-point) where Derrida tells us that deconstruction is neither an analysis nor a critique, he even suggests that, in certain texts of his, 'deconstruction' is replaceable by 'hymen' (Derrida 1991, 275). In attempting to introduce Derrida's work then, as a source for critical–interpretive insights, it is clear that we must come to terms with 'hymen'.

Geoffrey Bennington stresses that 'hymen' 'names "*economically*" the relation between inside and outside . . . "hymen" says separation *and* the abolition of this proximity' (Db 226; first emphasis mine). The term 'hymen' therefore figures in a certain manner that which is between apparently definable concepts while simultaneously naming both their separable spheres and their interdependent connectedness. (Consider for instance Derrida's remark that the history of literature constitutes 'the hymen – *between* literature and truth' [Derrida 1991, 65].) Bennington also tells us that the term also has an immediately comprehensible 'sexual register' (Db 226), while Peggy Kamuf states that Derrida's use of the term acknowledges a certain thinking about the subject of femininity on his part (Derrida 1991, xxxix–xl). The term has of course led feminists to question Derrida over the use of the term. Derrida has however cautioned, in 'Choreographies', that '"hymen" . . . no longer simply designate[s] figures for the feminine body' in his work (Derrida 1985, 181). Indeed, in *Dissemination* Derrida pursues the Latin and Greek etymology of 'hymen' and related words to show how hymen is related to stitching, tissue, sewing, weaving, textile, spider-web, net, the text of a work, the weave of a song (a wedding song or song of mourning) (Derrida 1981a, 213). So, the 'meaning' of the hymen for Derrida is in the fact that its complex semantic and textual relations mean that it cannot be pinned down or confined to a single meaning. Neither simply sexual nor nonsexual, hymen itself comes *between* the two places, as it were, complicating our understanding once more. The hymen does not simply name something and cannot be defined as such.

For Derrida, then, hymen is marked by a double meaning. It is, in his words, '. . . a sign of fusion *between* identities' (Derrida 1991, 209; emphasis mine). This figure marks the difference, and also the connectedness, between two places, two identities, between, let us say, as Bennington does, outside and inside. Hymen in Derrida's writing is the graphic expression of the margin, limit or border which connects opposites, binary oppositions such as inside and outside, and allows their meaning to be understood in relation to one another, while reserving to itself a non-determined place which a univocal meaning cannot be given. Absolute meaning cannot be found in the figure of the hymen and interpretive acts cannot control its meaning. If we think of the actual tissue of the hymen, the 'veil-like tissue across the vagina that remains intact as long as virginity does' (Derrida 1991, xxxix), we understand how it connects the 'inside' to the 'outside' of the female body, and yet is neither, strictly speaking.

The hymen is thus *in between* and hymen names this in-betweenness. In making and marking or re-marking such a connection (to name 'hymen' is always to re-mark its betweenness), and in being 'in between', hymen names its own betweenness. At the non-place of the margin, the border, the limit not simply of one but of both figures in opposition – the hymen is the limit of both inside *and* outside – hymen betrays the fact that inside and outside are never simply or completely separate: Edie's writing is hymeneal in that it betrays the connection between pairings such as gift and property, gift and economic exchange, between the dependence on economic exchange for maintenance of the *inside* the household and the functioning of economics *outside* the house. In fact, because the continuing economics of the house depend on the transfer of Edie as property, Edie is what connects the inside and outside of the house, and the inside and outside of economics. 'Edie' is thus the name of the hymen named otherwise; her writing folds back the various economic inter-weavings, the network or web of interdependent economic functions, and thus reveals her hymeneal function as a written trace (Edie is written *between* the reader and the character, between herself as diary-keeper and the other characters of the narrative) and her writing as a *hymenography*: a *text*-ile weave which traces for the reader the numerous interconnections. And, ironically, it is Edie's hymenography which both traces Edie's identity for us while also leading, seemingly inexorably, to the partial erasure of Edie's identity – an identity which she spins for herself (you'll recall Derrida's etymological web of connected terms, above) – in promised marriage, an act which will lead to the rupturing of Edie's hymen.

This hypothesis on my part becomes clearer once we remember that marriage is the joining of two identities and that hymen is an archaic synonym for marriage itself, as Kamuf points out (Derrida 1991, xxxix). The act of consummation will abolish the hymen by breaking the virgin's membrane. Once the economic agreement is reached and Edie is to be married to Phillip her writing, her self-engendered act of creation, is stopped. Edie will no longer weave together her dangerous supplemental connections and her hymen will become only memory.

However, as long as Edie writes the outside and inside, the external and internal, remain connected. And because she writes in a diary, with its potentially infinitely iterable dates, the hymenography remains intact; hence my lengthy focus on the title its possible functions and Edie's subversive inscriptions of the words 'Snowed Up' which confuse the 'inside' and 'outside' of the text. For Edie to write those words was nothing less than an act of making explicit the hymeneal trope which informs all her writing and which brings back to us insistently the constant network of associations.

So far, in discussing the hymen and Edie's diary, I have named only the spatial relationships which Edie's writing grafts through being between. It is important that we acknowledge that Derrida also insists on the *temporal* spacing effected by the figure of the hymen.

As well as being a spatial figure of undecidability, the hymen is also a temporal trace. The difference between virginity and non-virginity is defined by the temporal spacing. The hymen, writes Derrida, is the figure of 'a series of temporal differences without any central present, without a present of which the past and future would be but modifications' (Derrida 1981a, 210). Here we have what amounts to a possible definition of the structuration and writing of a diary, and my principal reason for understanding Edie's diary as a hymenography. The very form of the diary itself – of any diary – accords to this description of Derrida's. There is no central present moment either in a diary or in keeping a diary. Each day is a temporary present, with each previous and succeeding day being past and future modifications of the idea of the present. No single day can be said to be an absolute present, the origin, source or organizing, generative moment from which all others are engendered. Even the act of writing on a given day only serves to announce not the present as such but the memory of the present as past narrative. With a diary, the 'future (present) and past (present)' have no 'mother-form' (Derrida 1981a, 210) of a constant present which gives birth to them. Writing a diary reduplicates this deconstruction of the idea of a constant, central present, which the blank pages of the diary have always already implied. Writing only serves to re-enforce the deconstruction of a centre, a presence. And Edie emerges as a series of identities out of this writing. Her acts of writing to herself about herself guarantee that she is no more a presence to herself than she is to us, but always already a trace. The diary, and thus Edie's identity, is hymeneal therefore precisely because of the dated sequentiality of the diary, each date signing the never-being-present of the present.

The text of Edie's diary is hymeneal in another fashion also. Her writing is woven together out of what is, at times, an apparently quite crude stitching-together of culturally accepted foreign phrases, literary or semi-literary phrases, terms, quotations and paraphrases, clichés and modish terminology, all of which form the textile network of both her writing and her identity. As the figure of the hymen folds outside and inside onto one another, so Edie's writing folds into her identity numerous traces, connecting Edie's identity to the text of the 'outside world'. The word and the world are sewn together in the folds of writing. Edie's writing is thus hymeneal not only because it traces the margin between 'exterior' and 'interior' 'worlds', but also, importantly, it shows those 'worlds' to be textual. Her writing refers to all writing and performs her identity while making it possible for the reader to see that identity – in this case Edie's – is not a source or origin from which a truthful representation of the world emerges. Rather, Edie is seen as performed herself, composed out of a web of traces. Edie, in writing her diary, and in writing of her 'self' in her diary, is a character in that narrative which is performed from memory in the act of keeping a diary.

In effect then, Edie's 'hymenography' unsettles the very idea of stable origins, centres sources or meanings whether these are sought after 'locally' in literature or in the desire of a full presence; indeed, as we have already seen with the title, her writing plays with the very idea of fixed meanings, a play which is echoed in her use of the word 'poor' (20, 22, 24, 25, 26, 27, 28) which, in Edie's usage, is itself a graphic re-marking of the hymen, making connections as it does between the economic sense of 'poor' and the sympathetic use of the word in response to others' hardships. At the same time as she unsettles (her writing causing little tremors which expose semantic dependence on hymeneal traces), her diary entries connect places, times and events. Her writing does this in the place of the diary, across the blank pages which may also be considered as margins or spaces, the spacing of the hymen *between* the signatures of the dates. Her writing connects and, in so doing, partially erases the difference between '[n]onpresence and presence' (Derrida 1981a, 209). Her name, if it is a name for 'hymen' is also a name which names *différance*. The figure of the hymen, like that of the date, gives us to understand the following: in writing of her self – her Being, you remember, not her existence – every day, Edie not only writes of her self as always other than herself, but also she writes of her identity as a series of supplements without an originary starting-point, each inscription of identity being yet another 'nonsynonymous substitution', to recall Derrida's phrase for the hymen-function. Her writing, her identity, thus promises through its hymenographic movements a supplement or overflow beyond interpretation.

We should pause however, to consider the hymen further, rather than accepting it uncritically as an unproblematic figure which explains who Edie is, and what she does. Were we merely to do this, we would be falling back onto an economical theorization of the 'hymen' useful for explaining Edie's diary and narrative technique. We would thus institutionalize the figure, making it a safe tool for literary analysis in much the same way as some have done with the term 'deconstruction', and it is precisely against such institutionalizations in acts of reading and writing that Derrida warns us.

If the blank pages figure the figure of the hymen, then they – like the figure of the hymen – are only to be recalled after the act of writing, after the act of penetration. For the act of writing effectively abolishes the blank page, leaving it only as a memory. If we can think the possibility of blank pages to come in the future, it must also be possible to imagine them as being no longer blank. Similarly, for us to imagine Edie married to Phillip we must also be able to imagine Edie as having had her hymen broken. Edie's writing is paradoxical, then (as is the very figure of the hymen itself), especially, it would seem, with regard to its temporal spacing; for, in writing on the blank page, Edie abolishes the hymen; in writing of her future marriage, Edie writes of the future when her hymen will be already broken, writing once again of herself as an other Edie. Edie's writing is thus not a form of representation which can be described in hymeneal terms; it is, rather, hymeneal because it confuses and connects; it offers continuity between the supposed signifieds, the exteriority of which it confuses by re-marking them as signifiers, *in writing*. We read of Thrigg, Bilberton, the snow as signifiers, as written traces before any supposed reality they might have, and this is clearly most visible in Edie's acts of writing (about) herself. Indeed, the double function of Edie's writing – the doubling of the narrating and narrated narrator, the analyst and actor – is the confusion of the hymen between positions through and through, because such spatial and temporal confusion means that we can no longer differentiate between poles, between signifier and signified.

This confusion-effect is intensified by Edie's references to literature and the literary, to the belletrist's techniques. Her writing is thus a constant folding, veil after veil, tissue after tissue which is, to quote Derrida, 'located between present acts that don't take place. What takes place is only the *entre* [between], the place, the spacing, which is nothing' (Derrida 1981, 214). And it is precisely because the hymen figures the *between* that it carries within it the possibility of opening up a gap in coherence, logic, identity and meaning and explains *why* we can comprehend it, following Derrida, as a marginal figure, a figure of the border. This also explains *why* the hymen is, like snow (albeit nonsynonymously), an *aneconomic* figure. Edie's 'hymenography' 'snows up' the distinctions between poles, between inside and outside, text and reality, imitation and representation, signifier and signified, economics and pleasure. Writing does not 'outline' or 'trace' a portrait, image or representation; it obscures, covers up, hides.

All of which leads us to further considerations of 'hymen' in

Derridean thinking. Let's look at three different expressions taken from different texts on the function of the hymen, in relation to writing and economic value:

> The graphics of the hymen withholds *a margin* from the control of meaning. (Derrida 1991, 371; emphasis added)

> This entire syntax is made possible by the graphics of the margin or the hymen, of the border and the step. . . . (Derrida 1991, 544)

> Anything constituting the value of existence is foreign to the 'hymen.' And if there were hymen . . . property value would [not] be . . . appropriate to it. (Derrida 1985, 182)

We can discern a certain movement of thought here across these texts which we must acknowledge if we are to comprehend the ways in which Derrida approaches questions of interpretation. As has already been stated, for Derrida the figure of the hymen is one possible name of a margin or space wherein what is written, what is signified by that space and spacing, does not allow itself to be fully interpreted or translated. With this in mind we can say that the final 'marginal' comment by Richard Jefferies at the close of 'Snowed Up' seeks to close down the play of meaning in Edie's writing, for which play the words 'snowed up' are, once again, a suitable motif. Jefferies' comment desires control of meaning over the marginalia of Edie's diary. In desiring such control, Jefferies' commentary also betrays a desire for the location of a centre or origin from which writing issues, in this case a 'lady's fright' (29), which explains how the writing came to be and thus displaces the diary on to a marginal place, putting it, we might say, *in its proper place*.

However, Derrida's second remark suggests that, for meaning to be possible at all, for the syntax to be in the least significant there must be the margin, border, the movement or oscillation *between* which allows us the possibility of discerning any meaning between positions or statements. In order to understand the meaning or value of the 'gift' in 'Snowed Up' there must be the oscillation between the furs-as-gift and Edie-as-gift. And what makes interpretation at all possible is the undecidability, a certain question of force and tension, between, say, Edie's writing and Richard Jefferies' editorial commentary. Jefferies tries to locate Edie's writing properly, as I have just said; this involves him in trying to turn the diary into his own property through his final comment (how did he come to have possession of it?), and concealing this act through his presentation of the diary as a gift to us, as readers. The diary has to be presented as a diary for consumption, its meaning controlled by the omission or censoring of pages and the limiting of its entries to the economical form of a narrative to which all the events *properly* belong. Thus the potentially infinite process of writing day after day is halted through the imposition of narrative economy and the rendering of the diary as property. In the form presented to us, Edie's writing has been given an existence-value and property-value, both of which are alien to the hypothetical figure of the hymen, as Derrida's last quotation suggests. And all this is achieved through the placing of the final remark signed 'Richard Jefferies'.

I want to emphasize an earlier point, folding it back into the discussion if you will. You should understand that I am not referring to a real person here. For our purposes, Jefferies' name at the end of the text is one more textual sign, albeit it of a possibly different order than other signs (Jefferies himself acknowledges this by writing 'Author of 'A Midnight Skate' etc.'. As Derrida puts it: 'proper names – are not real references but indications for the sake of convenience and initial analysis' (Derrida 1991, 173). This does not mean that there was no Richard Jefferies, but that his name, attached to the text in this manner, is open to interpretation itself; it is not the truth of the text. Accompanying the commentary as it does we might be forgiven for assuming that he wished it to be printed (even though we have no evidence for this), thereby hiding his authorial role in favour of an editorial function which, interestingly, seems to provide him with a greater potential power over the 'truth' of Edie's text. Yet – and this is why we must read Edie's writing as a hymenography, against the issues of property and truth, and other economic figures – we must recall, along with Derrida and *pace* Richard Jefferies, that

> . . . the effects or structure of a text are not reducible to its 'truth,' to the intended meaning of its presumed author, or even its supposedly unique and identifiable signatory. (Derrida 1985, 29)

I am not suggesting that we naively or simple-mindedly take Edie's side against Richard Jefferies but that we read the writing effects which produce the undecidability of the text. Were we to do so Edie would become the signatory as centre or presence to which we have reduced the text through our reading.

What I am suggesting, developing from the previous section the idea of Edie's otherness, the otherness within being which writing expresses, is that Edie's writing as hymenography constitutes her nonsynonymous identities through the diary entries as a series of supplements which serve to mediate against the truth and univocity which Richard Jefferies' authorizing signature desires. Edie's 'performances' of narrating and writing acts unfold for us the excessive overflow of endless positions which all writing implies in itself. The spatial and temporal deferral and differentiation of meaning which any act of writing enacts mediates against all desires for presence, truth, origin and uni(voc)ity. Edie's writing of her own identities and her performances announce the conditions of both writing and identity, announcing nothing less than the writing *of* identity, writing *as* identity, and the identity of writing. And we are given a particularly cogent demonstration or performance of this in the writing of a diary, in the writing in Edie's diary. For the diary form announces the hymeneal condition of identity's writing.

Edie's writing is, then, a writing of identity, a writing always enfolded into itself. It is a writing which announces the act of writing *as* an act of performing the subject. Edie's subjectivity is provisionally given, contingent upon context, and without a permanent presence, without a centre. Edie doubles her identity through writing, dividing that identity and re-stitching it. All her entries are therefore not about her 'reality' but about the inscription of Being, Being's trace.

Nor is this merely a metafictional device, as some poststructuralist critics might suggest, as though the term 'metafictional' were in some way an adequate explanation of the story's relationship – we might say its *marginal* relationship – to the nineteenth-century realist tradition. The hymen of Edie's diary, a double-hymen of identity and inscription, ignores the tyranny of mimesis which dominates the reading of the classic realist text. Each diary entry, each dated page is another fold of the hymeneal tissue, folding back on itself at one and the same time the acts of temporally, spatially self-differing and self-deferring inscription and the deft spacings of identity as difference. Even as Edie writes to keep the hymen intact, so she penetrates it once again, leaving at once both memory and future anterior possibility, the possibility of the blank page, the blank margin of the page, awaiting annotation: and is that, after all, not exactly what a diary is, the annotation of identity in all its differential re-markings?

Edie's diary therefore offers us a series of interwoven *betweens*, broken and re-made, re-marked as so many hymeneal figures; figures which all of the essays have been forced in their reading to comment on, more or less: *between* writing and the psyche, *between* writing and gender; *between* writing and culture, writing and ideology, writing and identity, writing and history, writing and structure, writing and form. Between writing and reading. *Between writing and literature.* Edie's diary has come to us, and between each of us and our theoretical knowledge, as the other of our own writing and reading. Perhaps more than anything it has brought to us the *between* which connects – and is the difference between – writing and literature, literature and non-literature. Edie's writing is the border, the limit, the margin, the blank page, the *snowed-up* space which makes the place between so undecidable, which creates a tension and a play between places we call the literary and non-literary. Edie's writing is that marginal, aneconomic figure which confounds such definitions and any supposed certainty which 'literary theory' might believe it brings to interpretation. Edie's diary ~~is~~ that ill-named ~~thing~~ deconstruction, that escapes the instituting question of literary theory: 'what is . . .'? the diary being marked as it is by (and announcing) the always deferred, always already absent presence of Edie.[24]

Thus what we are left with is writing – and reading. Without presence, without institution, without programme. Edie is always already a kind of writing and a kind of reading. There is a passage from Derrida's *Dissemination* which, although a discussion of Mallarmé, is pertinent to Edie and to the writing and reading of 'Snowed Up'. As you read this passage, think of Edie's diary entries, her story, her various allusions and references:

> There is writing without a book, in which, each time, at every moment, the marking tip proceeds without a past upon the virgin sheet; but there is also, *simultaneously*, an infinite number of booklets enclosing and fitting inside other booklets, which are only able to issue forth by grafting, sampling, quotations, epigraphs, references, etc. literature voids itself in its limitlessness. (Derrida 1981a, 177)

Edie's diary is a writing which has no formal opening, no formal closure, no deliberate narrative device motivated by particular characters. At best the snow is only a chance, freak occurrence, without narrative or psychological motivation or cause. This diary is thus a writing without a book, without the formal properties of literature. Yet, at the same time, as Mark Currie has demonstrated so eloquently in his chapter above, there is sampling, quotation, reference, and so on. Even as Edie's writing verges on the edge – the border or margin – of the literary, even as it is a *writing at the margins*, as my title suggested, it also plunges literature into its own limitlessness, placing 'literature' under erasure.

WRITING AT THE MARGINS: INCONCLUSION

I have only been able to comment on a few motifs in 'Snowed Up'. And this is due to Edie's diary, having what Derrida calls a 'certain fold . . . [which] definitively escapes any exhaustive treatment' (Derrida 1981a, 173). However, we might now recognize, in relation to what we call 'literature', that Edie's writing is indeed a writing at the margins. Culturally and 'historically' 'Snowed Up' exists at the margins or limits of realist fiction, if we identify the moment at which it was initially written down. Simultaneously, and because of this initially identified marginal position, Edie's diary also stands at the margins of what we call 'modernism' (with its metafictional devices and arbitrary form it is clearly an antecedent of certain types of writing from the early years of the twentieth century). Third, it bears a marginal relationship not only to Richard Jefferies' published work but also to the so-called canon of 'great works' (in this last marginal relationship, 'Snowed Up' becomes a form of synecdoche for its author, whose literary reputation was also marginal and whose signature on the final line reduplicates the synecdochic relationship). Edie's triple marginality allows her the possibility of performing the inherent instability of all identity positions which rely on the inscription of concomitant, apparently stable economic positions, whether those 'economic' locations be 'wealth' or 'literature' (great or otherwise).

One of the inherent destabilizing factors which adds to the tension of undecidability is the diary's being a fabric woven out of a potentially endless number of citations. Edie refuses to admit the authority of the fathers of literature, alluding and citing imperfectly, and playing a game with referentiality akin to a gambit in a game of chess. In this way Edie's writing thus rejects the economy of literature in favour of the overflow of writing which is always already implied in the diary form. We may see Edie's diary as, in Derrida's words, a 'Babelian performance' (1985, 175), wherein there is no pure literature. So we, who write about 'the literary', can make no conclusion, no economically theoretical statement which closes the book on Edie, which finishes off her story definitively or with authority, even though this is what someone who signs himself 'Richard Jefferies Author of etc.' would clearly desire, as we have seen. I can make no final statement, either on Edie Audeley or Jacques Derrida, both of whom in any case amount to no more than a web or tissue of traces, filaments, threads, woven together and signed in this place, paradoxically enough, in my name.

We cannot deconstruct 'Richard Jefferies', Edie's writing cannot be 'deconstructed' because this writing is already haunted by the deconstructive, the supplementary, the excess and overflow, the hymeneal weave in language. Edie's writing, like 'deconstruction', resists theory because both, to paraphrase Derrida, demonstrate the impossibility of closure (Derrida 1990, 86). Were I to try and effect closure, I might just as well sign myself 'Richard Jefferies'. I cannot read Edie's story 'theoretically' because I am not reading theoretically; I am only, like Edie, reading, writing, and citing; making allusions, drawing comparisons, seeing similarities and responding to writing by writing in an unprogrammed, aneconomical fashion.

Both Edie and I use citation and self-reference. This locates us both as readers in our acts, our performances of writing. But such citation and reference does more:

- It suggests that identity and subjectivity are subject to, structured by, fictions, discourses, narratives, *writing.*
- It suggests that there can be no presence behind writing; nor can there be an original, originary writing, no source or ur-text (a suggestion we might apply to the lack of a definitive title).
- It suggests, through being located in this manner, by being subject to discourses, structures, institutions, and so on, that

Richard Jefferies – or Jacques Derrida for that matter – is also 'constructed', written in a double sense: (i) by the discourses both 'literary' and 'non-literary' which trace 'his' composition, and (ii) by the acts of criticism such as those carried out here for the reader in the performances of 'Richard Jefferies' (and 'Edie', and 'Roland Barthes', 'Jacques Lacan', 'Michel Foucault', 'Karl Marx' . . .).

Such citationality and referentiality has a profound and radical import. In Edie's case, we read her as breaking with the tradition of quotation which, up to the end of the nineteenth century, had been largely a tradition of citation for the purpose of illustration, ornament or authoritative support, as Claudette Sartiliot argues in her study of the uses of citation in modernist writing (1993, 3–33).

Sartiliot, a Derridean critic, points out that conventional citation was a mark of the author's temporary relinquishment of mastery over her own discourse in favour of an already acknowledged authority more eloquent, more respected, more recognized as an institutionalized authority than the author (Sartiliot 1993, 5). If you look at any George Eliot novel you will see such practice in action where Eliot defers authority and authorizes the 'truth' of each chapter with an epigraph, usually drawn from some writer, philosopher or critic. Eliot's mode of citation belongs to the tradition described by Sartiliot.

Edie, on the other hand, is no George Eliot; her practice is different. Her throwaway acts of citation and reference refuse to acknowledge the importance of tradition, convention, institution, practice, authority and mastery. Instead she carelessly folds her references – like that other Edie, who no one in this collection has been able to identify! – into her acts of writing, so that in the act of performing for herself in that highly self-referential fashion, Edie's writing, her use of apparently trite phrases, obvious literary devices and the banalities of everyday language allow no due place or respect to any supposed authority which 'literature' might have been supposed to have (you know, the authority accorded the 'greats' by literary critics). Edie shows us how reference can be turned away from the restricted economy of 'literature' to the unreserved aneconomy of writing. Nowhere does she perform this for us more strongly than in her double citation of the title 'Snowed Up', a double citation as if to comment on the necessary and interwoven actions of reading and writing. Edie's double citation divests the title *as* title – and therefore the idea of the title – of all its power, its property, its entitlement to claim the text as its property. She thus announces its simultaneous singularity and iterability, that condition which marks the title, the proper name, the signature, the date as both absolutely singular and endlessly iterable.

•

I cannot pretend to conclude this essay on 'Jacques Derrida' or 'deconstruction', 'Edie Audeley' or 'Snowed Up' with any definitive statement. But perhaps what I imagine is Edie Audeley reading Jacques Derrida before Derrida has written, and emphasizing with that wayward, giddy pen of hers writing over literature, difference over centre, text over source or origin, to emphasize those inversions one more time. Edie's writing, like Jacques's, resists both theory and closure. Her writing carries within it a possibility which exceeds its narrative, day after day. What that possibility is remains a secret. Nothing either Richard Jefferies or I, or, for that matter, any critic can say will be able to reveal that, or bring such writing to an end.

NOTES

1. I would like to thank Beryl Tanner and Christopher Stokoe for giving this essay generous and scrupulous attention through their various acts of reading, questioning and criticism.

2. As a principle, one should distrust introductions, my own included, and especially those which claim to provide potted versions of a body of thought or discipline. However, there are one or two 'introductions' to the thought of Jacques Derrida which are worth considering: John Lechte, *Fifty Key Contemporary Thinkers* (1994), 105–10. This is a brief dictionary-like entry which avoids possible error through the constraints of brevity, even though, in its brevity, it can hope to do no more than give the briefest of glimpses into some of the most profound developments in thought in the twentieth century. The other 'introduction' is Geoffrey Bennington's, 'Derrida-base', in *Jacques Derrida* (Bennington and Derrida 1993, 3–317). Throughout this essay, I shall have recourse, either through direct citation or reference for clarification on the part of the reader, to

various sections of the 'Derridabase', hereafter referred to paren-
thetically as Db, followed by the appropriate page(s).

3. The abbreviations used by Bennington refer to texts by Jacques
Derrida: GR: *Of Grammatology*; POS: *Positions* (full bibliographical
details of these and other texts appear in the Bibliography).

4. 'Writing', as I have suggested, is an important figure in Derrida's
thinking (Bennington Db, 42–64), and it's worth bearing in mind
what Derrida means by the term. For he has a far broader definition
of the term than the conventional interpretation, meaning the script
produced by the hand on paper or some other similar substance.
For Derrida, 'writing' is a metaphor, a figure which names, in the
words of Gayatri Chakravorty Spivak (one of Derrida's earliest
translators and commentators), 'an entire structure of investigation,
not merely ... "writing in the narrow sense," graphic notation on
tangible material' (Spivak, 'Translator's Preface' in *Of Grammatology*
[1976, ix–lxxxix]). Spivak, in providing a summary of Derrida's
argument in *Of Grammatology*, points out that Derrida is not merely
opposing writing to speech, in the process of reversing a binary
opposition (Speech/Writing), so as to give precedence to a term
which is traditionally considered in our thought to have a secondary
role, while speech is then relegated from its important role to a
secondary position. This requires a brief explanation involving a
provisional definition of what is taken to be 'deconstruction' (as
a technique or methodology) and why this is a misrecognition of
Derrida's processes of reading.

It is true that, in Derrida's early writing, there has been dis-
cerned a process of identifying binary oppositions (figures such as
Good/Bad, Day/Night, Man/Woman, Speech/Writing, Reason/
Madness, Truth/Falsehood, and so on) which are important conceptual pairings in the history of Western philosophy or that branch
of philosophy which is identified as metaphysics (this belongs also,
more or less directly, to Derrida's critique of linguist Ferdinand
de Saussure in his early writings [see chapters 1 and 2 on structuralism and narratology, above; importantly – and this is a sign
of the influence structuralist and poststructuralist thinking has had
on critical thought over the last thirty years – nearly every chapter
in this book reflects on the function of binary and oppositional
terms]). For Derrida, the reason for identifying such oppositions
is to show how, despite the fact that the terms are supposed to be
equal pairs, in our thought, the first, or left-hand term, is always
given greater value or priority than the second term, which,
concomitantly, is assumed inferior. Furthermore, in the history of
our thought, all the prior terms are used as substitutes for one
another in the proof of some absolute Truth. This privileging and
substitution Derrida terms *logocentrism*. Logocentrism is a word

coined by Derrida to bring together two ideas, that of the *logos*, the Greek term for The Word or Truth (as an unquestionable and desired value, i. e. the Word of God) and *centre*, the concept of a central or originary point, a moment of absolute beginning or origin from which everything springs and around which all ideas circulate or to which they refer. In observing this reiterated structure in Western thought, and in observing how the value of the terms was uneven, Derrida also noticed that the first term was always in some manner related to the natural, the organic, the seminal, and other senses of centre, origin, essence, source and so on; all such terms hide the fact that they are structured by other thoughts, ideas, concepts, *structures*. There is no original term or concept, which is not in turn constructed by other ideas, as I have already said; there is no original term, which does not in fact operate as a metaphor for, or which can be substituted, supplemented for, other similar terms. Once we recognize this, we can then see how all terms are part of structures, and how all terms prove the structure (or structurality) of structure.

One of Derrida's suggestions was that the reader should invert the binary opposition, placing the secondary term in the place of the primary term, and vice versa, and, in so doing, see how such an initial inversion or displacement revealed structure, whilst also showing how the meaning of any term is only produced by its difference from other terms (that is to say, how meaning is not inherent in the term); and how there was no absolute centre, which was not also, already, a supplement itself. It is this process, of first identifying binary oppositions and then inverting them in order to reveal how a text is structured through the privileging of certain metaphors over others, which has come to be known as 'deconstruction'. What is in fact merely a strategy at a certain time in Derrida's reading has become the basis for a certain methodology which, at the extreme, has been used to suggest how, because meaning is not fixed, all textuality is infinitely interpretable, and all texts are composed of an endless free-play of meanings.

For an example of such reductive misinterpretation see Charles E. Bressler's *Literary Criticism: An Introduction to Theory and Practice* (1994, 71–87). Bressler, in an undergraduate, introductory textbook, puts forward the entire 'binary opposition reversal' theory as the methodology of 'deconstruction'. It is precisely because I wished to avoid such a misrecognition of Derrida's strategies of reading in all their complexities that I have relegated such a discussion to the margins of the text in this footnote. Before concluding this lengthy digression, however, I would like to return to the Speech/Writing binarism, with which I began, in order to give one specific example of why a reading of Derrida such as Bressler's is fundamentally incorrect.

As Spivak points out (above), 'writing' is a key figure in Derrida's writing (certainly his earlier texts), but as a figure which announces structure, and not merely as the opposition to speech. Writing, once again, says Spivak, is a 'broader concept than the empirical concept of writing' (Spivak xxxix). Writing becomes a term for Derrida (and for which he owes Freud, amongst others, an enormous debt, which he has always acknowledged) which announces both the structured ('written') condition of all forms of text, including human identity and also the idea that all such writings are never completely logically coherent or homogeneous, but are in some way marked or traced by what we term *alterity* or *otherness*; moments which subvert, contradict the logic, figures, traces, conceptualizations for which we cannot account, which our reading cannot make fit in with the overall structure, and which, because of their heterogeneous nature, announce the structure they inhabit *as* structure. But once more, it is important to insist that the term 'writing' not be given a central importance, any more than the term 'deconstruction'. As Spivak cautions us, Derrida 'does not hold on to a single conceptual master-word very long ... such important words ... do not remain consistently important conceptual master-words in subsequent texts' (lxxi). Such words are not 'congealed', to use Spivak's term, but remain constantly on the move, their definition being altered by their subsequent use in various, different contexts. And it is for this reason, if for no other (although there are others too numerous to go into here, each requiring a rigorous analysis in their own right), that we should not accord 'deconstruction' a privileged place. This refusal of privilege on Derrida's part is actually a performance, as well as a demonstration of how writing is structural, and how meaning is not fixed but is always provisional, always a condition of *différance*.

This is another term, worth referring to at this point, itself related to 'writing' and 'deconstruction', and used by Derrida in his early writings. This is another neologism, this time in French. Clearly this term bears a resemblance to the English word 'difference' and the French 'différence'. But you will notice that Derrida's neologism is spelt with an 'a'. However, this is silent, and, in French at least, 'différance' sounds no different than 'différence'. Derrida coined the term for several reasons, amongst these being a critique of structuralism and Saussurean linguistics, which had always privileged voice over writing in the study of the structural production of meaning. The silence of the written 'a' and its phonic 'in-difference' to its conventional counterpart are, for Derrida, a demonstration of the alterity that always inhabits writing. But this is no mere pun or word-play for Derrida, for his neologism combines the possible writing of two concepts, these being deferment and differentiation, both of which are implied in Derrida's term, and performed for him in the silent 'a'. The first implies a temporal displacement, while the second announces a spatialization; which two ideas, temporality and spacing, are key in Derrida's understanding of writing as a notion incorporating a recognition of structurality, and the differences which articulate it.

But what to do once we recognize structures? How do we dismantle them? I shall give the last word here to Gayatri Spivak who, in illuminating the difference between Derrida's approach to reading and traditional methods, states that '[t]raditional textual interpretation founds itself on . . . [the] understanding of metaphor [as] a detour [or path] to truth' (lxxiv). Derrida's performances dismantle 'metaphysical and rhetorical structures which are at work, not in order to reject or discard them [which Bressler puts forward as the purpose of 'deconstruction'], but to reinscribe them in another way' (Derrida cit. Spivak, lxxv). Words, metaphors, Spivak points out, operate not as keys which unlock the way to truth (yet another reason why we should not trust a single term such as 'deconstruction'), but as a lever which, in being jiggled, loosens up the text enough to show it not harbouring the absolute truth at all, but being merely a structure which in various ways produces various meanings which we mistake for the truth. As Spivak suggests, if words or metaphors in texts seem to harbour unresolvable contradictions or suppress implications, we should grab hold of those words and metaphors, following their workings in order to 'see the text come undone as a structure of concealment' (lxxv).

5. The previous, lengthy expository note, immediately before this one, contains summary and précis of many of the supposedly 'fundamental' arguments which seek conventionally to explain what 'deconstruction' is, what it does, how you 'do it', following along the lines of a 'here's how to do deconstruction' prescription. Following ironically Derrida's early 'practice', I have taken the idea of inverting 'primary' and 'secondary' processes or positions in this essay and employed this gesture by subordinating 'deconstruction' (as a supposed literary theory) and its 'definition' to the place of an annotation, a secondary commentary not immediately germane to the analysis at hand. In place of a deconstruction-by-numbers approach, I am offering in the 'primary' place of this essay (that is to say, not in the endnotes) an exploration, in a non-thematic or programmed manner, of those figures, ideas, tropes, structural elements in 'Snowed Up' which appear in other literary forms or genres and on which Derrida has written. In sticking throughout this essay to elements within the short story and analysing the ways in which they function, I am seeking to avoid setting out a programme of 'how to read'. The other essays in this collection already pursue such gestures to greater or lesser extents. In doing

so, they ignore those elements of the text which their readings find inconsequential or unimportant.

Doubtless there may be those who would argue against such a practice as the one pursued here, especially in a place such as this, an undergraduate textbook; such critics would contest that one needs to lay out a fundamental set of rules from which to begin, especially for a non-specialist readership. Such an argument, it strikes me, is both misleading and condescending, assuming that the need of the undergraduate is best met by making that reader into a 'professional reader', one who is equipped with a range of theoretical tools which, once learned, can then be applied to, let us say, *Wuthering Heights*, *Hamlet* or, even, a short story by Richard Jefferies. 'Theory' in this thinking is a competence or skill which the student achieves to a greater or lesser degree. This argument places us back amongst binary oppositions, this time theory/practice. As the critics gathered together in this collection demonstrate, there are no longer – if there ever were – separable spheres. As the interrelatedness or contamination between essays shows we are all, in some measure, 'theorized'.

6. This is the substance of a famous, but often misunderstood, line from one of Derrida's early books mentioned in the footnote above, *Of Grammatology*, which in the French reads: '*Il n'ya pas de hors-texte*' (1976, 158; italics in the original). Translated as 'there is nothing outside the text' (a translation admitting to the impossibility of exact, precise, true translation, whilst also acknowledging that other translations are possible), the phrase has lead to misinterpretations of Derrida's thinking, which suggest that Derrida suggests that there are nothing but texts and that there is no such thing as reality. This is completely incorrect, and stems not only from the difficulty of translation (we may also translate the phrase, either as 'there is no outside-text' or 'there is no outside-the-text'; see the sections from *Of Grammatology* entitled 'The Outside and the Inside' and 'The Outside is the Inside' (1976, 30–44, 44–65), where Derrida argues that, if one comprehends the system of writing in its proper sense, one comes to understand how concepts such as 'inside' and 'outside' become, at the very least, problematized, not least for the fact that inside and outside are not strictly separable, always being connected to each other, being part of each other, as with the figure [used by Derrida] of the hymen, which, strictly speaking, is neither inside nor outside the body; for further discussion of the use of the 'hymen' see below, in the reading of 'Snowed Up'); but also the problem arises from a misunderstanding of Derrida's use of the term 'text' (another figure for Derrida with a broader meaning that its merely conventional sense, and a term which Derrida uses alongside others such as 'writing', 'trace', 'hymen', 'différance', and so on. Texts are the 'chains, the systems of traces'

emerging out of and constituted by differences (1976, 65). These chains and systems – also announced in Derrida's writing by the term 'writing' – are constructed and articulated by both temporal and spatial deferment and differentiation. Hence 'voice', that which in traditional metaphysics has been the guarantor of presence and, therefore, truth, is also, always already, for Derrida, a writing because voice can only operate temporally and spatially. Even in the time it takes to hear one's own voice – this hearing which announces one as both addresser and addressee, as both self and other, always already divided from one's own presumed unity of identity – presence is announced as absent, not there, because of the spacing in articulation, a spacing which is also a temporal deferring. And this is the nature of writing, being a fabric of traces, comprehensible as writing due to spatial and temporal relationships, which make the fabric (and the comprehension of the fabric) possible (see the note preceding this note).

7. 'Always already': this phrase implies that no truth, no 'starting-point' was ever original or simple; the 'always' implies a constant temporal space without beginning or end; the 'already' implies historicity, or an unspecified anterior moment in time for which, because of the action of 'always' in the phrase, can never have had a prior moment of origin. Meaning cannot settle.

8. I have coined the term 'aneconomic' with various etymological sources for the prefix 'an-' in mind, and as a term with which to counter the economic discourse of the text. According to the OED 'an-' can mean, depending on the context of its use, possibly 'against', 'towards', 'in return for'. It can also imply 'not', 'without', or 'about'. Thus the possible sense of the term 'aneconomic' may be 'against economics', 'towards economics', 'in return for economics', 'not economics', 'without economics', 'about economics'. It is such possible meanings that I am playing with in relation to the figure of snow in the text; also this is the homonymic play in the title of this essay: 'An 'economics' of Snow', which also sounds like 'Aneconomics of Snow'. The point here is that I am reading snow 'against', 'without' economics. There is not an economics of snow, snow cannot be an economic figure, so what we find is that instead of a false binarism, say economics/snow, what we have is snow as the overflow, the excess or supplement which cannot be economized in the text.

9. 'Theological' in the sense of a reading or interpretive process which attempts to reveal – is endowed with the desire to reveal – absolute knowledge. As Derrida suggests in 'Circumfession', there is always the unpredictable which can derail the theological enterprise (Bennington and Derrida 1993, [3–315] 26–31).

10. See Db 104 ff. on the proper name.

11. See also Bennington (Db, 148–66) on the related subject of the signature. As Bennington points out, 'Derrida's work' demonstrates how the signature should guarantee a presence, an origin or *telos* (an end, purpose, ultimate object or aim), the end or object as origin. Thus the signature is mistaken as a teleological guarantee, a guarantee of an absolute point or presence at which our interpretation aims and with which we can close our interpretation. However, as Bennington's analysis shows, the signature, being written, carries in its inscription the trace of the absence of the author, and, therefore the trace of the impossibility of absolute presence: 'Like every sign, including "I," the proper name involves the necessary possibility of functioning in my absence' (148). Furthermore, the signature, the proper name, in naming the absence of the one who signs, marks the death of that person, '[i]t already bears the death of its bearer' (Db 148) because the signature as writing will outlive the bearer of that name. The proper name and signature are certainly issues of some importance in relation to 'Snowed Up'.

12. This is discussed throughout Derrida's essay 'Circumfession'.

13. Can we say this, can we 'return' to something from which we have yet to depart? Indeed, I would suggest that we have never really left 'Snowed Up', never left it alone, having constantly worried at it like a dog with a bone. In effect, a reading of 'Snowed Up' is already implied in all that I have so far written. It has never been far from my thoughts, and, as you may ascertain for yourselves, it is acknowledged in some manner on most pages.

14. Ruth Robbins comments above to a limited degree on the function of the signature (Ch. 4, n.9).

15. The various essays in this collection have all, in one way or another, touched in a limited fashion on one or more of these themes. In Chapter Four Ruth Robbins touches on binary oppositions, as does Julian Cowley in the first chapter; while John Brannigan and Jessica Maynard write in various ways around questions of power and economics, in the context of the nineteenth century.

16. On the nature and the law of the title, see Jacques Derrida, 'Before the Law' (Derrida ed. Attridge 1992a, 181–221). There are several texts by Derrida which talk about the (question of the) title, many of which are named in abbreviated form by Bennington (Db 241–58). The question of the law aside for a moment, the title, its functioning, is significantly complicated by its relationships to inside/outside binary thinking, by its very condition of being a title, as (Bennington points out) Derrida points out. The

function of the title is to act as marker of the beginning of the text, as I suggest above. It is thus a marker of the outside limit of the text. At the same time, however, it is also *of* the text, if not exactly *in* the text, conventionally speaking (we certainly don't read the title as we read the body of the text; we submit the title to a different reading). It is therefore at the outer limits of the inside that is the text. Effectively, outside/inside distinctions are shown to be not as clear-cut or discrete as we had previously believed; outside and inside are shown to be connected, part of a 'hymeneal' flow (again, on the figure of the hymen in Derrida's writing and its importance to this reading, see the section of this essay entitled 'hymenographies'). Derrida's essay 'Before the Law' takes its title from a parable, also entitled, 'Before the Law', which is to be found in Franz Kafka's *The Trial*. In taking the title as his own Derrida brings to our attention the laws of literature governing the use of titles, including those laws which determine the placing of titles and our understanding of the place of the title. Derrida uses this process of questioning the title as a way of raising the question 'what is literature?', a question he has constantly addressed. As Derek Attridge puts it in his introduction to the essay, Derrida 'focuses on the institutional, ethical, and juridical implications of any such question' (1992a, 181). What makes matters more complicated is that the words 'Before the Law' (in the original German as well as in the English translation) appear as the first words of the first sentence of the parable; thus the meaning of the words – as used in the sentence, as used by Kafka as a title, and as used by Derrida, also as a title – shifts according to the various laws they have to obey in their relative placings. The destabilization which occurs because of this shows for Derrida how, again in Attridge's words, '[t]he strict notion of the law [which] is predicated upon its absolute separability from anything like fiction, narrative, history, or literature... cannot be sustained' (1992a, 182). This means that the Law is 'contaminated' by fictionality, narrativity, textuality; there is no pure essence to the Law, no originary status. The problematic (function of the) title (of) 'Snowed Up', if not disproving the desired status of the Law directly, does serve to question any supposed certainty we may have about the laws of literature, especially when Edie comes to use the title as a common-or-garden phrase within her diaries.

17. Derrida discusses the placement and suspension of the title, and its functioning, in 'The Double Session', in (1981a, [173–287] 177–80). Barbara Johnson's 'Introduction' to her translation offers a useful, if problematic account of 'deconstructive reading practices', with an outline of Derrida's thought in the tradition of interpretation (vii–xxxiii). Although this is not the place to go into a lengthy analysis of Johnson's introductory essay, it is worth taking note

of a 'problem' typical of English-speaking critics who work with Derrida's material. Despite Derrida's constant remarks that deconstruction is not a critique, Johnson insists that deconstruction is in fact a form of critique (xv). She even implies that this type of critique has a long tradition. Even as she attempts to render Derrida's thought faithfully, something gets lost along the way, and it is this very gesture which I am seeking to avoid.

18. Jacques Derrida, 'Le Facteur de la vérité' (1987, 411–97). A shorter version of the text, under the title 'The Purveyor of Truth' (trans. Alan Bass) is to be found, along with Poe's and Lacan's texts, in *The Purloined Poe: Lacan, Derrida, and Psychoanalytic Reading*, ed. John P. Muller and William J. Richardson (1988, 173–213), a useful source of essays on the issue of psychoanalytic literary criticism. Extracts from the text are provided by Peggy Kamuf in her *A Derrida Reader* (466–84), which version retains the French title with its play on the French word 'facteur', which can mean postman/factor/element. Also there is the sense of 'purveyor' as used in the Muller/Richardson version. There is also the possible translation in some contexts of 'facteur' as 'risk'. Derrida's essay is a rigorous, lengthy analysis of the strategies of Lacan's reading of Poe's text, whilst also unveiling the blind spots in the Lacanian text and providing an alternative reading of 'The Purloined Letter'. In their preface, Muller and Richardson summarise Derrida's critique in the following words: 'In his critique Derrida argues that Lacan has ignored the story's literary context and idealizes the notion of the letter as signifier' (xiii). Kamuf expands this point in her introduction to the text, commenting on how Derrida's essay constitutes a resistance to those who wish to assimilate 'deconstruction' to Lacanian psychoanalytic theory (464–5). As Kamuf suggests in conclusion, 'Le Facteur' marks a connection between the earlier Derridean analyses of logocentrism and phonocentrism begun in *Speech and Phenomena* and *Of Grammatology*, and the type of analysis found in 'Envois' and 'To Speculate on Freud', both of which are in *The Post Card*. Any further references to 'Le Facteur' will be taken from the full text in *The Post Card*.

19. Those essays which are ostensibly formalist in orientation in the first part of this collection, present a series of differing formal concerns. Further, we can see how the 'form' is never simple, nor fully traceable; neither is it exhaustible.

20. 'De*cap*itate: the root of 'cap' is the Latin *caput* or *cappa*, meaning 'head', hence, to cut off the head. *Cap* in French also means heading, so, in the sense that the title is cut off, the story has both lost its head and lost its heading, this being suspended by the absence of a definitive title.

21. For a discussion of the temporal and spatial privatization of the body as traced in writing through the diaristic form in a reading which draws on the work of Michel Foucault, Jacques Derrida and Jacques Lacan, see the reading of the diaries of Samuel Pepys by Francis Barker in *The Tremulous Private Body: Essays on Subjection* (1984, 3–14).

22. Violently because suddenly, unexpectedly. Such a move should make us hesitate in taking it at face value; we should be suspicious of such gestures.

23. Other terms used by Derrida are 'archi-writing', 'archi-trace', 'spacing', 'supplement', *pharmakon*. We cannot go into detail here about the meaning of all of these and their function within Derridean writing. What is important to remember, however, is that they are, for Derrida, *nonsynonymous* substitutions. While no term has any precedence over any other, each term can be substituted for any of the others. However, this does not mean that they carry with them the same meaning. Each figure describes a certain movement or spacing, both spatial and temporal, by which any signifying system comes to be constituted. Such figures in Derrida's writing point to the ways in which the production of meaning is spatially and temporally organized.

24. The first part of this sentence is in imitation of a famous sentence of Derrida's from *Of Grammatology* in the section named, appropriately enough, given my discussion, 'The Written Being/The Being Written' (1976, 18ff) (itself within a chapter entitled, equally appropriately, 'The End of the Book and the Beginning of Writing' [6–26]; in writing this section of the chapter, I had recalled Derrida's sentence which I have paraphrased, but not the titles of either section or chapter. Honestly!). The sentence runs: 'One cannot get around that response, except by challenging the very form of the question and beginning to think that the sign ✗ that ill-named ~~thing~~, the only one, that escapes the instituting question of philosophy: "what is...?"' (19). Derrida is responding to the inappropriate question 'what is the sign'? The question is inappropriate because it requires that you respond 'it is...' implying a presence to the sign which is never simply there as such. The sign is always marked by *différance*, that spatio-temporal differing and deferring. Derrida puts certain words *sous rature*, under erasure, to show us that presence is absent, is not 'in' the thing, 'in' the sign, while also marking those particular terms as having exhausted their significance. However, both the word and the erasure are kept as a sign that some trace remains of signification.

I have borrowed this phrase and the practice of placing something *sous rature*, in this case the diary of 'Snowed Up', to show how it escapes definition, either as literary or non-literary, and yet, simultaneously, is traced by both literary and non-literary figures and inscriptions. It is thus a marginal, hymeneal text which exposes that which deconstructs any certain definition, and certainly the idea that a text – especially one such as this – can be enclosed within the institution of literature, literary criticism or literary theory by asking the question 'what is this text'? The ability to ask such a question is predicated on the notion that we can find a central presence, whether in the form of the author, or a supposedly central character such as Edie. The conventions of literary criticism and much of 'literary theory' are based on such metaphysical misconceptions. Yet, as I am arguing, Edie is only ever the subject of her writing, a writing which is potentially endless and which always refers to the practice of writing. Furthermore, and a much simpler point, Edie is never a central character in terms of dominating the action. She merely observes from her marginal position the actions of others.

Bibliography

Anon. 'Report of the Meteorological Committee of the Royal Society, for the Year ending 31st December 1874'. London: Eyre and Spottiswoode, 1875.

Anon. *Reports from Commissioners, Volume XXVII* (13), 1875.

Austen, Jane. *Pride and Prejudice* (1813), ed. James Kinsley and Frank W. Bradbrook, introduction by Isobel Armstrong. Oxford: Oxford University Press, 1990.

Barker, Francis. *The Tremulous Private Body: Essays on Subjection* London: Methuen, 1984.

Barthes, Roland. *Image, Music Text*, trans. Stephen Heath. London: Flamingo, 1977.

Barthes, Roland. 'The Reality Effect' (1968), *French Literary Theory Today: A Reader*, ed. Tzvetan Todorov. Cambridge: Cambridge University Press, 1982; Paris: Editions de la Maison des Sciences de l'Homme, 1982, 11–18.

Belsey, Catherine. 'Literature, History, Politics', *Literature and History*, 9, 1983. Also in *New Historicism and Renaissance Drama*, ed. R. Wilson and R. Dutton.

Benjamin, Walter. *Charles Baudelaire: A Lyric Poet in the Era of High Capitalism* (1976), trans. Harry Zohn. London: Verso, 1992.

Bennington, Geoffrey. 'Derridabase', trans. Geoffrey Bennington, in *Jacques Derrida*. 1993a, 3–315.

Bennington, Geoffrey and Jacques Derrida. *Jacques Derrida* (1991), trans. Geoffrey Bennington. Chicago: Chicago University Press, 1993b.

Bowie, Malcolm. *Lacan*. London: Harper Collins, 1991.

Bressler, Charles E. *Literary Criticism: An Introduction to Theory and Practice*. Englewood Cliffs: Prentice Hall, 1994.

Brontë, Charlotte. *Jane Eyre* (1847), ed. Q. D. Leavis. Harmondsworth: Penguin, 1966.

Brooks, Peter. 'The Idea of a Psychoanalytic Literary Criticism', in *Discourse in Psychoanalysis and Literature*, ed. Shlomith Rimmon-Kenan. London: Methuen, 1987.

Brunette, Peter, and David Wills. 'The Spatial Arts: An Interview with Jacques Derrida', in *Deconstruction and the Visual Arts: Art, Media,*

Architecture, ed. Peter Brunette and David Wills. Cambridge: Cambridge University Press, 1994, 9–33.

Cavendish, Lady Frederick. *The Diary of Lady Frederick Cavendish*, Vol. II, ed. John Bailey. London: John Murray, 1927.

Chernak, Kim. *The Hungry Self*. London: Virago, 1986.

Coward, Rosalind and John Ellis. *Language and Materialism: Developments in Semiology and the Theory of the Subject*. London: Routledge and Kegan Paul, 1977.

Derrida, Jacques. *Speech and Phenomena, and Other Essays on Husserl's Theory of Signs* (1967), trans. David B. Allison. Evanston: Northwestern University Press, 1973.

Derrida, Jacques. *Of Grammatology* (1967), trans. Gayatri Chakravorty Spivak Baltimore: Johns Hopkins University Press, 1976.

Derrida, Jacques. *Writing and Difference* (1967), trans. Alan Bass. Chicago: University of Chicago Press, 1978.

Derrida, Jacques. 'The Double Session', in *Dissemination* (1972), trans. and introduction by Barbara Johnson. Chicago: University of Chicago Press, 1981a. 173–287.

Derrida, Jacques. *Positions* (1972), trans. Alan Bass. Chicago: University of Chicago Press, 1981b.

Derrida, Jacques. 'Deconstruction and the Other: Dialogue with Jacques Derrida', in *Dialogues with Contemporary Continental Thinkers: The Phenomenological Heritage*, ed. Richard Kearney. Manchester: Manchester University Press, 1984, 107–26.

Derrida, Jacques. 'Choreographies', trans. Christie McDonald, in *The Ear of the Other: Otobiography, Transference, Translation*, trans. Peggy Kamuf *et al.*, ed. Claude Levesque and Christie McDonald. Lincoln: University of Nebraska Press, 1985.

Derrida, Jacques. *The Post Card: From Socrates to Freud and Beyond* (1980), trans. Alan Bass. Chicago: University of Chicago Press, 1987.

Derrida, Jacques. 'Some Statements and Truisms about Neo-Logisms, Newisms, Postisms, and other Small Seismisms', trans. Anne Tomiche, in *The States of 'Theory': History, Art, and Critical Discourse*, ed. David Carroll. New York: Columbia University Press, 1990, 63–95.

Derrida, Jacques. 'Letter to a Japanese Friend', trans. David Wood and Andrew Benjamin, *A Derrida Reader: Between the Blinds*, ed. Peggy Kamuf. 1991, 270–6.

Derrida, Jacques. 'Before the Law' (1982), trans. Avital Ronell and Christine Roulston, in *Acts of Literature*, 1992a, 181–221.

Derrida, Jacques. *Acts of Literature*, ed. Derek Attridge. London: Routledge, 1992a.

Derrida, Jacques. *Given Time: I. Counterfeit Money* (1991), trans. Peggy Kamuf. Chicago: University of Chicago Press, 1992b.

Derrida, Jacques. 'Circumfession: Fifty-nine periods and periphrases *written in a sort of internal margin, between Geoffrey Bennington's book and work in preparation [January 1989–April 1990]*', trans. Geoffrey Bennington, in *Jacques Derrida*, 1993, 3–315.

Derrida, Jacques. *On the Name* (1993), ed. Thomas Dutoit, trans. David

Wood, John P. Leavey, Jr., and Ian McLeod. Stanford: Stanford University Press, 1995.

Eagleton, Terry. *Literary Theory: An Introduction.* Oxford: Basil Blackwell, 1983.

Engels, Friedrich. *The Condition of the Working Class in England.* (1845). Moscow: Progress Publishers, 1973.

Everest, Kelvin, ed. *Revolution in Writing: British Literary Responses to the French Revolution.* Milton Keynes: Open University Press, 1991.

Felman, Shoshana, ed. *Literature and Psychoanalysis: The Question of Reading: Otherwise.* Baltimore: Johns Hopkins University Press, 1982.

Fliegel, Zenia. 'Half a Century Later: Current Status of Freud's Controversial Views on Women', *Psychoanalytic Review,* 69: 1, 7–28.

Foucault, Michel. *Madness and Civilization: A History of Insanity in the Age of Reason.* London: Tavistock, 1971.

Freud, Sigmund. *The Interpretation of Dreams: Penguin Freud Library* Vol. 4 (1900), trans. James Strachey, ed. Angela Richards. London: Penguin, 1991.

Freud, Sigmund. *The Psychopathology of Everyday Life: Penguin Freud Library* Vol. 5 (1901), trans. James Strachey, ed. Angela Richards. Harmondsworth: Penguin, 1975.

Freud, Sigmund. *Jokes and their Relation to the Unconscious: Freud Penguin Library* Vol. 6 (1905), trans. James Strachey, ed. Angela Richards. Harmondsworth: Penguin, 1991.

Gallop, Jane. *The Daughter's Seduction: Feminism and Psychoanalysis.* Ithaca: Cornell University Press, 1982.

Genette, Gérard. *Narrative Discourse: An Essay in Method* (1972), trans. Jane E. Lewin, foreword by Jonathan Culler. Ithaca: Cornell University Press, 1980.

Greenblatt, Stephen. *Renaissance Self-fashioning: From More to Shakespeare.* Chicago: University of Chicago Press, 1980.

Greenblatt, Stephen. 'Invisible Bullets: Renaissance Authority and its Subversion', *Glyph,* 8, 1981, 40–61. Also in *New Historicism and Renaissance Drama,* ed. R. Wilson and R. Dutton.

Greenblatt, Stephen. 'Professing the Renaissance: The Poetics and Politics of Culture', in *The New Historicism,* ed. H. Aram Veeser. London: Routledge, 1989.

Greenblatt, Stephen. *Learning to Curse: Essays in Early Modern Culture.* London: Routledge, 1990.

Greene, Gayle, and Coppélia Kahn, eds. *Making a Difference: Feminist Literary Criticism.* London: Methuen, 1985.

Heath, Stephen. *The Sexual Fix.* London and Basingstoke: Macmillan, 1982.

Humm, Maggie. *Feminisms: a Reader.* New York, London: Harvester Wheatsheaf, 1992.

James, Henry. *The Turn of the Screw and Other Stories.* Harmondsworth: Penguin, 1972.

Jefferies, Richard. *After London, or Wild England* (1885), introduction by John Fowles. World's Classics. Oxford: Oxford University Press, 1980a.

Jefferies, Richard. *The Open Air*. London: Chatto and Windus, 1908.

Jefferies, Richard. *Jefferies' England: Nature Essays by Richard Jefferies* (1937), ed. and introduction by Samuel J. Looker. London: Constable and Co., 1947.

Jefferies, Richard. *Chronicles of the Hedges and Other Essays*, ed. Samuel J. Looker. London. Phoenix House Ltd, 1948a.

Jefferies, Richard. *The Jefferies Companion*, ed. Samuel J. Looker. London: Phoenix House Ltd, 1948b.

Jefferies, Richard. *Field and Farm*, ed. Samuel J. Looker. London: Phoenix House Ltd, 1957.

Jefferies, Richard. *The Hills and the Vale*, introduction by Edward Thomas. Oxford: Oxford University Press, 1980b.

Jefferies, Richard. *Landscape with Figures*, ed. Richard Mabey. Harmondsworth: Penguin, 1983.

Jefferson, Anne and David Robey, eds. *Modern Literary Theory: A Comparative Introduction*. London: Batsford Academic and Educational Ltd, 1982.

Johnson, Barbara. 'Introduction' to Derrida, *Dissemination*, vii–xxxiii.

Kamuf, Peggy, ed. *A Derrida Reader: Between the Blinds*. New York: Columbia University Press, 1991.

Keuchtwanger, E. J. *Democracy and Empire: Britain 1865–1914*. London: Edward Arnold, 1985.

Klein, Melanie. *The Psychoanalysis of Children* (1932), trans. Alix Strachey. London: Hogarth Press, 1980.

Klein, Melanie. 'Some Theoretical Conclusions Regarding the Emotional Life of the Infant' (1952), in *The Writings of Melanie Klein* Vol. 3. London: Hogarth Press, 1985. 61–93.

Kristeva, Julia. *The Kristeva Reader*, ed. Toril Moi. Oxford: Basil Blackwell, 1986.

Kristeva, Julia. 'On the Melancholic Imaginary', in *Discourse in Psychoanalysis and Literature*, ed. Shlomith Rimmon-Kenan. London: Methuen, 1987.

Lacan, Jacques. *Speech and Language in Psychoanalysis* (1956), trans. Anthony Wilden. Baltimore: Johns Hopkins, 1975.

Lacan, Jacques. *Ecrits: A Selection*, trans. Alan Bass. New York: Norton, 1977.

Laplanche, Jean and J. B. Pontalis, eds. *The Language of Psychoanalysis* (1967), trans. Donald Nicholson-Smith (1973). London: Karnac Books. 1988.

Lechte, John. *Fifty Key Contemporary Thinkers*. London: Routledge, 1994.

Leech, G. and M. Short. *Style in Fiction: A Linguistic Introduction to English Prose*. London: Longman, 1981.

Macherey, Pierre. *A Theory of Literary Production* (1966), trans. Geoffrey Wall. London: Routledge Kegan Paul, 1978.

Marks, Elaine and Isabelle de Courtivron, eds. *New French Feminisms:*

an *Anthology*. New York, London: Harvester Press, 1980.

Marx, Karl and Friedrich Engels. *Selected Works in One Volume* (1968). London: Lawrence and Wishart, 1980.

Matthews, Hugoe and Phyllis Treitel. *The Forward Life of Richard Jefferies: A Chronological Study*. Oxford: Petton Books, 1994.

Miller, J. Hillis. 'Heart of Darkness Revisited', in *Heart of Darkess: a Case Study in Contemporary Criticism*, ed. Ross C. Murfin. New York: St Martin's Press, 1989.

Mitchell, Juliet. *Psychoanalysis and Feminism*. Harmondsworth: Penguin, 1981.

Moi, Toril. *Sexual/Textual Politics: Feminist Literary Theory*. London: Methuen, 1985.

Montrose, Louis. '*A Midsummer Night's Dream* and the Shaping Fantasies of Elizabethan Culture: Gender, Power, Form', *Representations*, 2, 1983, 65–87. Also in *New Historicism and Renaissance Drama*, ed. R. Wilson and R. Dutton.

Muller, John P., and William J. Richardson, eds. *The Purloined Poe: Lacan, Derrida and Psychoanalytic Reading*. Baltimore: Johns Hopkins University Press, 1990.

Mulvey, Laura. 'Visual Pleasure and Narrative Cinema', in *Visual and Other Pleasures*. London: Macmillan, 1989, 14–29.

Porter, Carolyn. 'Are We Being Historical Yet?', *The South Atlantic Quarterly*, 87: 4 (Fall), 1988.

Prince, Gerald. *Narratology*. Berlin, New York and Amsterdam: Mouton, 1982.

Read, Donald. *The Age of Urban Democracy: England 1868–1914* (1979). Harlow: Longman, 1994.

Rimmon-Kenan, Shlomith. *Narrative Fiction: Contemporary Poetics*. London: Methuen, 1983.

Rivière, Joan. 'Womanliness as Masquerade', *International Journal of Psychoanalysis*, 10, 303–13.

Said, Edward. *Orientalism: Western Conceptions of the Orient*. (1978). Harmondsworth: Penguin, 1991.

Sartiliot, Claudette. *Citation and Modernity: Derrida, Joyce, and Brecht*. Norman: University of Oklahoma Press, 1993.

Saussure, Ferdinand de. *Course in General Linguistics* (1916), trans. Wade Baskin, introduction by Jonathan Culler. London: Fontana, 1981.

Scholes, Robert. *Structuralism in Literature: An Introduction*. New Haven: Yale University Press, 1974.

Selden, Raman. *Practising Theory and Reading Literature: An Introduction*. Hemel Hempstead: Harvester Wheatsheaf, 1989.

Shakespeare, William. *The Tempest*. Harmondsworth: Penguin, 1968.

Shannon, Richard. *The Crisis of Imperialism 1865–1915*. London: Hart-Davis, MacGibbon, 1974.

Showalter, Elaine. *Sexual Anarchy*. New York: Viking, 1990; London: Bloomsbury, 1991.

Sinfield, Alan. 'Four Ways with a Reactionary Text', *Journal of Literature Teaching Politics*, 2, 1983, 81–95.

Sinfield, Alan. *Faultlines: Cultural Materialism and the Politics of Dissident Reading.* Oxford: Oxford University Press, 1992.

Spivak, Gayatri Chakravorty. 'Translator's Preface', in Derrida, *Of Grammatology,* ix–lxxxix.

Thomas, Edward. *Richard Jefferies.* London: Faber and Faber, 1978.

Tillyard, E. M. W. *The Elizabethan World Picture: A Study of the Idea of Order in the Age of Shakespeare, Donne and Milton.* London: 1943.

Todorov, Tzvetan, ed. *French Literary Theory Today: a Reader.* Cambridge: Cambridge University Press, 1982.

Veeser, H. Aram, ed. *The New Historicism.* London: Routledge, 1989.

Veeser, H. Aram, ed. *The New Historicism Reader.* London: Routledge, 1994.

Waller, P. J. *Town, City and Nation: England 1850–1914.* Oxford: Oxford University Press, 1983.

White, Hayden. *The Content of the Form: Narrative Discourse and Historical Representation.* Baltimore: Johns Hopkins University Press, 1987.

Wilden, Anthony. 'Lacan and the Discourse of the Other', in Lacan, *Speech and Language in Psychoanalysis,* 159–311.

Wilson, Richard and Richard Dutton, eds. *New Historicism and Renaissance Drama.* Harlow: Longman, 1992.

Wimsatt, W. K., and Monroe Beardsley. *The Verbal Icon* (1958). London: Methuen, 1970.

Wollstonecraft, Mary. *Maria: or, The Wrongs of Woman* (1788, 1798), ed. Gary Kelly. Oxford and New York: Oxford University Press, 1976.

Wright, Elizabeth. *Psychoanalytic Criticism: Theory in Practice.* London: Methuen, 1984.

Yeazell, Ruth Bernard. 'Nature's Courtship Plot in Darwin and Ellis', *Yale Journal of Criticism,* 2, 1989, 33–53.

Notes on Contributors

William Baker is Professor of English at the Department of English at Northern Illinois University. He is the editor of *George Eliot – George Henry Lewes Studies* and has recently completed work on an edition of the letters of George Henry Lewes. In addition, he has published numerous articles on bibliographical study.

Jill Barker has a BA from the Australian National University and teaching qualifications from the University of Melbourne. Her doctoral thesis from the University of Warwick investigated attitudes to the nature of humanity, to women and to class in sixteenth-century theatre. She currently lectures in Literary Studies and Women's Studies at the University of Luton. Jill's academic interests range from postmodern critical theories (in particular psychoanalysis and feminism) through feminist readings of Shakespeare, to the rhetorical strategies of sixteenth-century 'popular theatre. Several publications are forthcoming, including 'Testaceous Androgyny: The Meaning of the Snail Image in Sixteenth Century Theatre' and an edition of William Turner and William Punt's semi-staged polemical dialogues of 1548.

David Blomfield is an author, historian and book editor.

John Brannigan is a researcher in the School of Literature and History at the University of Luton. He is currently working on a study of writers of the 1950s, including John Osborne, Brendan Behan and Sam Selvon, and a study of the relationship between marginality and writing. He is co-editor of *Applying: to Derrida* (Macmillan, 1996) and *French Connections: Literary and National Contexts of the Thought of Jacques Derrida* (State University of New York Press, forthcoming 1997).

Julian Cowley is Senior Lecturer in Literary Studies and Field Manager of Literary Studies in English in the Department of Literature and History at the University of Luton, he has published several articles on twentieth-century American literature.

Mark Currie is a lecturer with the Department of English at the University of Dundee.

Jessica Maynard is completing work on her doctoral dissertation at King's College, University of London. She is currently researching into discourses of terror and terrorism in nineteenth- and twentieth-century fiction, and representations of the city.

Ruth Robbins is a lecturer in Literary Studies at the University of Luton. She has research interests in late nineteenth-century literature and has published articles on Housman, Wilde, and Vernon Lee. She is the editor, with Julian Wolfreys, of *Victorian Identities: Social and Cultural Formations in Nineteenth-Century Literature* (Macmillan, 1995), *Applying: to Derrida* (Macmillan, 1996) and *French Connections: Literary and National Contexts of the Thought of Jacques Derrida* (State University of New York Press, forthcoming 1997).

Julian Wolfreys teaches in the Department of English at the University of Dundee. He is the author of *Being English: Narratives, Idioms, and Performances of National Identity from Coleridge to Trollope* (State University of New York Press, 1994), *Writing London* (Scolar, forthcoming 1997), and *Victoriographies* (Macmillan, forthcoming 1999). He is the co-editor of *Victorian Identities* (Macmillan, 1995), *Applying: to Derrida* (Macmillan, 1996) and *French Connections: Literary and National Contexts of the Thought of Jacques Derrida* (State University of New York Press, forthcoming 1997).

Index